CHINA
UNDERGROUND

CHINA
UNDERGROUND
ZACHARY
MEXICO

Soft Skull Press
Brooklyn

Library of Congress Cataloging-in-Publication Data

Mexico, Zachary.
  China underground / Zachary Mexico.
    p. cm.
  ISBN 10: 1-59376-223-2
  ISBN 13: 978-1-59376-223-0

Includes bibliographical references and index.
  1. China—Social life and customs—2002 2. China—
Social conditions—21st century. 3. China—Description
and travel I. Title.
  DS779.43.M49 2009
  951.06—dc22

                                    2008045319

Cover design by Fogelson-Lubliner
Interior design by Beth Kessler, Neuwirth & Associates, Inc.
Printed in the United States of America

PopMatters

www.popmatters.com

Soft Skull Press
An Imprint of Counterpoint LLC
2117 Fourth Street
Suite D
Berkeley, CA 94710
www.softskull.com
www.counterpointpress.com

Distributed by Publishers Group West

10 9 8 7 6 5 4 3 2

CONTENTS

INTRODUCTION

IN 2004, WHEN I returned to New York from a two-year stint living in Kunming, China, I spent a few months without a job, reading, writing music, catching up with old friends, and trying to figure out what to do next.

After the initial buzz of excitement from being home had worn off, I began to feel that I had made a mistake. I missed China, terribly.

In the beginning of the twenty-first century, it is hard to imagine a more exciting place than China. The country's economy is growing by more than 10 percent a year. The lives of Chinese citizens in every stratum of society are changing; indeed, the very rules that define the parameters of their lives are changing. One-point-two billion people are hustling simultaneously, trying to figure out what's going on, trying to carve a place out for themselves in the new China.

My life in China had been colorful, unpredictable, and

spontaneous; comparatively, New York seemed humdrum, boring, played out.

I began to spend hours a day reading books, flipping through magazines, and combing the Internet for China-related material. The majority of what I found in the mainstream media focused on China's booming economy and its role as the next "global superpower." Other heavily reported-on issues included human rights, social unrest, income inequality, the stability of the Communist Party, and the plight of the migrant workers. Some of these stories I found useless, and others compelling. While most journalists were focusing on these kinds of macro-level, socio-economic situations, others, most notably the sublime *New Yorker* correspondent Peter Hessler, were publishing narratives about their own experiences in today's China.

But I wanted to read something different. I wanted to read about the crazy people I'd met in China and the even crazier people they'd introduced me to. I wanted to read about the streets that hum with the energy of constant change, and how that change affects the young Chinese of my generation.

□ □ □

TWO YEARS LATER, I was fed up with waiting: instead of reading about the interesting people I'd met in China, I decided to write about them. These are their stories, and some of my own.

□ □ □

MANY OF THE names have been changed, at the subjects' request.

CHINA
UNDERGROUND

1

The Peasant Who Likes to Take Pictures

I'M STUCK IN Beijing's infamous traffic on the way to Capital Airport. It is the early evening: from the elevated ring road, I can see the sun setting through a thick gray haze. I have a ticket for an evening flight, the sixty-five-minute short hop to Shenyang, an industrial city in the Northeast of China, to meet up with the mysterious photojournalist Maohair. He has an MSN Spaces website, which he calls "The Little Monkey King," and he recently set the Chinese Internet world abuzz by posting a series of his controversial photographs on a bulletin board.

I posted a comment on his blog and he sent me a text message agreeing to meet with me if I came to Shenyang; I have no idea what he looks like, as the images of himself on his website show him only in shadows.

I only know the photographs I have seen on the Internet, a series of snapshots that are both deeply fascinating and profoundly disturbing. One photograph shows an old man, his face contorted in pain, sobbing in front of a wedding picture of his son and daughter-in-law, who have been killed in a car crash. In another picture, a coal miner has been taken to the hospital after an accident; his entire upper body has been charred jet-black as the result of an explosion. There are oxygen tubes up his nose and his hands are clenched into gnarled, blackened fists. A third photo shows the victim of a car crash, covered by a tarp, and a group of people standing around gawking at the dead body.

□ □ □

IN THE HALF hour since I hailed the cab, we've traveled about a mile, and it looks like I'm going to miss my flight. I'm not looking forward to waiting around at the terminal for hours, drinking $6 coffee, until I can catch another plane.

The driver belches and I catch a faint whiff of garlic and vinegar. He mumbles in a thick Beijing accent that he's going to take a shortcut. This seems like a terrible idea, and just as I start to voice my objection, my cell phone rings. It's a provincial number that I don't recognize.

"Wei?" I blurt, answering the phone with a slow grunting sound, in the traditional Chinese manner.

"Hello, are you looking to hire a handyman?"

"What?" I respond, somewhat taken aback. "I think you have the wrong number."

"How much does the handyman's job pay per day?"

"I think you have the wrong number. I'm not trying to hire a handyman."

"But this was the number in the newspaper ad."

"You must have the wrong number. Read the ad again."

There's a click, and the would-be handyman hangs up. The driver looks back at me quizzically. The garlic quotient of his breath has increased exponentially, and it's somewhat alarming that he's not looking at the road. A queasy, acidic feeling, born of halitosis and fear, begins to take hold in my gut.

"Why are you hiring a handyman?"

Suddenly, as if prompted by an invisible hand descending from the filthy sky, the traffic dissipates. The queasy feeling is gone as quickly as it arrived.

Once we get onto the airport expressway, our cab speeds along at a cool eighty kilometers per hour and I make it to the airport with twenty minutes to spare.

□ □ □

TWELVE HOURS LATER: I'm standing before a small night market set up on the sidewalk in front of a family-run restaurant in downtown Shenyang. It's very late. Maohair and I have been the only customers for hours. The restaurant's owner has gone to sleep with his head on a folding table, and his kids are bumbling about idly with heavy eyes, waiting for us to leave so they can all go to bed. In China, these restaurants don't close until the last customer's finished his meal, no matter what ungodly hour it is.

We're hanging out with an old man who has staggered over to our table, looking for a little late-night camaraderie.

The old man's teeth are yellow but even. A ratty brown jacket hangs loosely from his narrow shoulders, like a hobo scarecrow; attached to one of the sleeves with a safety pin is a red armband that indicates his status as a neighborhood watchman. He smells like a distillery but he's a pleasant fellow, with a playful, tireless smile superglued to his face.

"I was a driver," he grumbles, "a driver, back in 1980 when there were almost no cars. I drove all the government officials around. I was treated with respect everywhere I went."

He pulls a pack of cigarettes out of his pocket, lights up, and hikes his pantlegs up to his knees, exposing his lily-white legs, which are spotted here and there with uneven patches of coarse black hair.

He takes a swig of Snow brand beer. In China, every city has its own brewery: aside from Qingdao, there are no true "national" brands of beer. Shenyang Beer was recently taken over by Snow, a new conglomerate from Beijing that has been buying up breweries in second-tier cities in an attempt to create another national brand name. The resulting brew, predictably, has a different flavor in every city; in Shenyang it tastes like slightly rank beer-flavored water.

"I've been a pimp . . . and now I open casinos, because that's where the money is at . . ."

It's hard to believe that this shoddy old man is actually a casino baron. Either he's bullshitting, or he's in the throes of a transcendent bender and has entered an altered state where he owns casinos and draft beer rains from the sky. He is dressed like a bum and his monologues are straddling the thin line between humorously strange and embarrassingly incoherent.

He raises his bottle and smiles broadly at Maohair and me. "The two of you, are good friends to have, you two."

We hoist our beers and clink bottles with the old man. We drink deeply. It's six o'clock on a Sunday morning and we've been up all night talking. An array of half-eaten dishes from hours ago—tofu skin, cold tofu, lamb kebabs, boiled peanuts—lay scattered like battlefield carcasses on the folding table in front of us. An uneven procession of senior citizens strolls back and forth on the sidewalk behind us, taking their morning exercise. Dogs bark and birds chirp; the day's just beginning for normal people.

Maohair hands his business card to the old man. "Give me a call," he urges, "if anything's ever going on." The old man nods and grunts his assent, and we all take another hefty swig of beer, which has by now grown quite warm and foul.

Maohair winks at me slyly. He's drunk five bottles of beer to my two, but shows no sign of intoxication. His eyes are bright and his smile is playful. He's wearing a red shirt with white embroidery: the garment is characteristic of the ethnic minority regions of Southwest China.

The old man stumbles to his feet, crosses the street, passes by two middle-aged women walking impeccably coiffed dogs, fumbles with his zipper, pulls out his penis, and pisses against the wall of an adjoining building.

"You see my working style? Pretty effective, right?" says Maohair as we watch the old man. "You got to know what's up on the streets."

□ □ □

TO SAVE MONEY and to absorb the maximum amount of local color, while traveling in China I usually stay at friends' houses or shoddy government-owned hotels where the carpet is always slightly mildewy and dotted with cigarette burns.

In Shenyang, to preserve the illusion I felt I needed to give Maohair that I was a professional journalist, to help ease any concerns he may have about talking about his work, and to create a safe atmosphere for an open dialogue between us, I checked into a four-star hotel in the center of town.

As the clock struck midnight, I was sitting in my well-appointed room, drinking a cup of oolong tea and going over my notes from the previous day. My phone beeped. I had a text message from Maohair: "I am in the lobby of your hotel."

I put down my pen, hurried out the door, took the elevator downstairs and saw a man in his twenties, alone in the massive marble lobby, smoking a cigarette and sitting in a plush chair that seemed at least one size too big for his small, wiry frame. He was smiling, and his eyes were at once calm and lively. It's a rare quality, found in excited children, the spiritually enlightened, and psychopaths.

□ □ □

ON MAOHAIR'S WEBSITE, under the "About Me" section, he writes: "On my business card, it says I am a photojournalist, but I prefer to think of myself as a peasant who likes to play with a camera."

It's hip for many young Chinese artists from middle-class backgrounds to strive for "man-of-the-earth" authenticity and claim that they have "peasant" roots in "the countryside." When Maohair says he's a peasant, though, he's not trying to be cool or employ impressive hyperbole. He really does come from the *nongcun*, the impoverished countryside surrounding

Fushun, a small city near Shenyang, the capital of Northeast China's Liaoning Province.

Outsiders often fail to grasp the tremendously important dichotomy between those Chinese who live in cities and those who live in the countryside. For example, when I naively ask Maohair what his parents do for a living, he laughs at me: "What do you think they do? They're peasants! They work the earth!" He hesitates and then turns serious. "In China, being a peasant is not considered a job."

China's countryside is made up of a network of small, ragtag family subsistence farms. Commerce is relegated to one or two small shops per village, and many of these families have been living in the same place for a very long time. Last century, peasants were lauded as heroes by China's political revolution but, in this century, they have been largely left behind by China's economic revolution. Deng Xiaoping's famous words, "Some people will get rich first," led to a capitalist explosion that sparked massive growth and affluence in urban centers and coastal regions. While their quality of life has most certainly improved in the last few decades, the farmers are not driving new cars, eating hamburgers, drinking imported beer, or shopping at Wal-Mart. They are still in the countryside, tilling the dirt, waiting, wondering when their time to get rich will come.

□ □ □

IT WAS IN one of these villages, in 1982, that the Shi family was blessed with a boy. When the child was only a few years old, all the villagers agreed that he showed signs of exceptional intelligence.

As the boy started attending the village school, he became the number one student in his class. Every night, over their dinner of vegetables and rice, his father would say, over and over again, "Study hard, son, and then you can get out of the countryside, get a stable job in the city, and make the family proud."

The son listened to his father's advice, and studied with remarkable persistence and determination, achieving uniformly high test scores through primary school and middle school.

When he was in middle school, the Liaoning provincial radio station held a letter-writing contest for middle school students, and Little Shi came in first place. He won a camera, the old kind that had no flash or zoom; after taking each picture, you had to wind the film by hand.

At that time, in the early nineties, Little Shi was the only one in the village with a camera. Many of the older people had never been photographed in their entire lives. When villagers needed to get their pictures taken—at special occasions like weddings and graduations—they went to a photo studio in a neighboring village and paid five jiao (6¢) per photo.

When Little Shi received the box containing his camera, he had no idea how to use it. He followed the instructions to slide the chunky roll of film onto the black plastic holder; after he inadvertently exposed a few valuable rolls of film, he finally figured out how the camera's mechanism worked.

He learned how to take photographs like a child learns how to walk: by employing a crude method of trial and error. He photographed his family, his house, his friends. Film developing was expensive, though, and it required a long bus ride to the nearest city, Fushun, outside of Shenyang.

It's said that every city in China is famous for at least one thing: bean curd, vinegar, a special kind of noodles, whatever. Fushun is famous for its open-pit coal mine, which has been in operation since the twelfth century.

After a few trips to the developer, Little Shi had spent all his meager pocket money on his newfound pastime. But he had formulated a business plan: he would take pictures of his fellow villagers and sell them for a small fee.

Soon enough, word got around to the neighboring villages about Little Shi and his camera and the thirteen-year-old boy became the unofficial countryside photographer. Little Shi was developing his photographic skill and simultaneously earning a little bit of spending money. While his classmates ate the one jiao (roughly 1¢) "ice cream" which was just frozen sugar water, Little Shi had enough cash to eat the two-jiao ice cream, which contained a little bit of milk.

He was the big man on his middle school campus: not only did he have a camera and a thriving small business that allowed him to eat the good ice cream, but he consistently got the top score on all his examinations.

□　□　□

THE FOLLOWING YEAR, Little Shi left his village and went to Fushun to attend the city high school. The students in the school were mostly from the city with a few countryside kids like Little Shi thrown into the mix by the provincial government. Little Shi could not believe how knowledgeable the city kids were about life: they had spent their middle school years reading books, leafing through magazines, and watching television stations that weren't available in Little Shi's village.

While the city kids most certainly thought of Little Shi and his lot as country bumpkins, they were not mean or disdainful, and for this simple courtesy Little Shi was very glad.

His parents were spending a disproportionate amount of their paltry income on his school fees, so Little Shi once again turned to his camera to earn some spending money. He became a wedding photographer: on the weekends, Little Shi would go to the elaborate wedding ceremonies that are a hallmark of Chinese culture. He would receive 100 yuan per wedding—a tremendous sum for a teenaged boy in the midnineties—and also the traditional "red envelope" (a token gift of gratitude given out at weddings and holidays) stuffed with a few more notes.

The fringe benefits of the job were manifold: good meals at no cost, candy, and premium ten-yuan-a-pack cigarettes. For a few months, Little Shi brought the cigarettes home for his father to smoke. Then, he started to smoke them himself. At his high school, some of the older students had already started smoking, but they smoked the two-yuan-a-pack local brand and Little Shi felt very cool indeed when he handed around expensive cigarettes to the older boys.

Little Shi went to the Fushun secondhand market and bought a big, clunky camera made in the 1980s. The era of digital photography had not yet arrived in provincial Liaoning, but this camera—a comparably sophisticated piece of equipment relative to the plastic prize camera he'd been using—lent him an air of professionalism. He purchased some photography magazines and picked up a few tricks and tips.

After a couple months, he realized that the photographs he was taking were of more professional quality than all of Fushun's "professional" mom-and-pop photograph shops.

In his spare time, Little Shi wandered around the streets of Fushun and started to take pictures of things he found interesting around town: his classmates at play, people at work, and other minutiae of China city life. He pasted these photographs onto blank paper and added little paragraphs of commentary. After class was over for the day, he would circulate these sheets of paper among his classmates. "It was like a blog, before anyone used the Internet," he remembers. "You could say, in this way, that maybe I was the first blogger in China."

It was around this time that Little Shi acquired a new nickname: Little Monkey. He was often seen by his classmates climbing in trees to take pictures, and he was also very clever. The nickname made him happy: in Chinese culture, the monkey has long been respected as a symbol of intelligence.

□ □ □

BUT ALL WAS not well in the world of Little Monkey. He was caught in the tumult of adolescence, and this transition from childhood to adulthood confused and annoyed him. His high school classmates were focused on one thing and one thing only: preparing for the dreaded college examinations. But Little Monkey didn't feel like studying his schoolbooks.

He had started to read novels and books of poetry. He was getting into the philosophy of Daoism and it was changing his life. All of this stuff he was learning in school was worthless, he thought. His classmates, who spent all afternoon hunched over their schoolbooks, reminded him of robots that couldn't think for themselves. They were worried about studying but not about learning. Little Monkey knew there was more to life than memorizing arcane facts about Chinese history and making flashcards to pore over, again and again, in order to memorize stupid things like chemical formulas.

Since he was a kid his father had been hammering the same dull mantra into his head: study hard, go to college, get out of the countryside. Study hard, go to college, get out of the countryside. Study hard, go to college, get out of the countryside. Little Monkey felt sure that he wanted to get out of the countryside. But he thought that going to college wasn't the only way to go about it: there could be another way, a different way.

Little Monkey understood that his father meant well. His father was an uneducated man who wanted nothing more than for his son to succeed; to break the economic restraints forced upon farmers such as himself, and to attain the "respect" reserved for those who achieve financial success and social status. There is a Chinese proverb—"*wang zi cheng long*"—"you hope your son to become a dragon." All of the opportunities that Little Monkey's father had been denied, he wanted for his son.

Little Monkey told his father that he wanted to forge his own path, to live his own life. Little Monkey knew he was special. He could trust himself. But school and parental pressure were turning him into a product rolling off the assembly line at the factory, a piece of coal extracted from Fushun's open-pit mine and processed for export. He was done working within the rigid boundaries of the Chinese educational system. He wasn't going to get a university degree.

His father didn't agree; neither did his mother, his relatives, or the other people from his village. They begged him to reconsider. They protested that he wasn't showing appropriate respect to his family. They were disappointed, dismayed, devastated.

But Little Monkey was strong-willed, and he had made up his mind. Instead of going to college, he stayed in Fushun, and, in fine Communist Party tradition, he decided to serve his society by finding a position at a Community Welfare Center, a place where young people, in exchange for room and board, took care of those who couldn't take care of themselves: senior citizens, orphans, and incapacitated coal miners. Even though the place was staffed entirely by young people, Little Monkey, fresh out of high school, was the youngest of all. After a few weeks at the Community Welfare Center, he acquired yet another new nickname, due to his youth, one that would stick for a long time: Maohair, or "little kid."

□ □ □

ONE OF THE best things about spending time at the Community Welfare Center was the abundance of free time available, which Maohair spent taking pictures and reading books—his interest in philosophy, poetry and literature sparking a self-discipline to his studies that he couldn't attain in school. He devoured everything he could get his hands on: Confucius's *Analects*, Lao

Tzu's *Dao De Jing,* Mao Zedong's lengthy volumes of poetry and philosophy.

He knew little about Buddhism because it wasn't a popular religion in his village. But once Maohair picked up a book of sutras, he became instantly hooked. In his spare time, he scoured bookstores for Buddhist texts. During the day, he would play games with orphans and help the elderly go to the bathroom; at night, he would study Buddhism on his dormitory bed until they turned the lights out.

After a number of months at the Community Welfare Center, Maohair decided that maybe the Buddhist life was for him. With only the clothes on his back, and a book of Lin Qing Xuan's Zen poems, he climbed a mountain to take his vows at a monastery.

◻   ◻   ◻

AFTER JUST A few weeks of study and meditation at the monastery, Maohair shaved his head and dressed in monk's robes. He had made his decision: he was going to pursue a monastic life. First, though, he had to travel back to his village to get the blessing of his parents.

Back home, his father was irate. Buddhism was okay, it was sanctioned by the Communist Party and everything, but a monk was even lower in social status than a peasant! Monks made even less money than peasants! They had to beg for their food! No way are you becoming a monk, said his father, and Maohair reluctantly listened.

Maohair wanted to become a monk to seek intellectual and spiritual fulfillment. But now that he had reluctantly agreed not to return to the monastery, he couldn't stay in his village: there was nothing to do there except get pressured by his parents. He decided to travel south to Beijing, China's political and cultural capital, and expand his mind in a different way.

He had no friends in Beijing, and he rode the train still wearing monk's robes, carrying only a small bag containing his camera and a few books. When he got to the city, it blew his mind: enormous wide avenues, giant skyscrapers jutting into the sky, and people walking down the streets so fast it was almost as if they were running.

During his first few days in Beijing, Maohair wandered around the city, sleeping in empty stairwells at night. He couldn't believe how big the place was, and how expensive; he had a few hundred yuan in his pocket left over from his wedding photographer days, and his father had slipped him some money before he left, but he needed to find some work and a place to live.

He exchanged his monk's outfit for a T-shirt and jeans he bought at a secondhand market and found a hostel where a dormitory bed was only eight yuan ($1) a night. "It was at that hostel," Maohair remembers, "where I truly began to learn new things. The place was full of rock musicians, wandering artists, and wandering writers. Guys who played guitar in the subway to make money. That is where I learned about life."

At night, these bohemians would sit in the courtyard outside the hostel, eating peanuts and drinking Beijing's infamous and dirt-cheap Er Guo Tou rice wine from a communal bowl. They would stay outside, drinking and swapping stories, until the sun was about to come up and then they'd all go inside to the huge dormitory and try to fall asleep amid the cacophony of their roommates' drunken snoring.

Maohair enrolled at a cheap private arts school taught by moonlighting teachers from the famous Qinghua University Institute of Media Studies, near Beijing's China World Trade Center. A couple of China's most famous photography teachers were Qinghua faculty, and they would teach at this private arts school to make extra money on the side.

He didn't have enough money to go to the actual Qinghua but, he reasoned, the teachers were the same, and that was good enough for him. He would sneak into Qinghua University lectures, and students soon began to recognize him and even make small talk after class; they thought he was a classmate of theirs even though he hadn't paid Qinghua a cent. "I studied at Qinghua University," remembers Maohair with a grin, "but I was never a student there."

In order to make money to pay for the tuition at the private school, Maohair worked a variety of odd jobs. First, he handed out cards advertising travel agencies on the street for ten yuan ($1.20) a day. Once he'd saved up a little capital, he set up a small fried tofu stand, making sure to keep far away from neighborhoods where people he knew from school might see him. When such work was available, he joined other artists from the hostel as an extra on movie sets. The pay wasn't bad, and he didn't really have to do anything except sit still. Every night, no matter where he worked during the day, Maohair headed back to the hostel to hang out with his new friends, bullshitting and drinking until the sun came up in the hazy Beijing sky.

One day when he went to work as an extra, Maohair brought his camera along. He took pictures of the other extras, dressed up in their costumes, smoking cigarettes, talking on their cell phones, and adjusting their makeup.

He posted the photographs on the Internet, and soon enough they were picked up by a number of magazines and newspapers. Maohair realized that it might be possible for him to make a living as a photographer, again. One of his teachers saw his pictures, and encouraged him to enter a photojournalism contest, where he was awarded first prize. "Even though I didn't go to college, my pictures were better than the pictures of those who had graduated," the ever-confident Maohair recalls.

He adds, pointedly, "Maybe it was because I didn't go to college that they were better!"

Maohair decided that he was going to become a photojournalist. He said goodbye to his friends at the hostel and took the train north, returning home to Liaoning for a visit with his parents. After a few days at home, he walked into the offices of the *Morning News* in Shenyang and demanded a job. The boss looked at his portfolio and hired him on the spot at a princely salary of 3,000 yuan a month, twice as much as his parents made in a year.

□ □ □

AND SO THE wanderer has returned to his home province. Shenyang is inexpensive compared to Beijing, so his earnings allow him a comfortable life, materially, at least. He's bought an apartment pre-construction, which is still being built, and meanwhile he's renting a place in the north section of town.

He's also got a passion for motorcycles: he runs a motorcycle exchange website, and talks wistfully of someday owning a

Harley Davidson and starting a Chinese chapter of the Hell's Angels.

Every day, however, he rides his junky old motor scooter to the newspaper offices before heading out by car or bus to the mining areas and construction sites in and around Shenyang to take photographs of disasters such as mine collapses and construction accidents, and their aftermath: the dead and seriously injured. Sometimes, his photographs are taken on assignment from the newspaper. Other times, his network of local informants will give him a call about something gone wrong and he'll rush to the scene, or he'll be indulging in his favorite pastime—riding his motor scooter around Shenyang—and something will catch his eye.

Maohair grew up in mining country where just showing up to work in the morning can mean that you'll be killed by a mine explosion before the day is over. When he started working at the *Morning News*, taking pictures of industrial catastrophes that occur with frightening regularity, he became drawn to images of suffering and death. He has come to view himself as a crusader, exposing the corruption of society in his disaster photographs, and as an artist, making a statement about the moral vacuum that allows that corruption to exist.

When viewed individually, Maohair's photographs are deeply affecting and alarming. The pictures are remarkable: he's always *right there* with his camera at the scene of mining accident ("Victim of a mine explosion," the caption under the photograph posted on his website reads); a protest ("Migrant workers climb up construction towers at the site to demand their back wages"); a scene of environmental decline ("Scooping dead fish out of the contaminated river").

When viewed collectively, Maohair's photographs are a truly remarkable portrait of China's rapidly changing society, especially the dark side of tremendous economic growth. Despite a seemingly infinite series of government proclamations and laws designed to ensure the safety of workers, a combination of corrupt cadres and unscrupulous business owners ensures that regulation of factories, construction projects and coal mines is, in practice, virtually nonexistent.

He has taken photos of so many accidents that it seems inconceivable that he could be on the scene every time something goes disastrously wrong. When I ask him how he does it, he grins his trademark grin: "It's part luck, and part connections: I know all the people in the countryside and they all call me. Mostly, it's not that I'm in the right place at the right time. It's just that there are so many accidents and so many disasters. China has a lot of people, and it's very dangerous."

"My specialties are peasants, migrant workers, and coal miners," Maohair says, like a chef might say, "My specialties are cornbread, fried chicken, and collard greens." Since he grew up a peasant in a coal mining region, this affinity certainly makes sense, and he's a master of his oeuvre.

During the 1990s, an integral tenet of China's continuing economic reform included the closing of massive, money-losing state enterprises that existed only to provide tens of thousands of Chinese citizens with jobs. Liaoning, and Shenyang in particular, was a hub for such businesses. The sudden mass unemployment caused by their closure left a large percentage of the working population little choice but to take on dangerous jobs in the unregulated mining and construction industries. Also, peasants whose family farms earned but a meager income found that they could greatly increase their household cash flow if they went to work in the mines or on a construction site.

Maohair's photographs are, like all photographs, moments captured but since passed. But they make a very definite and lasting statement about the transitory nature of life in today's China. Callous factory owners dump their pollutants into rivers, destroying the ecosystem. Miners do not have proper safety training, and the mines themselves are often illegal, anyway. While around 80 percent of China's urban dwellers have some kind of health coverage, only a fraction of rural residents do. For those living outside the cities, China's government health care system is basically useless. When peasants are afflicted with disease, they often do not seek medical assistance, simply because they can't; they don't have the cash on hand to pay for treatment. People die every day from accidents and illnesses that should be largely preventable in such a thriving country.

The humanist primacy of individual rights over group obligation that is central to much Western social and political discourse is absent in China. In traditional, Confucian Chinese culture, the well-being of society is valued over the well-being of the individual. So the modern interpretation of that philosophy reasons that mining companies that produce more coal also make more money, and that a business's success is viewed as good for society. Construction companies build more buildings: the economy is developing and that is good for all of society. This economic growth increases political and social stability and that is most certainly good for society.

So while in the West, coal-mining deaths constitute a tragedy, in China, only a pittance is paid to the families of migrant workers who die in the coal mines and the very lives of those workers are written off as the financial and human cost of doing business.

Moreover, both in the public and private sectors, the conventional wisdom seems to be: China has way too many people. More specifically, China has too many peasants. Some of them must be sacrificed in order to increase the rate of development and the harmoniousness of society. In order to make a tasty omelet—or, in this case, a plate of *xihongshichaojidan*—you have to break some eggs.

Maohair's work is simultaneously an explicit acknowledgement of this philosophy and a condemnation of the system and the society that allows it to exist. His photographs are beautiful in their simplicity and shocking in their perversity.

◻ ◻ ◻

DURING HIS WORK as a reporter, Maohair has angered a lot of powerful people. His images have captured the existence of illegal casinos, the dangerous operations of unregulated coal mines, and the stories of families of migrant workers who have died on the job and disappeared without a trace.

"Today, when you were still in Beijing, you got a phone call from someone looking for a handyman. Remember?"

I do.

"That was me," smiles Maohair. "I had to make sure you were who you said you were . . . there are a lot of people who might want to find me and hurt me."

He is careful, yes. But he is calm. He is not scared. Maohair the crusader is too busy to be scared. He has more photographs to take. More stories to cover. More statements to make. More injustice to capture on the screen of his new digital camera.

2

The Black Society

THIS IS THE STORY of what happened one mild summer evening at a Qingdao karaoke parlor, as I heard it from those who were there. The story was told to me, rather raucously, over a typically lavish Sichuanese dinner that involved a lot of tongue-numbing peppercorns and equally fiery rice wine. My hosts were more than a little tipsy, their faces flushed with drink, and I had my notebook out, scribbling furiously and waiting for my mouth to cool between bites.

□ □ □

IT HAD HAPPENED very quickly: Liu Gang wasn't feeling terribly well. Everything in the room had begun to spin around, to become suddenly elastic: the walls, the soft leather couch he was sitting on, the naked young girl on his left, the naked young girl on his right, his friend Chen Yong, the naked young girl on Chen's left, the naked young girl on Chen's right, the massive dish of ketamine powder on the glass table in front of them. The six of them—Liu, Chen, and the four girls, *xiaojies* who worked at the club and were rented out to customers by the hour or the night—had been in this room for forty-eight hours, drinking Hennessy, taking pills, and snorting ketamine. Liu was strung out. He needed another hit.

Liu muttered something to Chen, who didn't respond. Chen's eyes were open, and his left hand was firmly planted on the breast of one of the naked girls. Liu repeated himself, louder, and shook Chen out of his stupor.

"What'd you say?" asked Chen.

Liu handed Chen a rolled-up 100-yuan note, and Chen used a knife to carve out six gargantuan lines of ketamine on a white porcelain plate. Chen handed the plate back to Liu, who handed it off to the naked girls by his side. After the four girls had each Hoovered down a line, Chen and Liu polished off the rest.

Liu closed his eyes and enjoyed the rush. It felt like he was floating in a warm bath; he smiled as the girls ran their fingers over his torso. He wasn't sure whether he was alive or dead. This was heaven. Liu thought he had just had a profound revelation. He had figured it out! This was paradise! He wanted to tell someone. He wanted to tell his best friend, Chen.

Liu tried to stand up, stumbled, and immediately sank back down onto the couch. What had he wanted to tell Chen? What had seemed so important? He couldn't remember, and now he felt like his mind had become detached from his body. What was his name? Who were these girls?

He placed his right hand over his heart but he couldn't feel a heartbeat. He tried again. Nothing. He did feel something else, though. Something hard. Liu pulled the handgun out of the inside pocket of his jacket and stared at it with wonder. He started to giggle and couldn't stop. This was amazing! He had a gun in his hands! He needed to tell Chen!

"Chen," Liu rasped, "check this out!" The words came out in a slurred burst of *Dongbei*—northeastern—dialect. "I've got a gun!"

On the opposite couch, Chen remained motionless, his eyes closed, his tongue hanging out of his mouth.

"Brother Chen!" Liu barked. "Check this out!" He didn't remember what he was asking Chen to check out until he looked down and saw the gun in his hands.

Liu was getting agitated. He wanted Chen to check out the gun but Chen was just lying there like a moron. Liu cocked the hammer but Chen didn't respond.

"Fuck this!" Liu said, and pulled the trigger. The bullet put a neat hole in Chen's designer pants and lodged into his left leg just below the knee.

The girls were too fucked up to even scream. Chen finally opened his eyes and looked down at the pool of blood forming at his feet. "Liu, you asshole," Chen said calmly, "What the fuck did you do?"

Wang Dalong was pissed off. He had been on his way to meet me for a beer that night in the new bar at the Shangri-La Hotel when he got the phone call from a very fucked-up Liu Gang, who'd handed the phone to a very freaked-out karaoke bar manager. Those morons Liu and Chen had gotten way too stoned again; somehow, one of them had smuggled a gun into the back room at the karaoke parlor and shot the other one.

Wang maneuvered his spotless white Lexus SUV through

the sparse nighttime traffic of Qingdao and arrived at the KTV (the Chinese term for karaoke bar.) He locked the car and bolted up the stairs where he was greeted by an apologetic, seriously nervous manager in a black suit. Wang peeled off a few bills from a wad of 100-yuan notes and handed them to the manager, who moved out of his way immediately.

Dalong made his way through the lobby of the karaoke bar to the staircase in the back that led up the stairs to the *baofang*, or private rooms. This particular karaoke parlor, a massive one by any standards, has over sixty of these rooms. They vary in size, from tiny to opulent, and are rented for 100 to 500 yuan an hour. The karaoke machine is included in the room rental fee; booze, girls, and drugs are extra.

Chen had wrapped his jacket around his leg in a crude attempt to fashion a tourniquet, but he was still too dusted up to do it effectively. Liu was sitting on the couch, his eyes glassy, stuck on the razor's edge that separates fantasy from reality. The girls had taken off as soon as they saw the blood.

Dalong couldn't take his eyes off the blood: the bloody jacket, Chen's bloody hands, the pool of blood on the floor. It made him feel ill, and he knew he'd have a hell of a time cleaning up the new leather interior of his Lexus.

This was not a good situation. But little brothers were little brothers, and you had to help them out, even when they fucked up, which Chen and Liu most certainly had.

Wang Dalong helped Chen to his feet, and they limped three-legged out of the room, Liu trailing behind. He walked them out the back door and into the backseat of his Lexus, cringing when he saw the first bloodstains on the cream-colored upholstery. He closed the door and left the two morons, still drugged up, in the backseat. He had to get them someplace where they could fix up this wound. Certainly not a hospital; in China, even possession of a firearm means a death sentence, and they couldn't risk getting the authorities involved. There was a doctor across town in the old city who wouldn't ask any questions in exchange for a few thousand yuan.

Before he took them to the doctor, Dalong ran back up the stairs to the *baofang*. He slipped the gun in his jacket pocket. He was about to leave but then he noticed a few ounces of ketamine that had been left behind on the table. He shook the pile back into its plastic bag, stuffed it into his pants pocket, then closed the door.

□   □   □

IN CHINA, WHERE the private and public economies alike rely on cash bribes, it is simple to slip a wholesaler or a veterinarian a few thousand yuan to look the other way while you purchase a couple thousand vials of ketamine. The illegal sale and distribution of ketamine is one example of countless rackets that are organized and controlled by the Chinese Mafia: the *"hei she-hui,"* or Black Society. These loose-knit criminal organizations rely on coercion, bribery, and *guanxi*—official connections—to make billions of yuan a year from such illegal enterprises.

For those not familiar with ketamine, it is a liquid inject-able solution that is used as a pre-operation tranquilizer for large animals like horses, bears, and big dogs. When the drug is converted to powder form, it becomes a powerful psyche-delic disassociative. Sniffing ketamine, while supposedly pleasurable, is also somewhat eerie. On ketamine, you feel disconnected from the temporal reality of "the self"; it renders you unable to remember what happened just moments before, and you can't be certain who you are or if you're even alive, anymore.

I've been at parties where the drug was being used and witnessed conversations between people on ketamine that were nearly Dadaist in their absurdity, because neither party could remember what the other one had just said.

"They have the best dumplings there."

"I want to buy a dog."

"What are you talking about?"

"I can't remember . . ."

"You're so beautiful."

"Thank you . . . wait, what?"

In June 2004, officials in Central China's Hunan Province discovered that nearly 3,100 cases of ketamine, containing 9.3 million vials of the drug, had somehow "gone missing" from thirteen different wholesalers. The wholesalers claimed that they had been defrauded by people posing as veterinary hospital representatives. This was the only reported case of missing ketamine in the last few years; the Chinese government notoriously reports only what it wants to report and often significantly alters statistics to fit their motives. More common headlines are: "Profit margins have become greater," "Air quality has improved," and "Less civil unrest in the provinces."

So if 9.3 million vials of ketamine had gone missing in the first half of *one* year, and in *one* province, it's easy to deduce that at the time of our dinner, the Chinese black market is absolutely flooded with illegal ketamine. In any big Chinese city, ketamine is readily available to those who have money and know where to look.

□ □ □

I MET WANG Dalong in passing over a year ago while visiting some friends in Qingdao. We ate dinner together on several occasions. In China, dinner is the most important part of the day. A typical greeting is "*Chifanlema*"—literally, "have you eaten yet?" Usually, when I'm out with friends, there will be at least ten people at dinner, maybe more, and a large amount of food and drink will be forced down my gullet to ensure that I'm "having a good time." Members of the Chinese middle class eat at restaurants very frequently, several times a week, if not every night, and they like to eat in large groups as it's more "*renao*": a word that literally means "hot and noisy," which is central to the Chinese idea of having a good time.

At first, Dalong seemed to be yet another in the seemingly endless series of Chinese businessmen that I've met at dinners over the years, the kind of guy that makes you drink too much and, when you're both good and sauced, wants to start talking politics and asking why America wants to dominate the world before engaging in a group hug and calling for more rice wine. It wasn't until later, when a friend told me that Dalong was a member of the *hei shehui*, that I began to look at him as more than just another potential argument.

Wang Dalong hails from Dongbei, the northeast region of China. Northeasterners are generally a hardy sort, used to drinking a lot to get them through the region's frigid winters. About ten years ago, Dalong had some trouble back home: he got in a fight and hit someone, more than once. The victim—by no means an innocent bystander—may or may not have died; Dalong didn't stick around to find out. As recently as last year, his name appeared on the government's online most wanted list. Now, it's disappeared; they didn't find him, and it seems they gave up.

He's a good-looking, well-spoken guy with a square jaw and a little scruff of beard on his chin that, in Asia, could pass for a five o'clock shadow. He likes to lift weights and play soccer and he's got the broad shoulders and tapered waist of an athlete. He favors expensive Japanese Evisu jeans and tight white Dolce and Gabbana dress shirts that show off his lean, muscular frame. To friends and business associates he is unfailingly polite and terrifically considerate.

Before we became friends, I asked some of his friends what he did for a living—in China, where the car import tax is nearly 100 percent, Lexus SUVs will cost over $100,000—I was told that he was "in construction." He doesn't smoke and he drinks moderately; he's just opened a smoothie shop next to a Starbucks Coffee in a local mall.

When talking to Wang Dalong, he seems like a genial and helpful guy. You might even believe that he's either the smoothie shop owner or the construction company owner that he claims to be. But Wang is the "*laoda*," or "Old Big," the boss of his own clan of the Black Society.

There are, of course, a few telltale signs of his status as a mafia boss, like his clothes and his car, which, not entirely incidentally, he drives like a madman, even by Chinese standards. Once, we were driving down the strip—Hong Kong Road in Qingdao. I was comfortably ensconced in one of the bucket seats in the back of his Lexus. A taxi was fifteen feet ahead of us. In the left lane, alongside the taxi, a large, dirty truck full of crushed stone and migrant workers belched smoke into the sky.

Dalong thought it would be a good idea to maneuver his massive SUV *between* the taxi and the wobbly truck. Without a second thought, he gunned the engine and went for it. Somehow, and seemingly in defiance of several of the basic laws of the physical universe, we made it. As my heart resumed pumping, I could feel a jolt of adrenaline hitting my brain. No one else seemed to notice; they just kept on talking as if nothing had happened. When I tried to bring up the incident later over drinks, the Chinese friends who had been sitting next to me in the Lexus seemed confused. They didn't even remember what I was talking about. They were used to it; near-accidents like this occur so often as to be commonplace.

After we left the Sichuanese restaurant, some of our party continued the evening over expensive pints of Qingdao beer in the sleek new Q Bar in the Qingdao Shangri-La, the preferred meeting place for the city's high rollers.

I asked Dalong exactly how he knew Chen and Liu. He referred to them as "his little brothers." However, since "brother" is a common appellation—friends, cousins, taxi drivers, bartenders—even the old guy selling watermelon on the street could be a "brother"—it was difficult for me to figure out their exact relationship.

Later, I'd query a mutual friend about Wang; my friend told me that several years prior, Dalong had moved fifty toughs from the Northeast down to Qingdao. He rented them apartments and paid their living expenses, including food, drugs, whores and, when needed, "doctors." In short, he transplanted and cultivated his own gang.

□ □ □

DALONG IS THE boss of his own branch of the Black Society, and the fifty toughs from Dongbei, including Chen and Liu, are his subordinates. This loosely-knit network of hooligans are small businessmen who use intimidation to enter the construction and real estate businesses and supplement those "legitimate" earnings with profits from selling drugs, girls, and guns. Other rackets controlled by the Black Society include shipping, bathhouses, car theft, pirated CDs and DVDs, and, strangely enough, seafood.

As in other countries, construction remains the most popular racket for aspiring criminals. This is especially true in these boom times, where the entire country seems to be constantly under construction. In order to build a new building, you need to demolish the old one, and then you need to dig a very large hole. If you're a property developer looking to redevelop some of your land, Wang Dalong or people like him will hear of it through word of mouth and contact you. They will express their interest in demolishing the old building and digging the hole for the foundation. They will name their price. If you decline, saying that you can get a better deal elsewhere, they will, for example, conspicuously follow your daughter home from school, or start calling your aging, fearful parents in the middle of the night, every night. They will get the contract, and they'll do the work. No one will mention any unpleasant incidents that preceded the work.

Karaoke parlors are also a lucrative racket for the Black Society. All karaoke parlors have prostitutes, which must first be rented by the hour; the owner keeps the lion's share of the women's profits. It's easy to sell ketamine, Ecstasy, speed, and other drugs out of private rooms, and it's always nice to have a karaoke parlor where you can loosen up a government official by treating him to a couple bottles of Chivas, to be mixed with iced green tea, and served with a side of a carton of expensive smokes, and a blowjob.

And then there's seafood. The Mafia gained control over the seafood market starting in the mid-nineties. At this time, the Chinese appetite for seafood triggered an increase in imports from Hong Kong and Vietnam. Since seafood is a highly perishable good, it has to be transported by air. In each city, a crew of gangsters would roll out to the airport and demand a "special local tax" on the shipments of seafood. If the importer refused to pay, the criminals simply refused to allow the shipment to be moved, and let it rot at the airport. After this happens a couple times, the importer is "glad" to pay the mafia tax. Eventually, the local gangsters realized that there was an opportunity to cut out the middleman: they traveled to Hong Kong and Vietnam themselves, tracked down the seafood exporter, and warned that selling to anyone but them would result in grave injury to the exporter and to his family.

Dalong used to own a seafood restaurant behind a Holiday Inn. Since he was already in control of Qingdao's seafood racket, it made sense to open a retail outlet. The concept of vertical integration exists even within the Chinese Mafia.

After the thriving restaurant had been open for a little

more than a year, the land on which the restaurant sat was sold to a developer; the building that housed the restaurant was to be demolished. For compensation, Dalong demanded 5 million yuan ($620,000). The developer refused, but when he came to the site with a surveying team, he was met by a posse of Dalong's little brothers wielding knives and chainsaws.

The developer appealed to the police, who were friendly with Dalong and his posse. The police told the developer to reach a settlement on his own. The next day, Dalong got his 5 million.

□ □ □

HONG KONG GANGSTER movies, popular all over the world, have led to many common misconceptions about organized crime. The Chinese Mafia is often referred to as "Triads": organizations with lengthy histories and boatloads of complicated rituals. These *tongs*—"clubs"—began during the early Qing Dynasty as the "Heaven and Earth Societies," which united a series of powerful underground forces all across the country against the Qing emperor.

During the civil war between the Communists and the Nationalists in the late 1940s, the leaders of these Triads, sensing the political instability to come, fled from the mainland to Hong Kong, where the Triads remain active to this day. However, just as the economic development of the mainland has led to a decrease in Hong Kong's importance as a financial hub, mainland gangs now far outnumber their Hong Kong counterparts. Criminal activity from the Hong Kong gangs is now concentrated in Hong Kong proper and Guangdong Province, the part of mainland China closest to Hong Kong.

These Hong Kong Triads, like the Sun Yee On and the 47K, are steeped in years of history and tradition, and they are controlled by some of Hong Kong's wealthiest businessmen who coordinate global arms and drug rings and have branch chapters in New York, Toronto, Sydney, and a host of European capitals.

Most Chinese mainland gangsters have no such organizational hierarchy or impressive history. After Mao took over and the reign of the Chinese Communist Party began, he cleansed the country of criminal elements and created his "communist utopia." In the early days of capitalist reforms in the 1980s, the Black Society began its re-emergence into mainland China. By the turn of the twenty-first century, when, in urban China, people were spending money like they were living their last day on Earth, a whole new host of opportunists appeared, seemingly from out of nowhere, using political and physical intimidation to get rich in the heady atmosphere of today's China.

No matter where one lives in the world, it helps to know people in power. Nowhere is this more true than in China, where the Communist Party has the uncontested ability to grant—or refuse—business licenses, construction permits, even Internet access.[1] *Guanxi*, the relationships one has with persons of importance, remains a necessity for economic transactions of all kinds.

China is currently in the throes of the largest economic and industrial boom in the history of the world. The sheer

---

1   See "The Uighur Jimi Hendrix."

scale of growth that's going on ensures that there are money-making opportunities to be had everywhere, and all the time. However, no one, not even the Black Society, can make money without connections in the government; therefore, CCP officials are often open to bribery. These bribes can take the form of cash or services. A police chief will accept a few cartons of cigarettes from a small-time shop owner in exchange for protection. A well-placed government functionary receives a penthouse apartment in a developer's new building in return for granting the construction permits. A well-connected businessman might accept a brand-new Porsche from the owner of the dealership for using his *guanxi* to help secure a business license. A few powerful government officials might be treated to a night out at a karaoke parlor or a lavish banquet complete with exorbitant delicacies like shark's fin and bird's nest by a businessman looking for a government contract. (Or, given the newfound popularity of Western food in China, the supplicant might spring for foie gras, escargots, and a couple bottles of vintage European wine.)

As a result, the Chinese business world is far from transparent. Government officials, legitimate businessmen with government connections, Black Society members with government connections—these are the people who really run China. And it's easy to tell who they are; like *nouveau riche* the world over, successful Chinese have embraced the material trappings of wealth, showing off Benzes and Bentleys, Versace and Armani, Rolex and Tag Heuer, the latest smartphones from Nokia and Motorola. While collusion between criminals, politicians, and police is an age-old phenomenon, in China it is increasingly hard to distinguish one from the other.

I remember one evening in Qingdao, I was sitting on the patio of a Western-style bar with some friends, playing a game of liar's dice and shooting the breeze, and a black Mercedes 300 series came zooming up to the entrance. A stocky guy, dressed in athletic clothing, got out of the car. He strolled up to us, produced a moist towel from his leather man-bag, and started wiping his forehead. He knew the people I was with, and started jabbering nonsense at them. He pulled out a tobacco pipe and lit it, still speaking nonsense. When he got close enough, I looked at his eyes. His pupils looked like saucers; he was clearly on some kind of psychedelic drug. After a few minutes he jumped back into his Benz and drove away.

"Was that a mafia guy?" I asked my companions.

"Nope," said one. "He's a police officer."

□   □   □

SEVERAL WEEKS AFTER the Sichuanese dinner where I learned about the karaoke joint craziness, I am invited to a party. It's Wang Dalong's birthday: A small restaurant has set up tables and a barbecue pit outside, next to a little patch of grass. It's like an ersatz backyard barbecue, and thirty or so people have gathered to celebrate. The crowd is eclectic: over the course of the evening I meet a real estate developer, the owner of an IT company, a nightclub impresario. The women in the crowd are dressed in tight clothing and high heels; some of them are wives, some are girlfriends, but it is understood that they are there "with the men." Dalong's businesslike, pretty wife, ten years older than he, hustles around making sure everybody's having fun. Liu, Chen, and the rest of Wang's hooligan crew are nowhere to be seen. I'm at the party with our common friends; Dalong and I have grown increasingly close over the past few months, and he's happy to see me, throwing his arm around my shoulder and introducing me to all his friends.

A guy in a baseball cap who, hours earlier, drove up in a GT racing jeep, now mans the grill. As is the custom with Chinese celebrations, the host has purchased way too much food. There are twenty-odd enormous sides of lamb, huge, bloody chunks with the skin still on, four multi-layer birthday cakes, skewers of tendon and vegetable, dozens of sweaty Qingdao beers, bottles of Chardonnay and Cabernet Sauvignon. Men and women alike hold massive lamb bones in their hands; they laugh and talk while loudly chewing meat and sucking out the marrow from the bones.

The guy in the baseball cap runs over to his jeep, hops in, and maneuvers it up next to the tables. He turns the stereo on full blast: the local radio station has given Dalong a birthday shout out and is playing a cheesy Mandarin-pop love song. The assembled crowd, swigging beers and sucking on meat, cheers and hoots.

The girls finish their meat and assemble a massive birthday cake out of four or five smaller cakes. The crazy policeman has shown up by this point, and he lights the candles. Though Dalong doesn't speak any English, we partygoers sing a pidgin "Happy Birthday." As soon as Dalong blows the candles out, the policeman scoops up a handful of cake and smears it all over Dalong's face.

Within moments, the whole affair has escalated into a full-scale cake fight. Men are smearing cake all over women.

Women are smashing handfuls of cake into their faces. The smell of the thick lamb-smoke, the roar of the laughter of a group of revelers coated in cake: it's an insane scene, and the crowd who are gathered inside the restaurant to watch the World Cup poke their heads out of the windows, staring at the party with a mix of wariness and jealousy.

Though there doesn't seem to be any kind of official at the party to rein in the behavior, a truce is called, somehow, and small groups of people take turns at the bathrooms to wash the cake off their faces and out of their hair. After everyone's face and clothes are free of frosting, it's time to *really* start drinking.

Chinese people—farmers and hipsters alike—are terrifically fond of their drinking games, which usually require an amount of imbibing that varies in dose from what would seem beyond the range of normal human possibility to lethal. (Literally: a case that made the headlines a few years ago involved a low-level government functionary who attended too many official banquets and drank himself to death.) These games usually involve a great amount of luck and a negligible amount of skill; every round entails the loser finishing his glass of beer or cup of rice wine or whatever. The goal is simple: get as smashed as possible.

And here, the games have begun. Eighteen people gather, standing, around the table, which by now is covered with an array of cake-smeared forks, empty skewers, and lamb bones in varying stages of existence.

The birthday boy rolls three dice on a clean plate. Eleven.

The person on his right becomes number one; the second person to his right is number two. Dalong points to each person, counter-clockwise around the circle, until he reaches the eleventh. Unlucky number eleven—the crazy policeman—knows he's lost, picks up the bottle of beer, and drains it in one go, with the crowd whooping and cheering with each swallow. The game goes on for a while, and everyone gets progressively more plastered.

Soon the restaurant's supply of cold beer has been exhausted, and we move on to Cabernet Sauvignon. After that, we move on to Johnnie Walker Blue Label, which costs 2,300 RMB ($290) a bottle. The Blue Label is smooth and oaky; it seems a waste to chug it, but no one's complaining. Dalong has gained major status points by buying such expensive booze. The assembled group finishes three bottles within an hour.

At this point, of course, everyone's hammered. The guy from the IT company staggers off to vomit in the bushes. The nightclub owner is passed out on a couch inside the restaurant. Everyone else still stands around the table, drinking slowly and toasting Dalong.

Dalong raises his glass in the air, and says, "Since I left home, I've never had such a fun birthday party with so many people. Thank you all for coming and for making this such a special day for me." He's twenty-nine, but the weight of his position is heavy, and he looks ten years older.

Everyone cheers. The crazy policeman grabs the carving knife and stands up on a chair whooping into the sky, like some demented wolf.

Suddenly we hear a massive crash. Across the street, a small minivan—the Chinese call them *mianbaoche,* or bread cars, because they are shaped like loaves of bread—has flipped over. A couple of the partygoers race over to stare at what's happened. The policeman just laughs and keeps whooping and waving the knife around.

A group of taxi drivers rolls the minivan upright; the van is undamaged and the passengers are somehow all right, and they drive away into the night.

It's getting late. Though drinking and driving is illegal in China, and signs along major thoroughfares warn against its danger—one of the funniest has a picture of a bottle next to a picture of a car with a line through it—anyone with a modicum of social status who is caught can get away with only a minimal fine. Tonight's party guests, representing a range of wealth and success, shakily get in their cars one by one and drive away.

I'm about to hail a taxi, and I clap Dalong on the back, wishing him a successful year. The day before, he told me, in private, that he wants to try to go straight. He's losing his soul, bathing in all this dirty money. He wants to forget about the intimidation racket and make less cash as a purely legitimate businessman.

But it will take serious willpower. He's used to the money and the car and the clothes and the freedom all of these luxuries bring to his life. The smoothie shop isn't exactly bringing in the buckets of money that will allow him to live the lifestyle to which he has become accustomed.

And these days, in China, the already-blurry line defining legality just keeps getting harder to distinguish. The government claims it's going to crack down on corruption; meanwhile, family members of high government officials make millions as "consultants" in land deals. The police and the generals keep getting their kickbacks and everyone, it seems, is "in real estate," making a pile of money. Everyone, from the kid selling yogurt on the street to the governor of the province, is trying to get theirs because they don't know if or when the proverbial shit—a change in the political climate, or a serious crackdown on corruption—is going to hit the fan.

At Pizza Hut in China, if you order the salad bar, it's not an all-you-can-eat proposition; you only get one trip with one little bowl. And just as the Chinese urbanites at Pizza Hut spend inordinate amounts of time packing the most possible salad into that tiny ceramic bowl, so Dalong and his contemporaries are trying to make as much money as possible in as little time as possible.

"You know, this year I'm going to make some serious money," he muses, without saying how he's going to accomplish this goal in a legitimate fashion. He pauses to think for a second.

"Maybe then I'll go to America. My wife's been over there. She likes it."

Then he climbs into his Lexus SUV and drives away, very fast, obviously drunk—just like a gangster.

3

The Chickens

ON A GOOD night, Xiao Li has sex with ten men in six hours. Each of her customers pays 200 yuan ($25) for a half hour of pleasure in the dark back room of a hair salon. Blowjobs, anal sex, sex without a condom: these are all options available for an extra charge. There is a menu to choose from, much like ordering a pizza.

Xiao Li has been a prostitute for a little more than three years; she says she cannot be sure how many men she has slept with in that period. Their faces blur together. As do, I assume, all the eyes, the lips, the fleshy stomachs, the aroused, uncircumcised penises. When I ask her to estimate, she wrinkles her brow: "Maybe 5,000? Maybe more?" I think of the old adage that when a doctor asks how much you drink, he doubles it to find out the truth.

Xiao Li is not a bad-looking girl, but she's not particularly attractive, either. Her eyes are spaced a little too far apart and her nose is bulbous and a little off-center. But she's got a nice smile, and she's bubbly and effusive. When I ask how old she is, she makes me guess. She looks about thirty.

"Twenty-two?" I venture, trying to stay on the safe side.

She snorts and curls her lips into an exaggerated scowl of displeasure. "*Wo shi ba liu nian de!*" she snorts. She was born in 1986. She is twenty years old.

"Are there girls younger than you here?" I ask, gesturing at the long row of identical blue-and-white striped barber poles that appear on both sides of the street, bored-looking girls lounging in plastic chairs in front of each pole. "Of course," she says. "*Shiwu sui, shiliu sui, dou you*, fifteen-year-olds, sixteen-year-olds, we have everything."

We're sitting in the lobby of a "beauty salon," a small, dimly lit room with a barber's chair and several shabby couches. In the back of the shop are the private rooms where Xiao Li plies her trade. The customers pay the madam of the place, a dried-out looking woman in her forties with sharp, intelligent eyes, and Xiao Li gets half the proceeds, after deduction for room and board—all the prostitutes live in the shop and eat communal meals from a small kitchen in the apartment upstairs. We are on a narrow little road that serves as one of Qingdao's beauty salon and barbershop districts by day, red-light districts by night; both sides of the street are lined with identical places. During the day, men come here to get haircuts and scalp massages; at night, they come for after-dinner quickies.

A young Chinese friend, Wang Gang, used to own a small CD and DVD shop in this part of town. Because he spent twelve or more hours a day in his store, he got to know a lot of the working girls, who would stop by his place to buy some music and movies. While most of the girls he knew had since moved on, he agreed to take me down to the red-light district, or as he called it, "*jinucheng*": "Whore City." In Chinese, the words "whore" and "chicken" are both pronounced *ji*, and the latter has become a slang term to refer to the former.

(And has generated bad puns, for example: A: "What do you want for dinner tonight?" B: "I don't know, how about we eat a couple chickens?" Hearty laughter ensues.)

On the way here, Wang Gang led me through a nearby pedestrian mall, a well-lit plaza full of urban high school students gossiping, shopping, and toying with their mobile phones as the smoke and smell of barbecued meat from street stands hung thick in the air.

As we made the turn onto the street where Xiao Li works, two red-faced businessmen, one's arm around the other, pointed at me and snickered "*Laowai*"—"foreigner"—before they scampered into a brothel across the street.

When I arrived at Xiao Li's place, the other girls twittered and whispered to themselves, but Xiao Li came up and sat next to me with a bemused half-smile on her face. We went through the standard conversational formalities: she complimented me on my Chinese, then I disagreed with her, saying that I speak very poorly. She complimented me on my Chinese again ("Really! You speak very well!") and I demurred ("No, it's nothing special.")

I explained that I was not a customer but an American writing a book about China, and asked her if she wouldn't mind speaking with me if I paid her for her time. She agreed; we sat in the lobby and chatted for about twenty minutes.

Then, I paid her 200 yuan and asked if she was available to meet me somewhere the next day to have a more in-depth conversation. Xiao Li agreed; she wrote down her cell phone number, and we made an appointment to meet at a nearby café in the old part of town.

□   □   □

THE NEXT AFTERNOON, I waited for half an hour, then an hour, and still Xiao Li didn't show up. I called the cell phone number she'd given me and heard the recorded bleat of the operator: "*Ni bo de haoma shi kong hao,*" and then, in shaky English, "The number you are calling does not exist."

That night, I went back to the brothel. I asked the other girls if Xiao Li was around; they told me she was inside with a customer, and so I left, walking through the narrow streets that make up the maze of Qingdao's old city, stopping on the way home for a bottle of beer and a plate of clams at a little stall in the night market.

□   □   □

A FEW DAYS later, some friends and I went out to an extravagant Sichuanese hot-pot dinner. These affairs are common in China—a group of friends or family sit around a large round table. In the center of the table is a large cauldron filled with stock. The ingredients that make up this soup vary from region to region: northern hot-pot comes with a mild chicken stock, while Sichuanese hot-pot comes pre-loaded with animal fat, enormous red chili peppers, and small round *huajiao*, a peppercorn that causes numbness in the mouth and tongue. Together, the chilies and *huajiao* form a famous flavor combination known as "*mala.*" First you feel the slow burn of the peppers, then the aching numbness of the *huajiao*. Then you start sweating and reach for your beer.

There's a gas burner built into the table, under the pot; the waiter turns on the gas and places plates of raw vegetables and meat on the table. After the pot has started to boil, you cook the food yourself, slowly, chatting with friends and drinking beer to quench the burning of the peppers. Our dinner that night lasted several hours, as hot-pot dinners usually do. Afterwards, our bellies were stuffed and in spite of our best efforts, still burning. In order to cool off and sweat out some of the peppers that were wreaking havoc on our collective digestive systems, we decided to visit a bathhouse.

Bathhouses, or saunas (*sa na* in Chinese) are a staple of Chinese cities. They are tremendously popular, for good reason; the *sa na* affords the average Chinese the experience of luxury for a few hours at an affordable price. In the first few apartments I had in China, we had solar-powered hot water. If the sun didn't shine, I couldn't take a hot shower. After a few cloudy days, my roommates and I would invariably hit the sauna. While all saunas have different features, the "sauna experience" is basically always the same.

First, you check in at a front desk, and stash your street clothes in a small, assigned locker. The locker room is staffed by a squadron of young fresh-faced men wearing poor quality suits (black pants, black vest, dress shirt, clip-on tie) who help you take off your clothes and hand you towels, plastic sandals, and a small plastic wristband with a number on it.

After you've stripped naked, you take a shower. The showers in most Chinese homes are low-pressure kind of affairs that involve a lot of nozzle manipulation in order to wash yourself as thoroughly as possible. The showers in the sauna are right-on: huge, powerful beasts that blast you thoroughly with hot water—much like a shower you'd find in a Western gym. After you've taken a shower and washed your hair, there are a number of Jacuzzi-style bathing pools in which to relax. Naked men lounge everywhere: some saunas have a separate section for women, but many are male-only. Often, drunk strangers, seeing a foreigner in their midst, approach me and make frank comments about the size of my penis.

These pools vary depending on the price of the sauna. Basic saunas have only two pools: hot and cold. More deluxe bath houses feature pools that are supposedly spiked with various kinds of healing herbs or skin enhancement products, et cetera. At one sauna I experienced a few years prior, they had a dizzying array of pools, the water in each dyed a different color: red, green, pink, purple, etc. The sauna also had a glass ceiling and the effect was so psychedelic that I wondered if the place's owner had been doing a lot of ketamine before meeting with his architect.

After you've relaxed in the pools, the young attendants, who have been standing silently watching you bathe and chat the whole time, come at you with another round of towels and you can sweat out all the toxins in your body in a series of saunas and steam rooms.

After a few minutes of exhausting your body of its water supply, it's time for another shower. Then, you move on to an anteroom where another set of attendants hand you a pair of paper-thin underwear, a baggy cotton pajama top and bottoms that are vaguely reminiscent of OR scrubs, and a small glass of cold water.

Then, once you're all dressed in your pajama getup, it's time to really *xiuxi*—relax. There's another room for this purpose, usually located on the second floor of the building. After padding up the stairs in your flip-flops, you enter a large hall with about one hundred enormous overstuffed chairs—rather like La-Z-Boys on steroids—arranged in rows. You find a vacant chair, and male and female attendants dressed in the same cheap but formal getup bring you whatever you might want: blankets, pillows, a choice of cigarettes in a mahogany box, bottles of mineral water, noodles, beer, sweet porridge.

For some patrons of the *sa na*, this is where the evening ends. Usually I sack out in the chair for a couple hours and let the rhythmic snoring of the other customers lull me to a gentle sleep, then wake up and groggily take one final warm, wonderful shower, and make my very relaxed way home.

For other patrons, however, after some time in the *xiuxi* room, the evening has just begun. In the back of the *sa na* there is a warren of little rooms with beds, couches, and televisions. These rooms can be rented by the hour or by the whole night: while the customer pays for the room, he receives a prostitute, *gratis*.

□　□　□

I RENTED ONE of the rooms, and was presented with the choice of ten girls. I explained to the staffer on duty that I only wanted to talk, and not to have sex, or *zuo ai*: literally, "to do love."

After he passed on my message to the girls, most giggled

and shook their heads. They didn't want anything to do with me, seeing as I was a foreigner who spoke Chinese—always a suspect combination. They formed little groups and giggled and a couple of them retreated back into the dark warrens of the *sa na*. One girl, chubby and younger than the rest, with a gleam in her eyes, stepped forward and agreed to talk with me. She introduced herself as Xiao Wang.

Xiao Wang has been working in the *sa na* for a year and a half, in a small room along a dimly lit corridor that smells of scented lotion and mildew. She has a bright and vivacious personality, and it seems she's well liked by co-workers and customers alike. When we met, she was wearing a shiny black corset-like piece of lingerie under a cheap-looking silk robe. She sat on the bed beside me.

"You really don't want to have sex?" she asked.

I nodded, and explained that I was an American writer working on a book about China and all I wanted was to talk to her. I asked when her next day off was, and she replied that she only gets one afternoon off a week and it was two days later. We agreed on a meeting place—Starbucks Coffee in the center of town—and I gave her my cell phone number.

"I'll buy you a coffee and see you then," I promised, and left the room to return to the comfort of my recliner and bowl of sweet porridge in the *xiuxi* room. On the way out I heard the fresh-faced sauna boys tittering—I had only been with Xiao Wang for five minutes. I guess they thought either I was a lightweight or I had lost my nerve.

□ □ □

TWO DAYS LATER, I sat in the summer sun at the Starbucks in the center of Qingdao. The Starbucks sits in front of a luxury shopping mall and a Porsche dealership. There are tables outside with nice umbrellas; when a breeze blows through the plaza, it's quite pleasant, and the luxurious atmosphere seems completely and strangely disconnected from the dirty beauty parlor or the dank *sa na*.

Starbucks set up shop in Beijing and Shanghai years ago, but in Qingdao it's still a novelty, and the place is always packed with young people trying to be fashionable, with the upper class spending their money on frozen drinks, and foreigners getting their coffee fix.

Xiao Wang strolled up to my table and sat down nervously. She had obviously made the effort to dress up—wearing a poorly cut metallic blouse under a white sweater, a short skirt, and high heels—and I smiled in spite of myself. I thanked her for agreeing to meet me.

"You're the first foreigner I've ever talked to. It's strange!" she giggled.

I asked her what she wanted to drink; she didn't know, so I bought myself a coffee and Xiao Wang a Frappuccino and I asked her to tell me about how she ended up in the *sa na*.

□ □ □

"I AM FROM Heilongjiang," Xiao Wang began, referring to the most northeastern province of China, which sits across the

Black River from Russia. Heilongjiang—literally, "black dragon river"—is famous for its arctic winters.

Like Xiao Li, she was born in 1986, in a small city called Jixi, which she says is "dirty and smelly but the people there are good people."

Her father was an alcoholic. At first he couldn't hold down a steady job, and then he lost interest in holding down a steady job and just sat at home all day drinking rice wine. Her mother worked in a factory.

I asked what kind of factory, and she said she didn't know.

Her father used to beat her mother, and they divorced when she was fifteen. After the split, her mother moved in with another man on the other side of town and she stayed in her father's cramped apartment, trying her best to clean up after him while attending middle school

"After I finished middle school," she explained, "I didn't want to study. I didn't want to do anything."

She moved in with the older brother of one of her classmates. He was the first man she slept with, and they spent a reasonably happy couple months together, but eventually he spent all his money on drinking and gambling. She decided to leave and move back in with her father.

In 2004, her "uncle"—a relative of her father's—was over at the house and suggested that she come to work at his massage parlor in Harbin, the provincial capital.

Her father thought it sounded like a good idea. She could send some money home.

Xiao Wang didn't know anything about massage parlors, but, she says, "all I wanted to do was leave Jixi." Her father called her mother, who agreed to let her go as long as she was in the care of her uncle.

The next morning, she packed all of her clothes into a small bag. Her uncle came to pick her up, and they took the bus to Harbin.

□   □   □

THEY DIDN'T GET off in Harbin. "My uncle didn't have a massage parlor," she tells me, with a trace of mournfulness. "We took the train to Qingdao, and he took me to a sauna that was owned by a friend of his."

After arriving at the sauna, Xiao Wang worked as a waitress for a little more than a year, but she was making only 300 yuan a month. Over time, she got to know what she calls "the masseuses," the girls selling their bodies in the back rooms. They were making a lot more money and it seemed like less work. She decided to try it.

She got the other girls to teach her how to give "massages." After a month or so, she thought she had the hang of it and told the boss that she was ready for her first customer.

But he didn't want his friend's niece working as a prostitute in his sauna. So, he did the logical thing: sent (or, more likely sold) her to *his* friend's sauna, where "ethical" rules regarding friends and family did not apply.

Xiao Wang's predicament was a common one. Many girls from the countryside and smaller cities in China are lured by relatives or friends of the family to the bigger cities with the promise of legitimate employment. When the girl arrives in the city, the job turns out to be not in a clothing store or a restaurant but in a brothel or sauna.

Her first night at the new sauna—the place where I met her—was the first time she was with a customer. That night, Xiao Wang says, "all she did was *da feiji*"—literally, "beat the airplane," the common Chinese euphemism for masturbation.

For a while, she continued the massage and masturbation routine. Eventually, though, almost without realizing it, she started to have sex with her customers.

"What was it like, the first time you did it with a customer?" I asked her.

She furrowed her brow. You could almost see the gears turning in her head. After a moment, she gave a little half-shrug and looked at me.

"I can't remember," she admitted.

□ □ □

WHILE PROSTITUTION IS technically illegal in China, it is also preposterously pervasive. Some estimate that one of every ten women in China earns her living as a prostitute, as she has few other equally lucrative options—that's nearly 70 million people.

First-time visitors to the country are often introduced to this reality in alarming fashion. No matter where you are in China, within minutes of checking into a Chinese-run hotel, male guests will invariably receive a phone call in their room; on the other end is a husky female voice, asking the guest if he's interested in *anmo* or "massage." I know plenty of naïve foreigners, tired from a long plane flight, who have accepted the offer and been surprised when a timid woman wearing garter belts knocks on their hotel room door.

Prostitution has become such a massive industry that Chinese police have adopted a seven-tier system with which to classify prostitution-related activity.

"Second wives"—more like the Western conception of a mistress. These women are kept by men with money and provided with an apartment and an allowance.

"Packaged wives"—like the Western conception of an "escort." These women accompany men when they're in unfamiliar cities, spend the night at their hotels, and receive payment.

"Girls of the three accompaniments"—these girls sit at tables or in private rooms with customers in karaoke parlors, nightclubs, etc. The club receives money from the customers for this service, and the girls take a cut; also, the club will give the "girls of the three accompaniments" a percentage of the proceeds from all the drinks they can get the men to buy for them. After several hours drinking and flirting with the customers, the girls negotiate a price for sexual intercourse which takes place either on-premises in rooms the club has constructed for this service or off-premises in a nearby hotel.

"Doorbell girls"—as mentioned above, the ones who work in hotels and solicit sex or all-night companionship. Many of these women work out of the hotel spas; others are freelance.

"Hair Salon little sisters"—like Xiao Wang and Xiao Li, they operate under the ostensible premise of providing health and beauty treatments in hair salons, saunas, etc.

"Street girls"—the name says it all.

"Down at the work shack"—women who ply their trade to the transient population of migrant workers from the countryside.

□   □   □

I ASK XIAO Wang if she knows about this hierarchy. She says no.

□   □   □

"I SLEEP WITH three or four men a day," Xiao Wang says, "for a few days, and then I'll rest for a day."

I ask her if she uses condoms. "Every time," she says, noting that a lot of customers offer to pay extra but she turns them down.

"How do you feel about the risk of AIDS?" I ask her.

"I have no feeling about it," she says casually, and I hope she was telling the truth about always using a condom.[2]

□   □   □

XIAO WANG WANTS to make one thing perfectly clear: she was not forced into prostitution. No one made her do it. She began selling her body because she realized that she could make a significant amount of money doing it, and she doesn't regret what she's done. Well, maybe a little.

"I took a wrong turn," she muses, "but really I just want to make money. If I keep doing this for one more year, I'll have

---

2   See "The Rabbit" and "The Journalist" for a more thorough discussion of AIDS in China.

tens of thousands of yuan, and then I can leave, maybe go open a store or something."

She finishes her Frappuccino and smiles at me. Our brief conversation is over. I thank her again for agreeing to talk to me, and promise that I will change her name in my article (not like it matters—"Wang" in Chinese is like "Smith" in America.) I tell her that maybe someday I'll run into her in that store she's going to open; we shake hands goodbye, and I watch her walk off, back to the sauna to get ready for a long night of work, remarkably steady in her high heels.

4

The Best and the Brightest

IT'S A SCORCHING, hazy August afternoon in Beijing. I'm standing just inside the enormous black west gate of Qinghua University, still coughing from the huge cloud of dust and dirt that emerged from yet another construction site and blindsided my lungs while I was walking up here.

I buy a bottle of water from a nice old woman who has set up her Styrofoam cooler of cold beverages just inside the gate. On the other side of the gate, and in front of the campus's other gates, blue-uniformed security guards stand watch in order to keep out unsavory characters–migrant workers, transients–anyone they deem unfit to stroll Qinghua's massive, luxurious campus.

Qinghua and its next-door neighbor, Beijing University, are the two best institutions of higher learning in China. They are China's Oxford and Cambridge, its Harvard and Yale. Additionally, Qinghua is often compared to MIT because of its top-flight science and engineering programs.

Nestled in the Haidian District, between the third and fourth ring roads in the northwest quadrant of Beijing, the two universities boast sprawling, gorgeous campuses. At Qinghua, numerous gardens bursting with flowers and a serene lake surrounded by water lilies create an escape from the bustling city outside its gates.

While there are a few buildings that were built in a traditional Chinese style, most of the university facilities are newer, Western-style structures. Just outside the campus gates, an enormous, futuristic steel-and-glass compound known as the Qinghua Science Park has just been completed. It's a huge monolith, housing the Chinese satellite offices for Western tech companies like Google and Sun Microsystems. There is even a Starbucks on the ground floor.

This area of the city once housed the imperial gardens of the Qing Dynasty; the magnificent Summer Palace, built by Emperor Qianlong in 1750, sits just a few kilometers north on the shores of the Kunming Lake. The Summer Palace, now a UNESCO World Heritage Site and a tourist attraction, was designed, according to the ancient Chinese concept of "harmony of man and nature," as a retreat for the emperor.

Qinghua was founded in 1911 as a preparatory school for students who were planning to go abroad to American universities. Its teachers were plucked from American high schools and colleges. After students had adequately honed their academic skills at Qinghua, they were shipped off to American universities, where they matriculated as juniors.

The gardens and lakes of the Qinghua campus, dotted here and there with clusters of utilitarian, modernized academic buildings, seem to be a modern archetype for this kind of "harmony between man and nature." Just as the emperor and his government inhabited the Summer Palace, so the twenty-thousand-odd Qinghua students walk around their campus with an unmistakable sense of clarity and purpose. Since their primary school days in whatever part of China they happened to come from, these students have been the best and the brightest.

China's one-child policy has spawned a nation where almost every child is an only child. One result? A whole lot of spoiled brats. The Chinese call these pampered tykes "*xiao huangdi*," or "little emperors." At Qinghua, this phrase takes on another meaning: these students are not necessarily spoiled, but they most certainly are "little emperors." They are the future leaders of China. Qinghua graduates make up almost half of the highest echelon of the Chinese Communist Party, the Politburo standing committee, including China's top leader, Hu Jintao.

□   □   □

I SPENT A SEMESTER as a foreign exchange student here in 2000, and I hadn't been back since. In the interim, the entire area has been transformed. New buildings are being constructed; old Communist-era buildings are being razed. The government has been on a serious mission to create a world-class educational-slash-technological zone before the 2008 Olympics.

So I'm standing at the gate, sipping my water, waiting for Mary Jones, a Qinghua graduate student in philosophy. I asked a colleague at Qinghua if he knew of any interesting and talkative students; he recommended Mary, and I called her on her cell phone. She said that she could meet up any time, except for evenings, when she has swimming lessons.

After fifteen minutes had passed, a young woman in her twenties came tottering up to me in a white sundress and high heels. She smiled and introduced herself hesitantly; we left the Qinghua campus and searched for someplace where we could sit and talk.

Qinghua and Beijing Universities are not the only two institutions of higher learning in the Haidian District. There are many others, such as the oddly named Beijing Normal University (a training ground for future teachers) and People's University; a large population of students—many of them foreign students—has created a feel to the whole area that is not unlike a shabbier version of a college town somewhere in America. There are cafes, chain restaurants, shopping malls, gigantic computer superstores, and bars that allow the penny-pinching collegian to get very wasted for very little money.

There are also several examples of a certain kind of Taiwanese coffee shop that's popular with younger Chinese people with a little cash in their pocket. These chains— Ming Tien Coffee Language and UBC Coffee are the two big ones—have hundreds of locations all across China. Theoretically, these places are supposed to be Western-style restaurants; the waiters and waitresses wear poorly-fitting dress-shirt-and-pants combos with clip-on ties, and the tables are set with fancy tablecloths and doilies. Often, someone will be playing the piano, albeit rather poorly.

There are artificial waterfalls everywhere. Customers snack on sweet popcorn and fruit plates. These coffee shops are not really Western restaurants, but the Chinese idea of what a Western restaurant might look like. They occupy some kind of bizarre yet fascinating cultural middle ground, the Eastern idea of the Western reality. And they offer very comfortable chairs.

Mary and I went into one of these coffee shops and sat across from each other in two enormous, cushiony chairs. She seemed very shy and unwilling to speak her mind. I asked her a simple question: "Do you like Qinghua?" She nodded and shrugged. "Yes, I like it," she said, nervously tapping on the table with her fingers.

Detecting her discomfort, I told her, "You know, I can use a fake name when I write about you."

She thought about it for a second and took a sip of her Lipton's milk tea.

She smiled and looked me in the eye. "Okay," she said, with a little nod, as if indicating: Okay. I'm ready to open up.

□ □ □

MARY WAS BORN in 1982 in a little town near Wuhan, an industrial city of some nine million on the Yangtze River.[3]

Her father had been a soldier in the People's Liberation Army; after leaving the army, he became a minor Party official, and went to work at a desk job in a government office. Her mother worked as a secretary in a state-owned

---

3   Note: more information about Wuhan can be found in the chapter "The Punks."

telecommunications company. Since both of her parents were affiliated with government work units, Mary's childhood was always comfortable. Certainly not ritzy—they lived a simple life, with a small apartment in a state-owned housing complex—but there was meat on the table every day, new clothes in Mary's closet, and the occasional gift from her parents.

"My father wasn't like the kind of people that are in the Communist Party now," Mary says. "He really believed it: that the CCP was glorious and that Chairman Mao was a hero, or a god." The family apartment was decorated with photographs of Mao and icons bearing the red-star logo of the Chinese Communist Party. "Since I can remember," Mary recalls, "I remember being taught that Chairman Mao was the greatest man."

She excelled at school from a very young age, winning an array of academic prizes and placing first in the Wuhan Math and Science Olympics. She aced her *gaokao* examination and ended up as a student of the humanities at Wuhan University.

"I wanted to go to Beijing at that time," she remembers, "but I wasn't ready."

After four uneventful years at Wuhan University, where, she says, "all I did was study," she graduated towards the top of her class. One of her teachers got in touch with the Graduate School of Philosophy at Qinghua, and she moved up to Beijing and enrolled in a master's program, with the goal of being a teacher.[4]

---

4   See "The Screenwriter" for more information about the *gaokao* examination.

□ □ □

SHE ASKS IF her childhood sounds boring; I respond that no one's life is boring because everyone's life is different.

Mary doesn't laugh easily. Like other very serious people, when she thinks something's funny, her eyes will get a little wider and she'll smile almost too widely for less than a second.

She does this half-smile-thing, and then a very intense look passes over her face. "I can remember when my entire life changed." It was when she got accepted to a study-abroad program in America. Mary and another Qinghua student were selected to spend a year at a small but respected liberal arts university in the Midwest, where they would take classes in religion and philosophy.

"I had seen America in movies," Mary remembers. "I thought, it's that way. Many Chinese people are like this. They see the movie, they think it's really how it is." Before she left for overseas, she went back to Wuhan for a visit with her parents. They were worried about Mary, and reminded her to be safe about a million times, but they were also proud of their daughter. She would be the first one in the family to take a trip outside of China. Before she left, her father pressed a stack of money into her hand and told her to take care of herself and to call when she got there if it wasn't too expensive.

Mary thought that in America she would be living in an alien and crime-ridden city. But when her plane touched down in Detroit and the school administrators drove her and other Chinese students outside of the city and into the heartland, she found something entirely different. "It was so peaceful," she says. "I couldn't believe it. It was the opposite of what I expected."

And so Mary Jones found herself in one of those little bucolic towns that populate the middle of America. She was staying in the biggest house she'd ever seen, with a couple who were both professors at the college. "They were Italian," she says. "Italians are good people."

It was complete culture shock: when most Chinese immigrants touch down in America, they land in coastal Chinatowns, where the ebb and flow of life is somewhat like China itself. Signs display Chinese characters, and other immigrants are speaking a mishmash of dialects. There are people everywhere, bustling to and fro, working, buying, selling. In this small college town in the boondocks of Michigan, there wasn't anyone out on the street most of the time.

It took Mary a short time to adjust to American life. For one, the food was different: "I got so fat," she scowls, tugging on her dress. "I'm still fat now. It was grilled cheese and pizza every day. The food in America is not fresh. That's why everyone there is so fat."

And of course, she missed her family, and she missed home and felt kind of lost. In the West, we're obsessed with the idea of the individual: in China, however, the sense of self is interwoven with the sense of one's place in a community, and in the Chinese nation.

But after she had become more comfortable with the cuisine, and with speaking English all day long, and with the way people looked at her (there weren't many Asians in that Midwestern college town) she began truly to realize American culture, to understand the essence of what living in a Western, Judeo-Christian society is all about.

Mary sat in the classroom with American students while the professor asked questions and stoked intelligent conversation. Mary sat down for dinner with her host parents. Mary went out for drinks with her classmates. Most of all, Mary watched the way people interacted with each other in everyday life.

And slowly, but inevitably, at the age of twenty-three, she began to discover herself.

◻ ◻ ◻

MARY JONES LOOKS and acts very much like an average, Chinese female college student. Despite her statements to the contrary, she's of slender build. While she makes an effort to be stylish, it's not entirely successful. Her dress doesn't quite fit right and her high heels are a little bit too high and don't really match with the rest of her outfit. Her bearing is reserved and even a little demure; she seems like a nice and mostly harmless person. She certainly doesn't seem like she would be bursting full of hatred and, if prodded, would go on a vitriolic rant detailing said hatred. Of course, that's exactly what she did.

When I previously discussed Mary's "self-discovery," I mean the stage of personal development that happens to most people where they begin to question certain assumptions that had previously defined a) the way they think about the world and, therefore, b) the way they think about themselves.

Mary's a very intelligent person; she's well-spoken and has

a quick critical mind. As far as she's concerned, though, up until she was twenty-three, "I knew nothing."

"China," she says, "is a terrible place in very many ways. People here are bad. They are cruel."

I ask her for an example, and the rant begins.

"There are no trees in the parks; we don't care about the environment. All we want to do with animals is eat them. Eating live rats? Eating the brains of live monkeys? Eating cats? My cat ran away. Was it eaten?"

While Chinese people do eat animals when they're still alive, it's a cultural tradition, and no longer a very widespread practice. I remind Mary of this, and she concedes her loathing of stereotypes, but then does that quick half-smile, again.

"I don't care," she says. "I'm angry!"

"In America," she says, "people give to charity. They care about people other than themselves. In China, that doesn't happen."

"In America," she says, "if you buy something at a store and something's wrong with it, you can return it. In China? That would never happen!"

"In America," she says, "people are good to each other! In China?" She snorts. By now, she's so worked up that she's shaking.

"Wow," I told her, "you really are angry!"

Her observations highlight an important point: in contemporary China, unlike the West, there is no shared moral code. Of course, every society has its share of selfish people who don't give two figs about others. However, the Confucian ideal of putting family first has combined with the uncertainty created by a tumultuous history to form a culture where the average citizen cares only about himself and his family. Hence, the societal manifestation of no universal health care, no subsidized housing for the poor, no recourse for labor issues, and precious few student scholarships.

In America, Mary found that most people were concerned about the welfare of society as a whole. At first, this humanism was disarming. And then, as she sat in her private bedroom in the Midwest (luxurious by Chinese standards: even graduate students sleep three or four to a room) she began to think very carefully about the differences between America and China.

□ □ □

BUT MARY SAVES her harshest criticism for the Chinese educational system. Before she was exposed to a Western academic situation, she figured that the Chinese way to learn things was the only way to learn things.

In China, she says, the teacher will say something, or write something on the chalkboard, and everyone will be forced to memorize it. If any academic discipline would invite teacher-student and student-student dialectic, it would be Mary's field of study, philosophy; however, in the Chinese classroom, there really is no place for discussion. Instead of really thinking about Heidegger or Nietzsche, the students just read the text and learn the historical data and theoretical terms necessary to examine the work from an academic point of view.

"It's terrible," she says. "Chinese students, they know more facts"—she was surprised that many of her American classmates had an ignorance of basic geography—"but they really don't understand anything."

The Chinese classroom environment, Mary says, has had an enormous negative impact on the country's academic culture. "Almost every student cheats," she says. "Graduate students! Ph.D. students!" I asked whether cheating was endemic even at Qinghua, the best school in the country. "Of course!" she responded.

When I asked her to give me some examples, she told me that all graduate students had to write academic papers. Because critical thinking isn't encouraged or even valued in the classroom, when it comes time to write a paper, students have no original ideas to discuss in writing. So they find essays written by Westerners in English and then pass off others' ideas—and sometimes even others' prose, translated into Chinese—as their own. Of course, cheating occurs in every country. But in China, since no school wants its name tainted by a plagiarism scandal, professors tend to look the other way.

And even when liberal arts students at China's best universities write their own essays, the freshness of the ideas often seems like something that would be found in an American high school paper. (You'll see this, for example, in the "journals of the humanities" that are released annually or quarterly by the most prestigious Chinese universities, such as Shanghai's Fudan U.)

Even more flagrant is the way that this potentially-plagiarized, often-sophomoric work gets published in academic journals. According to Mary—and many other critics of the Chinese educational establishment—most of these journals accept cash bribes in exchange for publication.

According to several recent, anonymous studies of Chinese graduate students, *more than half* of them admitted to plagiarism. Even at well-known institutions like Qinghua, the corruption of the academic environment has undermined the government's quest for prestige. Of course, officials at many Chinese universities and independent coalitions of scholars hold many conferences where they remind each other to be vigilant in exposing academic corruption. However, these same administrators and educators have no real interest, or incentive, at least, for rooting out this kind of academic fraud.

Identification and the subsequent punishment of cheaters requires a lot of time and resources. More importantly, if school officials unearthed evidence proving widespread corruption, it would reflect very badly on the school itself. This would be a catastrophe for two reasons. First, the school's government funding would probably be cut, and its top officials would be censured. Second, and perhaps more importantly, appearances are of paramount importance. In the West, perhaps, the school officials responsible for uncovering the scandal would be honored; in China, they would be ostracized by their colleagues for having brought shame upon the institution.

There are, of course, a few exceptions, among them Fang Shimin, a biochemist who resides in both Beijing and California and maintains a well-known blog[5] under the pen name of Fang Zhouzi, which exposes cases of Chinese academic fraud.

In a country where censorship constantly makes such resources "disappear," Fang's blog remains online, thus far, only perhaps because he makes a practice of targeting academics who don't have connections to high-echelon members of the Party; no one of importance has taken offense . . . yet.

---

5 http://blog.sina.com.cxm/fangzhouzi

"No one cheats in America, right?" Mary says.

I inform her that of course people cheat in America, and that people cheat everywhere.

"Everyone cheats in China," she says.

For a second, I wonder whether her meaning is that she, too, cheats. I don't ask.

□   □   □

MARY AND I left the coffee shop and strolled around the Wudaokou university district that surrounds Qinghua. We wandered along the sidewalk as the night came on. Every building seemed to be either new or under construction.

I offered to take her out to dinner and asked what kind of food she wanted. She admitted that during her time in America she had fallen in love with Italian food, using curious logic: "It's just like Northern Chinese food. They're both based on noodles."

She said that there was a new Italian place that had opened up nearby, and I suggested that we give it a try. We walked past little rows of cafés and shops. It was early evening, and the streets were jammed with students, holding hands, gossiping, hollering into their mobile phones.

Soon Mary and I came to an enormous, Western-style shopping mall that looked brand-new, as if it had opened the day before. The Italian restaurant, a brightly lit, fast-food style café, was on the second floor. Although we could see the restaurant from the wide-open plaza in front of the mall, when we entered the mall we couldn't find the restaurant anywhere. We left the mall and tried another entrance: no luck.

Mary asked a security guard for directions and we finally

found the correct manner of approach: a stairway hidden by a pair of enormous metal doors. It was a typical Chinese design flaw: a huge, beautiful building with an impossible-to-find entrance. Or, if the entrance is in the front, as would seem logical, the elevator to the upstairs restaurant would invariably not be working, and diners would have to seek out the nearly hidden stairwell, anyway.

Quite matter-of-factly, she called the waiter over and ordered fettuccine with cream sauce and ham. (I ordered a "plain" pizza; when it arrived, it was covered with chunks of canned pineapple.)

We started to chat again. "It's quite cheap here," she said and I nodded in agreement. "These dishes would cost much more back in America."

The restaurant was full with a mix of Chinese and foreigners: a professorial father trying to feed pizza to his infant son. A pair of overweight, tarted-up British girls sharing a table with a pockmarked Chinese youth.

I asked Mary how she thought China was changing and what she thought about its future.

"Every year," she replied, "it gets more international . . . well, especially here in Beijing. There is more money, and more foreign products, more foreign shops . . . now, if you have money, you can buy whatever you want. For example, I buy my toothpaste from Europe."

"How about the people?" I ask. "The way people think?"

Mary's response is scattered: she talks about how Chinese people know more things now, but only in the cities, and most people still don't know anything, because there's no freedom of the press, and then she sighs.

"What if you had a friend from when you were young," she asks me, rhetorically, "and you spent a lot of time with this person. You're always together. And you're so close that you don't know that this friend has grown up into a bad person."

The whole time, she's been looking down at the table, and now she raises her glance to look me in the face.

"That's how I feel about China," she says.

□ □ □

MARY TWIRLS HER PASTA around her fork. I ask if she likes it. "It's okay," she responds. "Not as good as America."

She pauses.

"Most things in China aren't as good as they are in America."

"How about Chinese food?" I offer, and she laughs, uncomfortably, and takes a big bite of fettuccine, chewing quietly, in the Western manner, not slurping her noodles like the Chinese do.

"When I was growing up," she says, "I believed a lot of things. I believed what I was told. I was taught to hate Japanese people. Once I even threw eggs at them. I was taught to worship Chairman Mao. We thought of him like a god. And now, after I came back from America, I know, logically, all the things he did were wrong. He was an evil man, like Hitler. When I see a picture of him, now, I hate him. But I still have this other feeling. My heart still swells with pride. Even though I know it's wrong, I can't stop it."

5

The Slacker

LIU JIANFENG HAS impressive hair. Most of the time, he keeps it hidden under a knit cap, which he only takes off when it's time to comb it, wash himself, and go to sleep. When he takes the cap off, his hair cascades like a waterfall, straight down to his ass: it is jet-black, shiny, soft and smooth. He uses a special wooden comb that is supposed to offer health benefits to both the hair and the scalp.

In a few hours, he'll let a few good-looking female friends take turns brushing his mane, but for now, it's hidden under his trademark cap—today's is black. Jianfeng is perched in a little nook in the second story of Cafeteria, a café where he's part owner. His joint is not really a cafeteria; it's a ramshackle but very comfortable little two-story restaurant in an old house.

Binoculars are pressed to his eyes, and he's staring out the window, looking down at the street, checking out the women walking along People's Road in the small town of Dali, which is nestled in the mountains of idyllic Yunnan Province.

There are a lot of good-looking ladies in this town, and Jianfeng's staked out the prime chick-watching spot. Girls who are coming back from swimming in the lake or from buying food at the little market down the street all stroll up this street on their way back to the center of town, right past this window.

Jianfeng has a contented smile on his face, like a cat that's just eaten its last bite of canary. He's singing a popular Chinese love song to himself in a barely audible, sweet falsetto. From time to time, he adjusts the focus wheel on the binoculars or takes a break to smoke a Red River cigarette. It's a lazy day; the mountain air is crisp, and the sun feels warm against my skin. I'm idly cracking sunflower seeds in my teeth and spitting them onto an empty plate, watching Jianfeng watch the girls, and debating whether to take a nap.

His patience is remarkable; on more than one occasion, I've seen him sit in this little nook for hours, combing the crowd. He looks through his binoculars at migrant workers in worn clothing, at elderly locals dressed in the blue traditional clothes of the Bai people, and at middle school students skipping down the street in blue-and-white uniforms. These are all extraneous presences in Jianfeng's field of vision, but he is quick to pounce when pretty girls walk by, fiddling with his binoculars quickly and following them up People's Road through his magnified gaze.

Jianfeng favors wearing his Levi's so tight that they look like they were spray-painted onto his skin. To complement the jeans, he wears equally tight T-shirts that he silk-screens himself. The shirt he's wearing today proclaims, in loud capital letters, WAR IS OVER IF YOU HEMP IT in the red-green-and-yellow colors of the Rastafarians.

He's wearing black Converse All-Stars which "fell off the truck" on the way back from the factory in Guangzhou and so cost only forty-five yuan instead of the retail price of 300 yuan. Around his neck hangs a massive necklace made up of stones, old coins, shells, and other little trinkets people have given him: reminders of friends he's had and people he's loved. I'm sitting next to him, idly skimming a copy of *On the Road* in Chinese and doodling in my notebook.

He's also very tall and slim for a Chinese man. Unlike most Chinese, who eat with relish every species in the animal kingdom—the more exotic the better—Liu Jianfeng adheres to a strict vegetarian diet. He credits his svelte physique to his health regimen: no meat, lots of vegetables, and a significant daily dose of grain alcohol.

The cumulative effect of his stylish clothes and the ultra-confident way he carries himself combine to form a kind of radioactive sheen of coolness, a mystical aura of kind indifference and individuality that earns Jianfeng the admiration of both men and women.

But there is trouble in paradise: time is running out for Liu Jianfeng. You wouldn't know it by looking at him—his manner could be the dictionary definition of "relaxed"—but underneath the appealing pose he's feeling some serious pressure. February 2007 marks the start of the Year of the Pig. His parents are getting older—hell, *he's* getting older—and it's finally time to find a wife and have a child. According to the Chinese zodiac, babies born in the year of the pig are lucky, smart, and clever. It's an auspicious sign. It's a good year to sow his seed.

Jianfeng's a serious playboy. He has more girlfriends than

anyone else he knows. But he needs to find his soulmate, the one he can spend the rest of his life with, the one who won't nag him to change his ways, the one he loves as much as she loves him. He knows it can take a lifetime to find a soulmate, but he's confident. The one thing he's absolutely certain of is that this chick has to be *perfect*.

He's already been married—and divorced—once. He chose the wrong girl, made a huge mistake, and is extremely wary of repeating it. Jianfeng lights a cigarette and furrows his brow. Maybe today will be the day, he says, and then nods to himself and says it again, like a Buddhist mantra or something out of a self-help book.

He is thirty-six years old but looks ten years younger.

□   □   □

LIU JIANFENG WAS born and raised in Jinan, the capital of Shandong, a province which is known for the richness of its soil, the mildness of its climate, and the kindness of its people. Chinese are very fond of making generalizations about people based on where they are from. For example, people from Shantou, in Guangdong Province, are known as skillful businessmen, while people from Henan Province are thought to be cheaters and liars. People from Shandong are kind; in Chinese, "*haoren*," literally, "good people."

Though all blanket statements like this must not, of course, be taken literally, I've spent a lot of time in Shandong and, for some reason—possibly due to its proximity to the coast—the people *are* nice. Liu Jianfeng could be the archetypical Shandong *haoren*. I met him several years ago, sitting around a fire in a mutual friend's house; after our first conversation, I was struck by his genuine concern and compassion for other people. (This is a quality lacking in too many of his self-centered contemporaries.)

His was a relatively comfortable middle-class upbringing. His mother was a doctor and his father was in the army and a local Communist Party official. "You would think that my dad would have hit me, 'cause he was in the army," Jianfeng says, "but I only saw him once a week—the rest of the time he had to be in the military compound—and so he was pretty good to me. Only my mother hit me, when I was bad."

He flashes a Cheshire grin. "I was a bad kid. She hit me a lot."

As Jianfeng grew older, he grew restless. By the time he was nearing the end of high school, he began to think that Jinan was a backwater. A hick town. So on weekends and during school vacations, he took the train up to Beijing or down to the seaside town of Qingdao, sometimes with a friend and sometimes alone, hiding in the bathrooms to avoid paying for a ticket, chain-smoking cigarettes out the window.

In those pre-reform days, Jianfeng remembers, it was rare for high school kids to be able to bum around; the other passengers thought he must be the son of some high official or something and they left him alone. Back then, eighteen years ago, the train from Jinan to Beijing took nine hours and cost seven yuan. Today, the same trip takes four hours and costs seventy yuan.

Like any wannabe hipster kid hitting the big city for the first time, Jianfeng became immediately and severely infatuated with Beijing. Compared to Jinan, Beijing seemed huge, and in those pre-Tiananmen days, the city was a hotbed of (relatively) free intellectualism. Jianfeng made his way up to the university areas and hung around trying to look cool. He listened carefully to pick up the local slang and started mimicking the harsh Beijing pronunciation to cover up his countryside accent.

But these trips always ended badly upon his return home: after a few days the excitement of Beijing wore off and Jianfeng was back in Jinan, the same dull place he started from. He decided to dedicate himself to the study of painting. He dreamed of attending art school in Beijing. However, the local art teachers' committee decided he didn't have any promise as a painter. His hopes were dashed: he was stuck in Jinan and condemned to a life of eternal boredom.

One November morning in 1993, Jianfeng was sitting around his parents' house, working on a painting (the compulsion to paint remained, in spite of the discouragement), when he decided that he was going to make a fucking break for it. In his youthful exuberance, he decided—he just *knew*—that he was good enough to make it as an artist. He called up Liu Bo, his best buddy, and said: We're moving to Beijing. Liu Bo said: When? Jianfeng said: Now. Liu Bo said: Let's do it!

They got on the train with only the clothes on their backs and a few hundred yuan between the two of them, and headed towards the big city, shaking with anticipation, listening to Bon Jovi through cheap, shared headphones.

□ □ □

WHEN JIANFENG AND Liu Bo arrived at the enormous, austere Beijing Railway Station, they had no friends and, therefore, nowhere to stay. They were dressed out in their best rock-and-roll regalia, padded leather jackets, long, straight hair. A policeman saw them wandering around the fringes of Beijing like a couple of lost dogs.

When the policeman approached the exhausted pair, they were scared shitless. Their first day in Beijing and they were already in trouble with the Public Security Bureau?

"Where are you guys from?" asked the cop.

"Shandong," responded Jianfeng, "Jinan."

The cop scratched his head, looking at their outfits. "Are you guys musicians?"

"Yes we are. That's us," said Jianfeng, and Liu Bo looked at him quizzically.

The policeman nodded. "Well, I know where all the guys that play rock and roll stay. They're pretty good guys. I'll give you a ride up there."

"It was funny," remembers Liu Jianfeng, "that cop saved our asses!"

□ □ □

DURING DENG XIAOPING'S "Southern Tour" in 1992, he made the famous statement "To get rich is glorious!" This was a tacit declaration to the people: you are free to open businesses and make money. That phrase sparked the madness also known as the market reform of the Chinese economy.

The People's Republic of China is ruled by an organization that calls itself the Chinese Communist Party, which owns most of the country's largest businesses and, theoretically, all of its land. China is, however, not "communist" at all; in fact, its remarkable growth in recent years has been largely due to this reform of the private sector economy.

From the teahouses in Chengdu to the restaurants in Beijing, people were meeting and scheming, trying to figure out how to get their piece of the action precipitated by China's rapid development. Those who already had some piece of the action were trying to figure out how to gain a bigger share. The percentage of conversations in China these days that revolve around cash and how to make it is staggering.

When this economic miracle was kicking into first gear, a small and mostly well-educated group of individuals in Beijing decided that making money wasn't for them. Instead of going into business or looking for work, they set up shop in Beijing's university district and spent their days sitting around, forming rock bands, and living off their families or off the kindness of others.

They were an artsy crew; the men grew their hair long and got tattoos of dragons, marijuana leaves, and English words like "Toxic" and "Danger" all over their bodies. They smoked dope and drank Yanjing beer out of green bottles. They read Kerouac and Burroughs, Marx and Krishnamurti. They listened to Sonic Youth, Soundgarden, Alice in Chains.

Soon enough, they came up with an ideology that ironically smacked of socialism: the freedom to make money leads to class differences, which leads to greed and corruption. In China, where speech against the government can lead to a serious jail term, there was no way they could fight against the system. Instead, they did the only thing they could do without risking imprisonment: drop out of the consumer society that all other Chinese embraced. Soon, this community of rebels had earned the name: *hunzi*. Slackers. Whether they gave themselves this moniker during a moment of stoned inspiration, or a frustrated passerby was heard to mutter the epithet and eventually some sociologist claimed to have coined the term, no one can remember, but it is commonly understood, now, to refer to people like Jianfeng.

□ □ □

THE PROGENITORS OF the *hunzi* movement were the "musicians" who were living on the outer edge of Beijing when the policeman dropped off Jianfeng and Liu Bo on that cold November night thirteen years prior. Jianfeng's a gregarious and pleasant guy, and he quickly made friends and found a crash pad. He checked out Beijing's nascent art scene, went to all the galleries, and decided that artists were assholes who only cared about money and, therefore, he certainly did not want to be one, after all.

Back at the pad, his new Beijing buddies were always playing the latest tapes from Tang Dynasty and Black Panther, the capital's emerging hip rock bands. Rock music was the in thing; Cui Jian—China's Bob Dylan, John Lennon, and Elvis Presley all rolled into one—had shot to fame after the 1989 student demonstration in Tiananmen Square when his single "Nothing to my Name" became the unofficial theme song of the student movement. New bands were starting every day. It was an exciting time for Chinese rock.

Jianfeng decided to become a drummer. In order to achieve this goal, he bought a pair of drumsticks. He did not, however, know how to play the drums.

Liu Bo took off, fed up with his friend's impressionable attitude and tired of never having enough to eat.

Over the next few years, Jianfeng embraced the *hunzi* life-style. He bounced around from crash pad to crash pad: he lived in a tent with migrant workers, he borrowed a house while its occupant was out of town, he slept on friends' couches and in lovers' beds. One day he ran into an old friend from Qingdao who was attending the Beijing Film University and living off-campus. This meant that the friend's dormitory bed at the university was empty; Jianfeng moved in the next day and stayed for two years.[6]

Now that he had a bed and, therefore, a semipermanent base of operations, Jianfeng was free to stroll around Beijing at his leisure, make new friends, romance eligible bach-elorettes, and continue in his quest to start a band. Around this time, a Harvard-educated American filmmaker, Irene Lusztig, made a documentary about Jianfeng, some of his friends, and their slacker lifestyle. The film was called *For Beijing with Love and Squalor.*

In the film, Jianfeng describes himself as a "professional parasite," living off the kindness of others, and offers up a superb statement of antiestablishment youthful ennui:

"All my friends' parents want their kids to find steady jobs. That way they can make money, find a girlfriend, get married, have kids . . . and be better off than their friends. My parents just go to work day after day. After work they come home and watch TV, make dinner . . . Then they talk about their jobs, the people in their work units . . . If it weren't for them, I

---

6 Note: Coincidentally, his bunkmate at this time was Shao Xiaoli from the chapter "The Screenwriter." The two are currently estranged: Jianfeng thinks Xiaoli has sold out by taking money to write commercial scripts, and Xiaoli thinks Jianfeng needs to get his act together and stop living off everyone else's dime.

wouldn't be this way. They put a kind of invisible pressure on me . . . I hate it."

A few years later, a friend of Jianfeng's opened up a clothing store on Beijing's Houhai, or Back Lake. The store's location was lousy—at that time, the Back Lake area had not yet become a nightlife destination—and the place closed after a few months.

Jianfeng's friend gave him the space, rent-free, and said: "Why don't you do something here? Open another store? Sell something?"

Jianfeng thought about the proposition and quickly agreed. The timing was impeccable: a few months later the Back Lake area became the hip place to go in Beijing, and Jianfeng had a storefront with a perfect location to capitalize on this new trend.

It was the turn of the century; Jianfeng, just shy of his thirtieth birthday, had yet to hold down a steady job. Then he did what many professional delinquents with a bit of money do: he opened a bar. But instead of selling drinks for a profit, he sold them at cost. He didn't even open the place on the weekend, preferring to go party elsewhere. From a business perspective, it was a colossally bad decision. For Jianfeng the *hunzi*, however, to make money would have been distasteful. He just wanted a cool place for his friends to hang out. And that's what he got. According to a few Beijing old-timers I spoke with, it was a great place: cool décor, an interesting mix of celebrities and bohemians, and drink prices that ensured everyone present was good and toasted.

The bar was legendary, despite (or perhaps because of) its lack of a name. Eventually, of course, the landlord kicked him out to make way for a business that would make some cash.

With the bar closed, Jianfeng had nothing to do. He couldn't, or wouldn't, go back to Shandong: "If I went home," he says, "I would have been too advanced. I was already a different kind of person. [In Shandong] you go to work, come home. Get married. In Shandong, you drink a glass down to forget your problems. In Beijing, you can choose. The pollution is terrible. The traffic is terrible. But you have freedom."

Then, the SARS crisis suddenly descended on Beijing. It was as if an enormous hand turned off an enormous light switch: the vibrant city became lifeless almost overnight as rumors of a strange disease circulated via text message and furtive cell-phone calls. Neighborhood stores closed, foreign companies sent their executives on holiday, and the government set up secret quarantine centers around the city. In China—especially in Beijing, where China's most concentrated and educated populace resides—average citizens certainly don't depend on the government to let them know what's going on when there are rumors of an impending catastrophe. And so they cloistered themselves in their apartments.

Some of Jianfeng's crew decided to split town. Liu Jianfeng and a few friends hopped on a train heading west toward the mountains of Yunnan, and that's where he's been living ever since.

□　□　□

AS IN ANY bohemian movement, ten-odd years later, many of its creators—the original *hunzi*—turned to embrace the very system they once scorned. They got married. They made babies. They got work as graphic designers, magazine editors, and record company executives to support their families. They started rapidly expanding businesses. They learned to enjoy going out to Beijing's fancy nightclubs and sip from bottles of Chivas Regal. They purchased cars and condominiums. As the bank accounts of the original *hunzi* swelled, their antiestablishment ideals shrunk until they were no longer recognizable.

Liu Jianfeng, however, resisted the siren song of the almighty yuan. While he theoretically has a job these days—along with two equally mellow friends, he owns this café, called Cafeteria—he succeeds in doing absolutely no work at the place. Neither do his two business partners. All the food is cooked and all the money is counted by the girlfriend of one of the guys. Dali is beautiful, but the rent is cheap, and no one (locals included) ever seems to be working very hard. No one except the girlfriends of these guys, that is. Jianfeng and his friends live for free in a luxurious house (rent $60 a month) that serves as a second home for one of his newly rich Beijing buddies.

In the daytime, when he should theoretically be working, Jianfeng and his mates sit in their little room upstairs at Cafeteria. The room has fantastic natural light, several ratty, comfortable couches, a TV, a computer, and a stereo; his posse lounges around all day, listening to Mongolian folk music or American indie rock, drinking cups of strong black tea and smoking joint after joint of green bud. (In Dali, this marijuana doesn't cost a single yuan; it grows wild in the nearby mountains and along the sides of mountain roads, and it's freely exchanged as a social lubricant.)

The scene at Cafeteria this day is oddly reminiscent of an American high schooler's ideal weekend: cheap weed, cool music, good friends, hanging out together, just enjoying the vibes. But it's not a weekend. It's a Wednesday afternoon, and Jianfeng and his posse aren't teenagers; they're in their mid-thirties.

They are idle, and proud of it. They study Eastern and Western philosophy, yoga, tai chi, and qi gong, but they have no interest in commerce or politics. They like music, beer, weed, and women; they like spending time with their friends, shooting the shit. They are affable, beautiful people who treat other people well. For this, they are supported: by their girl-friends, who keep their businesses running, by the other hip-ster business owners in town who allow them to run up tabs that will never be paid, and by the moneyed friends who take them out to eat and hook them up with a free place to live.

□   □   □

LIKE MOST CHINESE, Jianfeng has great respect for his parents. He goes home for vacation a couple times a year. He has a good relationship with his mother and his father, though they exist in a completely parallel universe from his. His mother and father are both retired. While Jianfeng's in Dali, hanging out and picking up women, his parents spend their time sitting at their home in Jinan, drinking tea and cooking Shandong delicacies; pictures of China's pantheon of Communist leaders adorn their walls.

"It's a changed society," remarks Jianfeng. "The old people, like my parents, they're all still citizens of the Communist Party, and we're the citizens of New China."

Jianfeng's parents can't be proud of his lack of stable

employment, but, like most passive Chinese parents, they remain generally resigned to his chosen lifestyle. There is one thing they want more than anything else, however: a grandchild.

□ □ □

EVER SINCE HE was a middle school student, Jianfeng's liked the ladies, and they've liked him right back. At the end of his penultimate year in middle school, a pretty, doe-eyed classmate from the grade above him was the only student in his school to achieve a high enough score to earn a place at Jinan Number One High School—the best high school in Shandong. Jianfeng wanted to join her at Jinan.

So in a rare period of determination and discipline, he dedicated the next year of his life to studying for the high school entrance examination. Every night he lay awake in bed, dreaming of himself and the doe-eyed girl as Jinan Number One classmates. At the end of the next year, Jianfeng was the highest-scoring student at his middle school, and he matriculated at Jinan Number One the next year.

The doe-eyed girl?

"It didn't work out," remembers Jianfeng, smiling.

Jianfeng is what Westerners call a serial romantic. He's enamored of the concept of true love, of finding the perfect woman. Of course, the concept of perfection means no flaws, which often leads the romantic into a trap: no woman is ever good enough.

"I average about one and a half new girlfriends a month: eighteen a year," Jianfeng says matter-of-factly. (I asked if he used condoms, and he said "of course," but I wasn't so sure he was telling the truth.)[7]

After the SARS scare and the successive short stint in Kunming, he moved to the mountain town of Dali. Educated, young Chinese flock to Dali in droves for vacation from the polluted mess that is Chinese urban life. This allows Jianfeng to choose from a steady stream of tourists: big-city girls, white-collar workers, and college students.

"Sometimes, these girls, at home they have boyfriends or whatever," muses Jianfeng, "but when they come to Dali, it's a romantic place, they feel like getting in touch with somebody, somebody that will listen to their feelings."

He laughs. "Someone like me."

□ □ □

THE DAY AFTER our hang session, I return to Cafeteria. Jianfeng's in the same position as he was the day before, perched on his little ledge with his binoculars pressed to his eyes, watching the girls go by. One of his friends is fiddling with some electronic music on a PowerBook. A couple other guys are slouched on pillows in the corner sharing a joint. Everyone, including me, is wearing black Converse All Stars. A waitress from the restaurant comes up with a tray of watermelon slices, and we sit around and slurp them.

The guy with the PowerBook changes the song: over a droning beat, a voice says in English, "Let go of worry and stress . . . down to perfect relaxation . . . down to peace."

---

7   See "The Rabbits" and "The Journalist" for a more thorough discussion of AIDS in China.

I translate, and everyone laughs and thinks it's very cool. Jianfeng picks up a bottle of Dior aftershave from the table and applies it to his neck. He reaches up inside his shirt and squirts some onto his armpits. He smiles and says "So sexy!" in broken English, drawing a chuckle from the assembled crowd.

I ask Liu Jianfeng if he wants to talk some more. He grabs a stuffed doll off the table, studies it intently, and smiles at me. "Later," he says.

The music changes to Pinback, an instrumental band from San Diego that's become a mellow Dali favorite, and no one really talks much for a while; we're just sitting back, enjoying a pleasant afternoon in a comfortable room in a beautiful town.

After a while of this quietude, we slowly realize the night is creeping in. Jianfeng hands me a large envelope full of hundreds of photographs, and I look through them carefully. Jianfeng appears in many of the photos, looking younger and, in some cases, older. ("That's before I became a vegetarian," he explains.) Most of the pictures are of people about his own age, in their teens, twenties and thirties. There are a few Westerners, a couple of older Chinese people, and a lot of long-haired, artsy-looking men wearing leather jackets. Most of the photos, however, are of beautiful women.

After I finish looking at the photos, I hand them back to Jianfeng, using both hands, as is the Chinese custom to show respect. He smiles and takes them back with both hands. "These are my past," Jianfeng says, "my history. They have made me, me."

He borrows the PowerBook from his friend to show me a

slide show of more recent photos, and I think that it's funny, how exponentially fast the world, and especially China, is progressing. One day, digital images replace photographs. Just like that.

Jianfeng excitedly pauses the slide show and goes back a few frames, stopping when he reaches the photo of a pretty, young-looking girl with light skin.

"She's a college girl from Chengdu," he tells me. "She's coming up here in a few weeks. To marry her . . . would be trouble. But she might be the one, I think."

□ □ □

LATER THAT EVENING, a few of us are still hanging around at Cafeteria, sharing a bottle of too-acidic Chinese red wine. In the best tradition of Tang Dynasty poets and drunks everywhere, the alcohol has turned Jianfeng philosophical and self-reflective. "New China is good," he muses. "It's a good thing. You can choose. You can decide what you want to do with your own life. In China, this is a new thing. But there are still too many things you're supposed to do. Buy a house. Go to the supermarket . . . there's too much garbage in today's society. Some of us want to change it. But we have no power . . ."

I sip my wine, wince at its acrid taste, and think about how much Liu Jianfeng's antiestablishment rhetoric reminds me of what he said in that movie ten years ago. Jianfeng's a charismatic guy; he likes to think of himself as a visionary, and perhaps he is. Most of his contemporaries have sold out, but his ideals are still intact. In the past fifteen years, he's taken full advantage, with the help of a tolerant support network, of the opportunities allowed him by China's newfound freedom of choice.

But he's unhappy. He's feeling pressure to get married and produce a grandchild. And if he does, his parents will probably have to support the child financially on their meager retirement. Or, even worse, he'll have to get a steady job.

6

The Uighur Jimi Hendrix

IT'S A WEDNESDAY NIGHT in Shanghai, and I'm at the Tang Hui Club, a four-story music venue just off Huaihai Road, the city's main shopping street. The Tang Hui used to be a scummy little dive on the outskirts of town; in the spirit of New China, it has been given a slick makeover, resurrected as a clean and modern music pub in an unbeatable location.

A World Cup game has just finished, and throngs of party-goers mingle around, waiting for the band to start. The group is called Alhambra, and they're a strange-looking crew: the drummer is a skinny Chinese hippie in a baggy T-shirt and Rasta hat. The rhythm guitar player is thick and well-built, with broad shoulders and flowing black hair. He looks vaguely like a Tibetan or another ethnic minority—stockier and darker than the average Chinese.

And then, at the front of the stage fiddling with his guitar, there's the kid. The superstar.

The kid's scrawny, with pale, white skin and the ethereal

beauty that is often bestowed by the hand of genetics on people with mixed blood. His deep brown eyes are partly hidden under a hairdo that's half Afro, half hippie-era Beatle shag. He wears a tailor-made, floral-print shirt, open at the collar, exposing his hairless chest. A silver medallion dangles around his neck. His jeans hug his skinny legs in true rock-star fashion, and simple flip-flops hang playfully off his feet. He twists his even features into a bad-ass expression, brushes his hair off his face, closes his eyes, and starts to play.

His hands are fast, insanely fast. Most amazingly—and like almost no other music in China—the kid's improvising. He's rattling off little motives from Spanish folk songs and then, without notice, shifting his fingering patterns and taking the music in completely new directions. Sometimes, the music seems so standard-flamenco that it wouldn't be out of place at a club in Barcelona; seconds later, though, the kid will shift into a darker, more psychedelic style.

Behind him, the drummer and guitar player are laying down a simple groove, and the kid's just going nuts, playing whatever he wants. It's easy for guitar virtuosos to descend into wankery, but the kid's so talented, so in the moment, so versatile, that the entire crowd is hanging onto each note he plays. Growing increasingly ecstatic, the audience starts clapping for the kid, hooting, cheering. He glances up at the crowd, for just a few seconds, curls his lips in disdain, and then returns to his music, moving his hands up and down the neck, firing off quick little riffs.

□   □   □

AFTER A LITTLE more than an hour, Alhambra finishes their set. The other house band comes on, a mediocre one with Cure covers and an American bass player, and the kid steps outside to get some fresh air. He breaks little mouse-dropping-size pieces of hash off the ball and mixes them with the contents of an emptied-out cigarette, then rolls the whole thing up into a joint with the dexterity of an experienced craftsman. He appraises his work like a jeweler looking at a freshly cut diamond, lights the joint and takes a long hit.

He sucks in a lungful of smoke, exhales a thin stream, and smiles, looking at me curiously. I've already asked if I can interview him; at first, he acted quite dismissive but I've explained that we have a good friend in common, this old travel buddy of mine who works for an English-language magazine in Shanghai. He's really looking at me hard now, judging me just like he judges everyone he meets: What can this person do for me? What can I get out of this guy?

"Okay," he says in accented but fluent English, "call me tomorrow. Here's my home phone number."

□   □   □

IT'S WELL INTO the next afternoon, and I've called several times and left messages on the kid's home answering machine, but that was hours ago, and so I am stuck, waiting for the kid's phone call, sitting in an air-conditioned café near Tang Hui on Huaihai Road, Shanghai's central shopping artery. The street is known as "The Champs Élysées of the Orient," as

Huaihai Road was originally constructed by the French who modeled it after their own most famous boulevard. Today, most of the old buildings are long gone, replaced by colossal shopping malls: Times Square, Hong Kong Plaza, Plaza 66. A Porsche dealership sits next to a park where migrant workers from a nearby construction site are taking their noonday break, chatting, picking their bare feet and sipping from thermoses of tea.

Both sides of the street are absolutely jammed with people, going to lunch, coming back from lunch, going shopping, looking in store windows, buying things. There's something for everyone, here, with stores selling tea and cigarettes next to stores selling international luxury products; "Gucci" next to "Shanghai Famous Cigarettes and Alcohol."

Right in front of the Pacific Ocean Department Store—a standard Chinese multi-story monolith with hundreds of tiny shops selling mid-priced consumer goods—and just next to the exit of the Huangpi Road subway station, a crowd has gathered around an old woman. The woman is dressed in a grey shirt that has Chinese characters handwritten all over the front and the back, like some kind of homemade sandwich board advertising. She wears a white hat which looks like a cross between a nurse cap and a dunce cap. The hat's also covered with messy black characters like her shirt—they are written all over her clothing with a marker.

The woman has what she wants, which is the attention of the crowd. She's addressing them in a series of pitiful screams: she punctuates the end of each sentence by thrusting her head forward ever so slightly, and streams of spittle fly out from the many gaps in her teeth. The bystanders, their hands toting shopping bags, are listening with a mix of interest and befuddlement.

Her rural dialect is very thick, and I can't understand what she's saying nor get close enough to read the sloppy characters that are written all over her clothes. A mall security guard who's way too young for his too-big blue uniform stands in the crowd near the woman, nervously running his hand over the peachfuzz on his upper lip. He knows that he should get her out of there, but he can't; there are too many people around her, and besides, she's a force, she's got some power, everyone in front of the Pacific Ocean Department Store can feel it.

"I HAVE BEEN INJURED!!!" She's screaming. "I HAVE BEEN INJURED! THEY KILLED MY HUSBAND! I HAVE BEEN INJURED! I HAVE BEEN THE VICTIM OF GOVERNMENT INJUSTICE! THEY KILLED MY HUSBAND!"

She takes a plastic bottle of water that's all crinkled and bent—it looks like it's been imported directly from the city dump—out of her purse, which is an old plastic sack, and she unscrews the cap carefully, takes a sip before slipping it back in her bag.

"I HAVE BEEN INJURED!!!" She starts to scream again.

By now the young security guard has called for reinforcements. Two Pacific Ocean Department Store blue-uniformed guards, Chinese rent-a-cops, take the old woman gently by the arm and lead her away.

Just as this drama concludes, my phone rings. It's the kid. He gives me his address, tells me there's a party going on, to come over to his house, he'll wait for me.

□   □   □

AS I GET OUT of a cab in front of the kid's house, I see him getting into the cab in front of me with the bass player from his band. I wave to the kid and he beckons for me to get into his taxi. I hop into the back seat and close the door behind me; from the front seat, he turns around and fixes me with an incredulous, wide-eyed stare.

"What the fuck took you so long, man?" He's wearing a sleeveless undershirt, and locks of his thick black hair stick out in every possible direction. It's well into the afternoon; clearly, the kid has just woken up and smoked a joint, before hopping into this taxi just as I was arriving.

"I thought there was a party going on," I say. He turns away without response.

We ride in silence for a bit before I ask him where we're going. A zany smile crosses his face, and he starts ranting in his speedy, stoner English: "We've got to get the Internet fixed, man, without the Internet, what are we going to do, man, we can't do anything, we can't download music, we don't know anything, man, you know?"

I nod, and he smiles, and repeats what he's just said over again. "We've got to get the Internet fixed, man . . ." Hyper, kinetic, he starts blabbing to the cab driver in Mandarin about the World Cup. Then he begins a long, impassioned speech in Uighur to Madan, his bandmate, who's been sitting stoically next to me, smoking Panda cigarettes, throughout the whole cab ride.

□   □   □

THE KID'S NAME is Hassan and he's twenty-two years old. He is Chinese, and he is not Chinese. He has a Chinese identity card; he is a Chinese citizen; and the place where he was born, the Xinjiang Uighur Autonomous Region, is part of China. But he looks like a Middle Easterner, not an Asian. His mother tongue is Uighur ("wee-gur"), a variant of Arabic, and not Chinese.

He considers himself a Uighur, not a Chinese. Indeed, one of his favorite things to do, it seems, is make fun of Chinese people. He's got, he claims, a beautiful Minnesota-born, California-bred girlfriend who taught him his English, which he speaks in a lazy drawl reminiscent of Sean Penn's character Jeff Spicoli in *Fast Times at Ridgemont High*. When Hassan gets impassioned while speaking English, he rants, talking incredibly fast and repeating phrases several times in a row; he doesn't lose the lazy pronunciation, though, so it gets difficult to understand exactly what he's saying. When talking about Chinese people—mostly about how he doesn't like them—he'll preface his statements with a quick drawl: "Chinese people, man . . ."

□   □   □

"CHINESE PEOPLE, MAN," he says, "they don't know how to dress. Look at them, they all dress the same." We're stuck in traffic in Shanghai's busy Xujiahui district. To our right, a steady stream of bicyclists and motorcyclists pass by. The women are dressed in floral-print blouses and too-tight pants, the men mostly in ill-fitting Western suit pants and dress shirts. He points at them and sniffs. One older man rides by wearing a massive white hat and no shirt.

Hassan thinks for a second, then smiles. "I do like his hat, though."

Since Hassan is from Xinjiang and carries a Xinjiang ID card, getting a high-speed Internet connection in his Shanghai apartment requires a series of tricks. He's borrowed a Shanghainese friend's identity card, and he's brought the silent Madan along because he bears more of a resemblance to the picture on the card.

We climb up a flight of stairs into a large room in the China Telecom building. "Oh, shit," says Hassan, and I understand why: there are hundreds of people waiting in line and only four tellers processing forms at small tables to the front of the room.

There are so many people waiting that it's almost funny. Just as the citizens of Moscow queued for hours in bread lines during the leaner days of the Soviet Union's communist empire, and the Chinese queued for rice during their past famines, so today's Shanghainese line up to register for home DSL connections.

The scene in the telecom office is emblematic of socialist bureaucracy: you have to wait for hours and present an ID card to get a form that says that you are a Shanghai resident and thus allowed to have broadband in your apartment. Then, sometime in the undisclosed future, a representative for China Telecom may or may not call you to set up an appointment to actually install the connection. In short: while more and more urban Chinese are acquiring the level of income needed to buy their own computers, the inefficiency of the state-run telecom services makes it difficult to use said computers. In the cab on the way over, in the middle of one of his rambling, semi-lucid monologues, Hassan told me that China "is not a communist country, you know?" Now, at China Telecom, I remind him of what he said.

He stares at the line of prospective DSL users from the foyer outside the room and lights a Panda cigarette. (He's not standing in the queue; instead, he's dispatched his bandmate Madan to endure the torturous wait.) The scene is grim: The people in the line all wear a uniform expression of extreme, numbing boredom, except for an older gentleman wearing an ill-fitting Western suit, slouched in a plastic orange chair, a wet yellow washcloth covering his face.

"Well, sometimes, it is, you know?"

❑   ❑   ❑

A MAJORITY OF the population of China is Han Chinese. However, China also has fifty-five "national ethnic minorities" including the Miao, the Zhuang, the Hui, and the Tibetan. Hassan's ethnicity is among these minorities. Uighurs are Turkic Muslims, native to Xinjiang, who comprise a little more than half of Xinjiang's population of 15 million. The other residents of Xinjiang are Han Chinese who have moved there from the east of the country.

Xinjiang—in Chinese, the characters mean "new frontier"—comprises the northwest quadrant of today's China. It takes up roughly one-sixth of China's total land mass and separates China from the Muslim countries of the Middle East: Afghanistan, Pakistan, Tajikistan. It also borders Tibet and

Siberia. Xinjiang is comprised of two large basins, the Tarim and Dzungaria. It is a land of desert and mountains, a remote, isolated corner of Asia.

An assortment of desert warlords controlled what is now called Xinjiang until the Communist Party's People's Liberation Army marched into Urumqi and "liberated" Xinjiang in October 1949. The native population of Xinjiang is, by definition, Uighur. Since "liberation," however, Han Chinese from the overpopulated east of the country have been flooding into Xinjiang in order to use its natural resources in search of a better life.

However, Han culture and Uighur culture are, understandably, natural enemies. The Han are secular and view Xinjiang as part of their country. The Uighurs are Islamic and view Xinjiang as their own country, not part of China. There are comparatively few biracial enterprises: most Uighurs work and live with Uighurs, while Han work and live with Han.

However, the Communist government has always been controlled by the Han. Almost sixty years after the first Communist troops arrived in Xinjiang, Han Chinese now run most of Xinjiang's largest businesses. Han Chinese also hold most of its government positions. The Han, in effect, control Xinjiang.

Due in part to Xinjiang's separation from the prosperous Chinese East Coast—its GDP is a fraction of that found in wealthy eastern provinces—and in part to the aforementioned economic imperialism perpetuated by the Han Chinese of the CCP, the Uighurs have been largely left behind in the recent Chinese economic boom.

Therefore, Uighur males often leave Xinjiang and go east

to China's big cities and more affluent coastal provinces in order to find work and make money to support their families back home. They hook up with other Uighurs, and, speaking their pidgin Mandarin, open restaurants, start small trading companies, change money on the black market, serve as interpreters, sell nuts and raisins, furs and hashish, and, in Hassan's case, play guitar.

Hassan left Urumqi, his hometown and the capital of Xinjiang, after high school, when he was eighteen. He had the chance to come to Shanghai because his father, a prominent Uighur in Shanghai, had been here for several years working in a government bureau before Hassan arrived. When he arrived in Shanghai, Hassan says, he felt "crazy": there were so many different kinds of music at his disposal.

The rich Uighur musical tradition dates back to Ancient Persia. Uighur music sounds like Middle Eastern folk songs touched with occasional Eastern European influences. The Uighurs are famous throughout Asia for their love of music, and it is a staple not only at holidays and festivals but also in their daily lives. Hassan started making music when he was only three years old. As his childhood progressed, he mastered the guitar along with traditional Uighur instruments, such as the tanbur, which is the guitar's ancient predecessor, and the first stringed instrument ever—there is evidence of its existence as far back as 600 BC.

In Shanghai, all kinds of international music is readily available on bootleg CDs, and there are live performances of all kinds of music on a nightly basis: rock at the Tang Hui or the Shuffle Bar, jazz at JZ, blues at The House of Blues and Jazz, for instance.

After he arrived in Shanghai and started checking out the music scene, Hassan knew this was a place where he could succeed as a musician. He had originally planned to pursue a university degree, which would have been tremendously difficult for a non-native speaker of Chinese. Instead, he decided to focus on playing guitar. Electric guitar, that is.

□   □   □

HASSAN LIVES IN a ground-floor garden apartment in the French Concession section of Shanghai, the area that was controlled by the French in the 1850s when Shanghai was the busiest international port in Asia. His front door opens onto a small, pleasant courtyard, filled with plants and flowers and his Pearl drum set, which he stores under a massive waterproof tarp.

We take off our shoes before entering the house. Hassan makes a point of emphasizing that he keeps his apartment clean, the subtext being that Chinese people are not clean enough for him.

The apartment is small; in between the kitchenette in the back and the sitting room in the front, Hassan has set up a basic home recording studio on the bottom level of a loft bed. He's got a rack of stringed instruments affixed to the wall: acoustic guitars, electric guitars, and some traditional pieces from Xinjiang, some of which he claims are hundreds of years old.

A cluster of microphones sits next to a sixteen-channel mixing board and two flat-screen PC monitors. The whole setup would be pretty standard for the West but, for China, his equipment is impressive, his space remarkable in its efficiency.

On the walls are pictures of Hassan's rock idols: Bob Marley, Jim Morrison, Jimmy Page. More prominent, in a telling testament to his rock-star aspirations, are pictures of Hassan himself at various stages of his adolescence: a skinny, scared-looking kid at eighteen, a tough-looking punk at twenty, and a fuzzed-out recent black-and-white portrait, which sits on a wall next to a picture of Jimi Hendrix. Hassan and Jimi look very similar; the hairdo, the lazy eyes, the cheekbones, the symmetry. I ask Hassan whether it would be fair to call him the Uighur Jimi Hendrix. "No, man!" he explodes. "I'm me, man, my music is my music."

Hassan takes me into the tiny front room. The furnishings consist solely of a mattress on the floor and another PC. Madan and Aziz, another Uighur in his forties, are sitting solemnly cross-legged on the tile floor. Seemingly from nowhere, Hassan produces a small wooden bowl containing what appears to be a gourd with a straw sticking out of it. He packs a fat wad of hashish into the gourd/bong, lights it, and sucks down the whole thing in one gulp. He exhales an enormous cloud of smoke and immediately starts rambling again.

"This place is so fucking ugly man, you know? Look at that (he indicates the shoddily constructed chest of drawers set back into a depression in the wall). Look at that (he points to the grotesque, bulbous fluorescent light fixture on the ceiling). These Chinese people, man, they always make their houses so ugly! Why do they do that? Hey why don't you check out some of my new stuff man, my new music."

He hands the bowl to Aziz, who's got a skullcap on his head and a crazy gleam in his eyes. Aziz stubs out his cigarette and pulls a chocolate-bar-sized baggie of hash out of his pocket. Aziz can't speak English or Mandarin, and I can't speak Uighur; he's staring at me and I'm growing increasingly uncomfortable.

A wicked droning arises from the speakers. It's one of Hassan's new tunes. While one guitar repeats the same haunting motive and the drums remain steady yet subtly threatening, Hassan kicks in with the electric guitar, spinning a crazy, hypnotic masterpiece. Though there's no bass on this recording, Hassan's tone is so full that the music's thick and symphonic. As the music swells, it sounds like an orchestra of paranoia and destruction, like the modern subsuming the ancient, like a powerful expression of the relationship between certainty and uncertainty in contemporary life.

After almost an hour of uninterrupted music, the song finally ends. A tiny kitten the size of a human fist pops out from behind the computer and dashes around the apartment like a rat on speed. Hassan packs up the bowl and hands it to me. I decline, vociferously, but they're not having any of it. In the Uighur culture, just like the Chinese culture, when people offer you food and drink, you take it, even if you're not hungry or a teetotaler, or, in this case, aren't in the habit of smoking hashish, especially when Aziz's cold stare and Hassan's insane music have created a cauldron of paranoia in your mind that might bubble over at any minute.

"Just suck," says Hassan, seductively, as he lights the pipe.

The hash tastes clean, earthy, and the smoke is smooth, filtered through the water in Hassan's pipe. Just a few seconds later, I'm out of my mind, stoned so violently that my foot is tapping out a steady, paranoid rhythm on the floor. Hassan puts on the new Tool album, and, in spite of myself I'm tripping, caught up in a terrible fantasy. These guys are gonna abduct me, bring me to some back alley, take my money, and then slit my throat in the name of Allah. Even though I know that my thoughts are irrational, that these are friendly people, the effect of the drug is so strong that I'm really no longer existing in the world of rationality; instead I've been punted into some kind of hyper-awareness where the massive FreakOut is lurking in the shadows, waiting just around the corner to fuck up my brain for a while . . . or maybe forever.

Hassan takes off the Tool album and throws on another one of his new tracks, while Aziz, who's been sitting in the corner wearing a devilish smile, scoots over to the computer and pulls out a steering-wheel style joystick from behind the monitor. He starts playing a driving game, maneuvering a race car down American city streets, crashing into light poles, wiping out pedestrians. Hassan teases him in Uighur; Aziz stares at the screen intently but is too stoned to control the car and he crashes it into a virtual Pizza Hut.

Hassan snatches the steering wheel from Aziz. "This is how you play the game, man," he says, and indeed, he's as skilled as Aziz is clueless.

The pixels on the screen are moving too fast, and I'm scared I'm going to be sick. I close my eyes and let the waves of that crazy guitar drown me in its radical sound. Somehow, the music, while still violent, now seems strangely comforting.

Hassan glances over at me and smiles goofily; he can tell that I'm gone, so gone.

"Now you understand, man? Now you understand this feeling, the feeling, my feeling, the feeling of my music?"

□   □   □

IF ROMANTIC LOVE remains the number-one theme of modern rock–and-roll music, alienation from society and from others must be a close second. Much of this music, somewhat incongruously, is made by middle-class white people from the United States and Western Europe. While these musicians can undeniably know what it's like to *feel alone*, or whatever, it would be hard to find a group more alienated from their own culture than China's Uighurs.

The Uighurs are a people without a country; soon, if the Chinese have their way, the Uighurs won't even have a region. Han Chinese are moving to Xinjiang at an unprecedented pace. In ethnically Uighur Xinjiang, the Han Chinese will outnumber the Uighurs within the next couple years. While government agencies have Uighurs on staff, the Chinese run the show, granting business permits and development rights in prime areas to other Chinese, pushing the Uighurs to the outskirts of the towns they've inhabited for centuries.

While Uighurs in Xinjiang have fallen on hard times economically, things are even more dire for those who dare to question Chinese rule. After September 11, the Chinese government sensed an opportunity to deal with their Muslim separatists in a manner which would be perfectly kosher in the paranoid atmosphere of the global "war on terror." They labeled the East Turkmenistan Liberation Front—a loose-knit coalition in Xinjiang that supports an independent Uighur state and a higher standard of human rights for Uighurs—a "terrorist organization" that was, purportedly, funded by al-Qaeda, and convinced the United States to do the same.

Of course, this was little more than a strategic maneuver to enable the Chinese government to gain legitimacy for its policies towards separatist Uighurs. Ordinary Uighur civilians who go public with their opposition to the Chinese Communist Party are subject to arbitrary arrests, lengthy sessions of torture, and summary executions.

It would be an understatement to say that things are not well in Xinjiang, and so while Hassan lives in China and speaks Chinese, he, like most Uighurs, has a deep-rooted hatred for the Han Chinese and their policies of economic genocide.

The cause of Tibetan freedom has been seized by Western musicians like Pearl Jam and the Beastie Boys, and concerts have been set up worldwide to benefit Tibetan exile groups and to promote awareness of the Tibetan cause. Uighurs are Muslim, and their religion—and, thus, their cause—lacks the hippie cool of Tibetan Buddhism. Therefore, their quest for equal recognition, if not outright independence, remains relatively obscure to the average otherwise "globally conscious" citizen.

Just like every other electric-guitar-wielding musician, Hassan wants to be a rock star. But he wants to be a rock star on his own terms. He wants to use his music to draw attention to Xinjiang and what's happening there. "I want to show people," he drawls, "what's Xinjiang, our *culture*, man, you know?" Though his music is not directly political—most of it is instrumental, so there's no opportunity for protest lyrics— he wants to become a superstar, a cultural ambassador delivering Xinjiang consciousness (or hashish unconsciousness?) to the international community.

"I just need to be able to make my music the way I want

to make it, man," he says. He's turned down offers from several Chinese record companies because "they want to tell me what to do, you know, and that's not the way it's gonna be. They need to pay for my hash, pay for my house, and let me do whatever I want. It's about the music, man, of course it's about the music, but it's about doing it *my way*. And that's the best way."

Part of "Hassan's way" is to stay put for a while in Shanghai with his band, just like the Beatles did at the Cavern Club, getting their songs tight and their skills even tighter. Later, they'll move on to other cities, and then the whole world. Unlike most young musicians, Hassan understands the importance of sharpening his skill and realizing his potential before gearing up for a shot at the big time. He's taking it slow, perhaps due in part to the massive amount of hashish he smokes, but he's happy that way. He can play his guitar all day, and listen to the new Tool record, and then play along with the new Tool record after listening to it just once (the kid's talented). He can go out to dinner with friends, indulge in halal meat at the local Uighur restaurant. He can play around the city three or four times a week and get paid for it, enough to support this lifestyle. Though he's far away from home—"I left my heart in Xinjiang"—he's got a good life here, while he hangs and waits for the day when he will make a move towards stardom, or whatever.

In the next couple of years, he will try to go abroad and look around, he says, to check out what's happening in California or maybe in Europe. "What's LA like?" he asks. "Is it like, driving around in cars, smoking joints, listening to Led Zeppelin?" Pretty close, I tell him, for some people at least. He smiles his beatific smile, translates what we said into Uighur for his friends, and reaches for his bowl.

Hassan's certainly been blessed with a formidable sense of egotism. Luckily for him, though, he is not only virtuosic but also blessed with a singular vision. The Chinese music scene suffers from a glaring lack of true originality: while trends come and go, bands by and large rely heavily on Western rock, pop, punk, and folk for inspiration. Hassan's on an entirely different trip: while his guitar playing most certainly contains Western influences, most notably Jimi Hendrix and Jimmy Page, he looks at music from the perspective of a kid who grew up in Xinjiang, immersed in the rich Uighur folk tradition, not a kid who grew up in Shanghai listening to Western pop. He's got the look, he's got the chops, he's got his own way and his own sound.

In the next several years, as the Han Chinese continue to colonize Xinjiang and the suffering of the Uighurs continues unabated, we may very well see the world's first Uighur superstar, emerging from a first-floor garden apartment, slinging an electric guitar, broadcasting the cause of his people to those who would otherwise never listen up and take notice.[8]

---

8   In September 2006, the Tang Hui Club and several other Shanghai live music establishments were shut down by the Ministry of Culture for lack of a "performance license."

7

The Rabbit

IT'S A HAZY summer day in Chengdu, the capital of Sichuan Province. I've shacked up in a newly opened branch of the American chain Super 8 Motel on the twenty-first floor of the SOHO Tower. It's a nice, functional, modern room that would pass for standard in a boutique hotel in some European capital: single bed, glass shower, high-speed Internet access, all for the low price of eighty-eight yuan ($11) a night. Ten years ago, a streamlined, design-conscious room like this would have been unimaginable in China.

Chengdu, a thriving city of ten million, is known as *di si cheng*, "the fourth city" after Beijing, Shanghai, and Guangzhou. It's the cultural capital of China's West, the gateway for tourists and travelers headed to Tibet, and the home of Sichuan Province's legendary spicy cuisine. The city is located at the bottom of a basin, surrounded on all sides by mountains. Except for the occasional storm, there isn't any wind to clean up the air: most of the time, it just stagnates.

Like many other cities in China, Chengdu is currently in the throes of a massive development boom. Old streets and buildings are being torn down and replaced with enormous steel-and-glass office towers and residential structures. From the window of my room at the Super 8, looking down on the city, there are so many buildings under construction that it looks like they're creating a whole new metropolis.

Even though the skies are grey and the air sticky and humid as a sauna, Chengdu feels healthier and more relaxed than the industrial cities of the eastern half of the country. Chengdu's teahouse culture is legendary: the city's thousands of teahouses, from little shacks to opulent mansions complete with spas and butlers, serve as social gathering places where retirees while away their afternoons playing mah-jongg and moneyed women gather for serious gossip sessions. Even businessmen use teahouses as makeshift offices where they conduct their business on cell phones and laptops, sipping steaming glasses of green tea as they work.

As the evening comes on, Chengdu's growing middle class and their extended families move the party from the teahouses to the city's restaurants. Chengdu enjoys a reputation for having the best food in China. Though new restaurants are opening up every day, the demand is so high that, at peak times, you have to wait for a table almost everywhere, from the swanky, modern joints downtown to the old hot-pot places and noodle joints that populate the city's fast-disappearing back alleys and old streets.

After their bellies are full of spicy food, Chengduers (Chengdudes?) like to head out to one of the city's "nightlife complexes" and get incredibly wasted on a mixture of Scotch and cold green tea, poured from icy pitchers into shot glasses and tipped back once every few minutes. While Chengdu has all the amenities and infrastructure of Beijing and Shanghai, its residents are more laid-back and hedonistic, and they're not shy about their partying ways.

An American colleague who's lived in Chengdu for years has mentioned that it has a famously wild and open gay culture—drug-fueled gay bars and parties, bathhouses every corner—and I'm here on his recommendation to do research into this scene. "It's crazy," he told me with a smile, "Communist Party members fucking each other in massive all-night orgies."

□ □ □

CHENGDU IS A very pleasant place to spend a few days, and so, armed with a cell phone full of contacts, I slowly attempted to make inroads into the Chengdu gay scene. Most of my Chinese friends, however, asserted that while there were plenty of homosexuals in Chengdu, they certainly didn't know any of them.

I stopped in at an address I had heard was a nightclub that served as Chengdu's gay epicenter and found instead a bar full of Chinese businessmen watching transvestites dance on a neon-lit stage. I stopped by saunas supposedly frequented by gay men and found only heterosexual saunas with the requisite bored-looking female prostitutes.

I hit all the big discos—the Empty Bottle, Club Mix, and Barbie—sipping overpriced beers and hanging around. While I socialized and interviewed several groups of young gay kids at these bars they were clearly high on Ecstasy or crystal meth. But they refused to be interviewed, preferring instead to ask me questions about America and, in the lewd manner of brash youth, make suggestive comments about the speculative size of my penis. I got a few of their phone numbers and set up meetings via text message, but come time to meet, no one ever showed up.

Finally, I called the friend who had told me that Chengdu was a gay hotbed in the first place and asked him what was going on.

"Don't sweat it, man. I have a friend called Nine Dragons," he said. "He's a sweet guy. He'll talk to you."

□ □ □

THE MYTH OF nine dragons goes back centuries to imperial China. The dragon is a symbol of luck, and nine is a lucky number that, in imperial times, also symbolized the emperor. The Chinese dragon has nine attributes; there are nine types of Chinese dragons; and the Chinese dragon has nine children. Back when the Chinese leaders wore embroidered silk robes instead of black suits and red ties, only the emperor himself and his most senior cabinet members were allowed to wear robes with nine dragons embroidered on them.

I was about to encounter the ongoing lore of the nine dragons. One evening, just thirty-odd years ago, there was a huge thunderstorm above a small village in the farming region of Sichuan. The sky was *tian hun di an*: a Chinese proverb meaning "in a state of chaos and darkness." And the people were terrified.

Suddenly, the clouds vanished, and the sky was bright, and it seemed that the dreadful storm never even happened at all. A few minutes later, a peasant woman gave birth to her ninth child.

The family saw the clearing of the storm as an auspicious sign that this baby would have a lucky life; since he was a male, and the ninth child, they decided to christen him Nine Dragons.

□   □   □

THIRTY-ODD YEARS LATER, Nine Dragons was sitting in his lofty graphic design studio in the southern part of Chengdu, trying to get his head around the incredibly complicated manual for the new version of Adobe InDesign and debating whether or not to log on to the Internet, enter a gay chat room, and try to get some action.

I called Nine Dragons while he was busy wrestling with the computer manual. About an hour later, we were on the first floor of the SOHO building, sitting across from each other in a back booth at SPR Coffee. SPR is a Taiwanese chain that's a blatant Starbucks ripoff: the sign features the same green, round lettering and a menu that includes not only coffee but perennial Chinese favorites like blended fruit drinks, fruit plates, and, of course, fruit pizza. While the coffee isn't nearly as good as Starbucks, many Chinese people prefer to meet at SPR for one simple reason: unlike Starbucks, SPR is owned by a Chinese company, so smoking is permitted inside.

□   □   □

"MAYBE IN A HUNDRED or two hundred years," Nine Dragons sighs in mock exasperation, toying with the sleeve of his T-shirt, "our government will have improved. But we'll all be dead by then, so it won't matter!"

The corners of Nine Dragons' mouth turn up in a wry smile and he lights another Pride cigarette, continuing his diatribe. "For now, we're stuck with what we've got. A lack of standards. Our government, our people, no one understands what 'quality' means. It's terrible."

He stops for a second, stirs his mango smoothie, picks up the glass and takes a sip through the straw, dimples forming in his hollow cheeks.

"And as for me," he considers, staring over his black-rimmed glasses with a coquettish look on his face, "in *my situation*, it's extra difficult. I don't exactly have a lot to choose from."

"What do you mean, your situation?" I ask.

At the beginning of our conversation, I had mentioned that I was interviewing him for a chapter on homosexuality. He looks me in the eye. "You know, what we were talking about before," he says, loath to use the word "homosexual."

"Rabbits?" I guess, using a Chinese code word for homosexuality.

He smiles. "How do you know what that word means?"

I tell him what I've heard about the gay scene in Chengdu and how it's supposed to be so wild. He laughs at me, and explains that it's not at all like that. Orgies full of Party members? Nope. Gay bathhouses? There are a few gay bathhouses, sure, but they have them all over the country. Gay clubs? Not so much.

I express my disappointment that Chengdu's not the gay mecca I had hoped. Nine Dragons laughs and takes a long drag on his cigarette.

"Don't worry. I'll tell you a few good stories."

□   □   □

THE NINTH CHILD of that peasant family has matured into a small, slender man. Nine Dragons is a blur of nervous movement: twitching, cocking his head to one side, tapping his fingers on the tabletop, smoking endless cigarettes. His cell phone buzzes every few seconds and, each time, without thinking, he reaches down and presses a button to silence it. When Nine Dragons speaks, however, he has an intelligent, articulate, condescending manner about him that's hard to reconcile with his constant fidgeting.

His clothes are expensive and stylish but not ostentatious: expensive-looking black-rimmed glasses, tight Yohji Yamamoto Y-3 T-shirt, designer jeans, black Italian loafers. He's got that cosmopolitan polish that could be found on any graphic designer living in Soho or Milan or London or Tokyo.

From the time he was young, Nine Dragons showed an unusual aptitude for his studies and a proclivity for the visual arts; he left the countryside to study at a high school in Chengdu, earned a place at a top fine arts college, and he has never looked back.

Over the years, using a combination of natural intelligence, serious self-discipline, and good old-fashioned hard work, he has made quite a name for himself as a skilled graphic designer. He often works eighteen-hour days, he explains. "Work and sleep: that's my life. It's very sad, my life in Chengdu. All work, no relaxation."

He has directed a number of high-budget advertising

campaigns for a tremendous range of clients: the government's new Arts and Culture Center, a luxury condominium development on the outskirts of Chengdu, even a nearby Buddhist temple that was breaking ground.

"This kind of work," he says, "is to earn money. It's helping bad people do bad things. Government, real estate . . . they are all cheaters."

I suggest that the government arts center seems pretty worthwhile and he looks at me like I've just said that the sky is green, or something equally preposterous. "Culture should be created by the artists, not the government. The artists have culture. The government? No culture."

Ironically, then, to supplement his income from freelancing—though he does well, more money never hurts—he's worked as a professor, on and off, at three government-run universities in Chengdu, teaching art and graphic design to undergraduates.

I ask Nine Dragons what he thinks of teaching. "The universities are failures," he sniffs. "The graphic design teachers don't know how to design. I have students that are doing better work than the other teachers."

He's one of those people who constantly grapples with his sense of self, trying to make sense of the myriad contradictions that make up his personality. He is obviously passionate about his work and friends, and he is clearly a kind, gentle, and sensitive person. Everything he says, however, is laced with a bitter streak of disdain: for China, its government, its present-day society, and its closeted homosexual culture.

◻ ◻ ◻

THE LEADING SPOKESPERSON for gay rights in China, the sociologist Li Yinhe, recently wrote a book called *History of Chinese Homosexuality*. Her monograph asserts that male homosexual love was in bloom during the early dynastic period in China and that many well-known traditional poems are actually about the love between the poet and his same-sex patron. In fact, homosexuality was not taboo in China until the Qing Dynasty (1644–1911) when Confucianism became the primary belief system. Confucianism asserts that the husband and wife must be involved in a "proper relationship" and that homosexuality goes against the natural way of the universe.

After the Communists took over and during the Cultural Revolution, homosexuals faced the wrath of the Chinese government. Homosexuality was classified as a "mental disorder" and those exhibiting what were perceived as "homosexual tendencies" (whether they were gay or not) were rounded up, tossed into internment camps, and tortured. Many died.

In 1997, sodomy was decriminalized; several years later, homosexuality was removed from the list of mental disorders (which still includes things like "excessive fear of the penis shrinking back into the body" and "psychosis brought upon by traveling").

Although homosexuality is no longer a criminal action, the social mode of "coming out" as a homosexual and defining oneself as such does not exist in China in the same way it does in the West. There is no "gay pride," no gay rights groups, no gay groups of any kind. Li Yinhe—although not gay herself—is the primary spokesperson for the homosexuals of the nation.

In the interest of social justice, Li Yinhe has proposed a same-sex marriage bill before the National People's Congress in 2000, 2004, and 2006. Understandably, however, she failed to receive support from any government delegates and so the bill was never even discussed.

In 2001, the Chinese government estimated that there were "5 to 10 million active homosexuals," a laughably low figure in a nation of nearly a billion and a half people. In China, if you happen to be a homosexual, it's a strictly private thing: as long as you hide it well enough and don't discuss your homosexuality with people who might have a problem with it, you can get by.

However, if your homosexuality is discovered, there can be problems, especially in less cosmopolitan cities. Unlike their counterparts in, say, America or Nigeria or any other of the many countries where anti-gay violence is routine, gays in China are not really at risk of physical harm. They are, however, at risk of social and professional ostracism. So while homosexuality is openly acknowledged to exist in an "official" sense, it is fiercely denied and protected by many homosexuals themselves.

A common threat to gay Chinese is blackmail. If they don't pay the ransom, the blackmailer will expose their secret. Admitted homosexuals can then be fired from their jobs, and disowned by their family members.

Also, when homosexual men reach a certain age and they still haven't found a wife, they give in to parental pressure and marry a female family friend. Of course, the man continues his lifestyle, in secret, hidden from not only his family but his spouse. Many of the gay men I've met in China have been married. (These days, the lucky few are married to lesbians, a practice that has been going on in Western countries for decades. These marriages tend to work out very well.)

This is the result of a post-communist shame-based culture where it is necessary to hide anything "different" about oneself from public view. You have a mentally handicapped child? Don't let him out of the house because it will bring you shame. Your kid suffers from psychological problems? Don't acknowledge them because to do so will bring you shame. You are a homosexual? Don't be open about it because to do so would bring you shame. (And your family, as well.)

And so, of course, Nine Dragons hasn't told his parents or any of his eight siblings about his sexual orientation. "My mother," he says, "she's seventy-five years old. She's a peasant. She's got no culture. What am I supposed to say to her?"

□ □ □

WHILE THE FATE of homosexuals in China is not as dire as in many African and Middle Eastern nations where male-on-male sex yields the death penalty, it's still tremendously hard being a homosexual in this kind of "don't ask, don't tell" environment.

It's especially difficult for guys like Nine Dragons, who is intelligent and discriminating, and who wants to meet other men like himself.

Unlike in the West, or even Japan and Korea, for that matter, there are few gay bars in China. There are a couple in Shanghai—where the atmosphere is more open—and a few in Beijing and Guangzhou. There's the gay bar I visited in Chengdu, but it features drag shows, and the patrons are largely straight guys who have brought along their women to gawk at the transsexuals strutting their stuff on stage.

Some Chinese discos—the kind where the watered-down house music is turned up so loud you can feel it reverberate in your chest cavity—have gay areas. These areas are usually to the left of the DJ booth: in China, right symbolizes male and left female, and so "left" has become code for homosexual. (I discovered this accidentally on my second night in Chengdu; seeing an open table at a disco, an older male friend and I staked our claim. Soon, we were joined by two cooing Chinese men in tank tops who kept trying to get us to buy them drinks.)

But these noisy, unpleasant discos are anathema to classy dudes like Nine Dragons, who would rather stay at home watching a foreign movie. Also, all the guys in the discos are on something or other, E or K or speed or some unholy cocktail of the three. Nine Dragons doesn't like druggies or party people, and therefore meeting other men is really difficult for him.

So Nine Dragons, and millions like him, turn to the Internet to scout out sexual partners. QQ, China's homegrown instant-messaging software, is now a ubiquitous form of social interaction. When I meet Chinese young people, they'll ask me for my phone number and my QQ address.

For Chinese youth, gay and straight alike, Internet dating has become a rapid and widespread phenomenon. One mischievous friend of mine in Qingdao explains it pretty simply—"it's easy. You just go online, find a girl, you exchange pictures, meet up, and fuck."

When Nine Dragons was a little younger, there used to be gay meeting places in public parks, often, ironically, next to Mao statues. But now China has rushed full-throttle into the Internet Age. The best—the only—place to meet other men is online, in the friendly confines of gay chat rooms.

□　□　□

NINE DRAGONS HATES—no, detests—this mode of interaction. In our conversation, he constantly uses the phrase "all the guys online" to refer to a class of gays that are only concerned about physical appearance and penis size.

"All the guys online," he says, "it's so stupid. All people care about is your body. Just the body! Then, you have to spend a lot of time chatting, exchanging messages back and forth. It takes so much time! I don't have that much time! And then, it's all about going to meet up somewhere, or checking into some hotel. People don't care about you, or what's in your mind. They only want to fuck a body, fuck a face. They don't care about your thoughts."

And then, he adds, you usually never see the guy again: "You meet up with someone once, and then it's over. These guys," the crazy ones, "meet up with three, four, five different guys a day."

These promiscuous sexual proclivities combined with the general lack of resources for homosexuals in China have led to skyrocketing rates of HIV infection. Most gay men are vaguely aware of HIV/AIDS, but are unsure about how exactly it's transmitted. It's a common misconception that "only foreigners have AIDS" or "only heroin users have AIDS." The absence of a strong and united gay community leaves a vacuum of misinformation, resulting in death sentences for many of China's gay youth.

While the Chinese government has started AIDS-awareness billboard advertising and outreach, it's not targeted towards homosexuals, but to IV drug users. Western NGOs like France's Medicins du Monde and the US-based AIDS Relief Fund for China have started outreach programs, but, again, the community infrastructure necessary to provide targeted, effective outreach just does not exist. There are isolated outreach centers in major cities, including Chengdu. These efforts are certainly commendable, but due to the social taboo about homosexuality, they reach only a fraction of their potential audience. They can't advertise, and there are few homosexual meeting places to distribute educational literature.

Nine Dragons is hyper-aware of AIDS, and the dangers posed by anonymous sex. In the end, though, Nine Dragons returns to the Internet because he's got nowhere else to meet other people.

"Some friends of mine [in the gay community]," he says, "they've been together for two or three years. I envy them . . . They play tennis together, go swimming, play mah-jongg . . . it's pretty cool." He stares off wistfully over my left shoulder and sighs.

Ideally, Nine Dragons is looking for a boyfriend, someone who respects him for his intelligence. He wants a partner, in the truest sense of the word: someone who he can have meaningful conversations with, someone who shares his interests, someone who cares about him for who he is and not what he looks like.

Nine Dragons imagines, perhaps correctly, that it would be easier to find a partner abroad, perhaps in Europe or Canada. Once we've talked for a while, and he's grown more comfortable, he peppers me with questions about what the gay scene is like in the West, be it Western Europe or the US. He's tried to learn French in hopes of securing a visa to go abroad, but it's proved too difficult and he doesn't have the language skills or high-level connections necessary to get him out of China, even just for a holiday.

He imagines—correctly—that everything would be easier for him in a society where people might be open about homosexuality, an open society where potential partners would understand the concepts of taste, class, and quality.

He picks up a piece of paper. "You have a piece of paper, okay? You should design the best piece of paper possible." He picks up his empty smoothie glass. "You have a glass. You should design the best glass possible. In the West, they understand . . . but not in China."

"Here," he moans, "there's no music, no art, no good museums. Only hot-pot. Teahouses. Mah-jongg."

□　□　□

NINE DRAGONS PULLS his laptop out of his bag. It's a sleek, silver MacBook Pro, the newest model that was just released a couple months ago. In China, this computer costs a fortune, almost twice what they cost in the States.

I ask if he has an iPod. He smiles and removes the also-expensive video iPod from his pocket. "I bought these for all my friends and gave them away as presents," he says. I wonder to myself where he got the money for all these gadgets.

On the screen of his MacBook, he shows me his portfolio. Among the advertisements for luxury goods and services is a poster he created for a French NGO that's started a needle exchange program in Chengdu. It's a haunting image of an enormous cartoon syringe. Unlike the other advertisements he's done, he actually seems proud of this one: he did something constructive and positive with his skills.

"In the future, I will do some more things for the gay community," he muses, stubbing out a final cigarette.

And then his cell phone buzzes. Someone he connected with on QQ wants to meet him. He slips his computer back into his bag and heads out in the humid Chengdu day to continue his fruitless quest for a caring boyfriend with whom he'll form a life partnership. So, for now, he anesthetizes himself against the pain of his loneliness with work. He wakes up every morning and starts to work, works all afternoon and into the night. He doesn't take vacations and accepts too many projects.

He works excessively, partly because he grew up in an impoverished area and he likes having money of his own, but mostly because as long as he keeps working, he doesn't have time to think. Nine Dragons is frustrated. He lives in an authoritarian regime that doesn't understand *culture*, goddamn it. He lives in a society where, in order to ensure a productive existence, he must hide a vital aspect of himself from the people in his daily life.

Nine Dragons, the lucky man born after the passing of a

storm, lives alone. After the boys he met on QQ have left, he spends his nights alone in his apartment, chain-smoking and fiddling around with graphics on his computer, finally falling asleep and then waking up again to continue his cycle of work.

8

The Most Polluted City in the World

"Environmental protection has been a basic national policy since the 1980s. The State Environmental Protection Committee was established in 1984 and the first Environmental Protection Law formally issued in 1989. After the United Nations Conference on Environment and Development in 1992, China was one of the first countries to formulate and carry out a strategy of sustainable development. In 1993, the Environmental Resources Committee of the NPC was set up. So far, the state has promulgated eight laws for environmental protection, fourteen laws for management of natural resources and thirty-five regulations on environmental protection. Environmental protection authorities have publicized over 100 national environmental protection regulations and more than 1,000 local ones.

Responding to stresses on natural resources caused by fast economic growth, development and urbanization, the state at the turn of the 21st century responded with a 'green strategy' that includes developing a revolving economy, increasing resource-use efficiency; developing clean production, reducing pollution cost in production processes; developing green consumption, reducing ecological impact of consumption; developing new energy resources, reforming production methods, moving toward ecological industrial civilization, and creating a balanced ecological environment."

—THE CHINESE GOVERNMENT WEBSITE, www.china.gov.cn, September 2007

"The scenery changes with the seasons. In the spring you can see hundreds of different flowers vying with each other in beauty. In the summer the whole city seems to be covered with lush foliage, sending off a delicate fragrance so charming and pleasant that the visitors are reluctant to leave. Linfen is a 'Fruit and Flower' city!"

—THE WEBSITE OF SHANXI NORMAL UNIVERSITY, http://www.sxnu.edu.cn/english/linfen.html, September 2007

□ □ □

BECAUSE MOST CHINESE don't yet use credit cards, certain industries that have been staples for years in the West—online shopping, online hotel reservations—are not yet established. Also, in certain parts of industrial China, the supply of luxury hotel rooms far outstrips demand. Often, with the aid of same-day Internet and telephone booking services, it's possible to score a plush luxury hotel room in a modern building for the same price as a dingy cubicle in a thirty-year-old government-owned hotel.

I get off the plane in Taiyuan, the capital of Shanxi Province in Central China, and take a cab to the Shanxi World Trade Hotel. The place resembles a small-scale model of its inspiration, the structure that used to tower over Lower Manhattan. Two enormous black towers surge up into the sky. The Shanxi World Trade Hotel was built in 2000, and, of course, New York lost its World Trade Center the next year.

I hop in the high-speed elevator. At the twenty-third floor, I walk down the silent, carpeted hallway, and into my room. The room boasts all the standard accoutrements of the international business hotel: satellite television, marble bathroom, and a mini-bar stocked with imported chocolate and booze.

□ □ □

SHANXI PROVINCE IS one of China's poorest. Much to its natives' displeasure, it is often confused with the similarly spelled Shaanxi, its more prosperous neighbor to the west, which is home to the ancient city of Xi'an and Emperor Qin Huangdi's famed army of terra-cotta warriors. While international tourists often visit Shaanxi, comparatively few make it to Shanxi. Its economy relies greatly upon heavy industry: coal mining, steel mills, and chemical production.

The Shanxi World Trade Hotel is virtually empty, and I sit in a comfortable chair in the lobby, taking advantage of the free wireless Internet access and staring out at the blank lobby.

After a while, a stream of German men, dressed in collared shirts and pleated pants like an engineering squad from a multinational company, pass by, speaking in hushed tones.

Most of them appear to be in their thirties, and move about in a big group, twenty deep, as if they're scared to be alone. They take the elevator up to their rooms. (I would find out the next day at breakfast that they were indeed an engineering team, stationed in Taiyuan for a couple months to set up a heavy-industry joint venture.)

More time passes; around eleven, a pair of country bumpkins in too-big suit jackets, presumably flush with coal revenue from the countryside, stumble into the lobby, each accompanied by a prostitute clinging to his arm. One of the prostitutes wears a white sequined baseball cap and a pair of camouflage hip-huggers. I watch the drama unfold: the men approach the check-in desk, pull huge stacks of 100-yuan notes from their pockets, haggle over the price of the room (even at fancy hotels, it's standard protocol to argue over the prices), slap wads of notes on the counter, and drunkenly lead their charges towards the elevator.

I feel tired but hungry, so I saunter over to SPR Coffee. They have a branch in the lobby. I'm the only customer, but there are eight young men working at SPR. In China, over-staffing runs rampant; unskilled labor is extraordinarily cheap. The waiters are all standing around with blank expressions on their faces, wearing green robes and black bandannas. They look like ersatz coffee ninjas.

Their leader—the headwaiter, or whatever—would be a handsome youth of about twenty, if not for a pair of incisors that jut straight out, almost perpendicular to his gums. He emerges from the pack, grins shyly, further revealing his bizarre teeth, and asks me in a soft voice what I want. I order a tuna sandwich and a large coffee.

The coffee tastes excellent. The sandwich, however, consists of a thin layer of still-frozen tuna buried under dollops of ketchup and mayonnaise sitting atop a stale baguette.

Still smiling, the curious headwaiter asks me what I'm doing in Shanxi, and I explain that I've come to visit Linfen. He looks at me with a come-on-you-can't-be-serious expression; I tell him that, yes, I'm going to Linfen.

"It is very polluted there," he says. His embarrassed grin grows larger so that his horizontal incisors are practically bursting out of his mouth.

□ □ □

THE NEXT MORNING, I get on the public bus. As we head south towards Linfen, heavy machinery makers and coal refineries line both sides of the highway. On the freeway, passenger cars, including public buses, are few and far between: enormous trucks carting loads of raw materials and finished product rumble along the road, spewing noxious black smoke into the air.

The one-year-old Taiyuan-Linfen highway was built with loans financed by the Asian Development Bank. It is clean, sterile and well-constructed, and looks like it could be a smooth stretch of road laid through Missouri or Montana.

The trucks, on the other hand, look like they've been recently salvaged from a junkyard in one of those states. They cruise along the brand-new highway, blue paint peeling, engines sputtering, gears and machinery groaning and clanking. Their cargo, whether it's steel or wood or coal or pigs, almost always seems perilously close to coming loose and causing an unpleasant accident.

On both sides of the road, enormous smokestacks rise up into the sky, spewing towering plumes of smoke into the air. The sky, the road, the buildings—everything is grey. From my window seat the world looks like an Eastern European art film, shot in black and white: bleak, sad, and hopeless.

We continue to travel further and further into coal country, and the air has gotten progressively palpably blacker, and then the highway ends and we're suddenly in Linfen. It's two in the afternoon but it looks and feels like dusk. Dusk, that is, in a blast furnace. The haze hangs in the air like soup-thick fog, and there's a circle of hazy light up in the sky where the sun should be.

Through the haze, I can make out the white surgical masks covering the noses and mouths of passing cyclists. It's so difficult to see that some of the cars on the main drag have their lights turned on in the middle of the afternoon.

The air has an acrid, chemical smell, like a mixture of sulfur and burning hair.

Xiao Liu, my seatmate for the two-and-a-half-hour trip, is a bespectacled, excitable student at Shanxi Normal University. He is from Taiyuan but attends school in Linfen. The entire trip down, he's been talking at me about the war in Iraq. At the beginning of the conversation, we managed to agree that we were both against the war, but since then I have barely been able to get a word in edgewise. He's been chattering on and on, blinking furiously and clearing his throat nervously, telling me how America shouldn't start wars and how the Iraqi people should be able to govern themselves without America meddling in their affairs.

It's an argument I hear a lot in China, with an obvious

subtext. The Chinese argue against America's hegemonic role in the world, but what they really mean is: China's a strong country, not a pushover, and America should not be able to tell us what to do.

"Is the air in Linfen always this polluted?" I ask him, eagerly changing the subject as we step off the bus into the exhaust-laden chaos of the bus station.

Xiao Liu hawks up a sizeable ball of phlegm and spits it onto the sidewalk in front of the station. His mucus is tinged with black. He pulls a pack of cigarettes from his pocket and lights up.

"It's not as polluted as it was before," he philosophizes, and invites me to lunch. I decline; in the typical Chinese fashion, he insists that I go. I apologize and lie to him that I have another appointment.

When he realizes that I'm not going with him, he politely excuses himself and leaves me alone, among a phalanx of enormous brightly-colored buses belching smoke, in the most polluted city in the world.

"Linfen is a famous city in China," Xiao Liu told me on the bus down. "Last year, we had the Miss Bikini China contest here!" We're in the industrial heartland of China: the nearest beach is hundreds of miles away.

□ □ □

CHINA PRODUCES ROUGHLY one-third of the world's coal, and Linfen is the country's coal capital. Most Chinese people I asked reckoned that Lanzhou or Taiyuan, two provincial capitals in the heart of the massive coal belt, are the most polluted cities in the country. However, in 2006, a study conducted by the World Bank showed that sixteen of the top twenty most polluted cities in the world in terms of air quality are in China. The three most polluted cities in the world are in Shanxi Province. And Linfen is the big kahuna. It has the most polluted air in the world.

Over the past ten years, I have traveled extensively in China. I've been to many major cities and an assortment of provincial ones. However, before reading the World Bank report, I had never even heard of Linfen. Indeed, many intelligent people I know, both Chinese and Western, asked, blankly, "Where?" when I told them my destination for this trip.

There are around four million people living here; in the West, it would be a notable place, but in China, it's just another mid-sized, prefectural-level, anonymous Chinese city. The number of cities with more than a million people in China is truly staggering: more than 150. By comparison, in Russia, only eleven cities are bigger than one million; in America, there are only nine.

China, as any of its denizens will frequently remind you, has five thousand years of history, and this long cultural heritage has given rise to more proverbs than it would be possible to count. One of the more famous of these states: "(One should) marry in Suzhou, live in Hangzhou, eat in Guangzhou, and die in Liuzhou," because Suzhou has the prettiest girls, Hangzhou has the best scenery, Guangzhou the best food, and Liuzhou the best coffin-making wood.

Apparently, there's also a saying about this city: "If someone is truly your sworn enemy, you should wish for them to live in Linfen."

◻   ◻   ◻

I STOP FOR LUNCH in a little noodle shop. It's the kind of place that I normally like—vaguely dirty interior, usually tasty food, a glossy photomural depicting a famous Chinese nature scene on the wall. (In this case the photograph is of nearby Hukou Falls, the closest thing Shanxi has to a nature paradise.)

But in Linfen, I feel none of the comforting rush I usually get when entering a place like this. Even inside, in the air conditioning, the smell of the city has begun a campaign of terror in my sinuses. The smell clings to everything: my T-shirt and jeans, my hair, even the bowl of beef noodles I've ordered.

The owner of the place and the two waitresses, unaccustomed to seeing foreigners in their restaurant, are gathered around, staring at me expectantly.

Looking down at the thick wheat noodles and chunks of beef floating in the broth, I think of what the groundwater must be like in this town. My stomach turns a cartwheel, but I don't want to be rude, and so I take a bite of noodles. They taste like salty wood, or maybe paper.

I ask for a can of Coca-Cola and crack it open, taking a greedy gulp in an attempt to wash the nasty taste out of my mouth. As I'm enjoying the soda, the thought that it might have been produced with local water flashes through my mind.

Panicked, I check the label, and I'm relieved when I see the Coke has been manufactured and bottled at a plant down south.

"Are you from Linfen?" I ask the pot-bellied proprietor.

He nods, smiles and offers me a cigarette, which I decline.

"It's very polluted here, don't you think?" I ask.

The proprietor shrugs and smokes.

"Linfen is a coal city," he says, and asks if I like my noodles.

I apologize, rub my stomach, and explain that they're very good but that it's too hot outside to eat. I put three yuan on the table, thank him, and walk out, back into the haze.

After a few blocks, I see a KFC. I duck into the restaurant, which is substantially more crowded than the noodle shop, and wolf down an "Old Beijing Chicken Wrap," which is basically the regular chicken wrap with a little bit of plum sauce and a few pathetic scallions. It tastes delicious.

My belly full, I leave and begin wandering aimlessly around Linfen, looking for something interesting, thinking that most of the time, I don't eat at fast-food restaurants because their food is not produced locally. Now, I'm eating at KFC precisely because their food comes from somewhere other than here. It's ironic, I think, and then I start to cough. My body shakes so hard I have to lean up against a wall. After what seems like forever, I finally, thankfully, stop coughing and catch my breath.

□   □   □

IN THE HILLS around Linfen, around 50 million tons of coal were mined in the past year.

Getting the coal out of the ground is difficult enough. Chinese coal mining is perhaps the most dangerous job in the world; many small mines operate without government approval and the workers are forced to work in dangerous conditions with few or no safety regulations. Fatal accidents occur on almost a daily basis.[9]

For all of its industrial output, for all the new buildings in all the rapidly developing cities throughout the whole country, for the new highway system which, when completed, will have paved more kilometers of road than all the roads in America, China relies on the burning of coal.

□　□　□

CHINA HAS LEAPT onto the world stage as a manufacturing power of gigantic proportions. Indeed, it would be remiss to write anything about contemporary China without mentioning that the whole country resembles one giant construction zone. This ambitious, too-rapid modernization drive has led to one of the fastest-growing economies in history and has lifted hundreds of millions out of extreme poverty into a somewhat more comfortable (if not ideal) existence.

However, the environmental fallout has been tremendous. The air in many Chinese cities barely qualifies as breathable. China's most famous river, the Yangtze, will soon become a "dead river": i.e., it supports no marine life and its water can no longer be used for bathing or for irrigation. The country's second-most-famous river, the Yellow River, no longer flows into the ocean because of the myriad dams constructed to provide hydroelectric power.

When I went to college in Beijing, people at home asked me what living in China was like. Similarly, Chinese people

---

9   See "The Peasant Who Likes to Take Pictures" for more on this.

often ask me how living in their country is different from living in the West. The differences are, of course, too many to name, and my responses to these questions vary depending on how I'm feeling. But I always make sure to mention the pollution.

Everyone who's ever been to Los Angeles knows that it's smoggy, and sure, if you're hanging around a factory somewhere in the States, the output can be annoying or inconvenient. But in most Chinese cities, poor quality air is just a way of life, a given: the sun is in the sky, the earth is on the ground, and the air is polluted.

□　□　□

THE CHINESE GOVERNMENT, the World Bank, a host of lesser international institutions and a broad range of NGOs have commissioned myriad studies to research China's environmental crisis.

They all agree: people are dying. The pollution created by the Chinese government's relentless quest for economic development is killing its citizens. Places like Linfen are the side effects, the collateral damage.

And these problems are not just happening in Linfen, but in cities like it all over China. As China's economy continues to soar, and its appetite for energy grows ever more voracious, the amount of destruction wreaked on the environment will surely get worse.

If you enter an apartment building anywhere in China, the homes themselves are usually clean and well-kept while the common spaces are filled with trash. People discard their garbage on the street, and don't even grasp the idea that there's anything remiss about this. Tourist sites from Mount Tai in the east to Jiuzhai Gorge in Sichuan Province are covered in trash: plastic bags, used beverage containers, shiny empty potato chip bags.

□ □ □

I WALK ALONG the wide boulevards of Linfen, checking out the Communist-era cement housing blocks and the new buildings under construction. I stroll past a brightly lit supermarket, past a computer shopping center. The Linfenites shuffling along the street seem grim and resigned, as if the pollution hanging in the city's air was a personification of its inhabitants.

I pass a Dicos, the Chinese McDonald's knockoff. I pass a movie theater and a furniture store. The more I walk, the more I realize just how *normal* the city seems. Except for the horrendous air pollution, I could be walking along the streets of Weifang, or Zibo, or Baoding, or any mid-sized, low-profile Chinese city.

After a while, I arrive at Yao Miao Temple. The temple is one of the city's most historic structures: though it has been rebuilt many times, it is over one thousand years old, and there are many well-preserved carvings from China's dynastic period.

Next to the temple, the city government has put a lot of yuan into creating a "town square" in a vain attempt to reinvent the area as a worthwhile tourist destination.

Apparently, the planning committee thought the best way to stir up tourism revenue would be to build an enormously tall red gate that towers into the sky, and to construct a selection of

Chinese monuments in miniature around that enormous gate. There's a tiny Great Wall, a diminutive Temple of Heaven, and a vaguely surreal micro-reproduction of Tiananmen Square.

Incongruously, a few amusement-park-style rides are scattered around these replicas. In front of the little Tiananmen, where in the real version the memory of the student protesters killed seventeen years ago burns in my mind, there is a dingy bumper car ride that wouldn't be out of place in a shabby county fair somewhere in Middle America. The government's plan to lure tourists isn't working; in fact, I'm the only tourist around. The bumper cars are empty.

My contact lenses burn and my stomach feels queasy. I pull my cell phone out of my pocket and check the time; I have been in Linfen for just under four hours. I decide to head back to the bus station to catch the bus back to Taiyuan.[10]

---

10 In June 2007, nearly a year after my visit, a Linfen child-labor scandal made the headlines in the international media. The owners of many brick kilns on the outskirts of town were "employing" hundreds of slave children as their workers. These children had been abducted from their homes elsewhere in the country, brought to the kilns, and forced to work making bricks. The children were barely clothed and fed.

9

The Bohemians

"Wherever you go, there you are."

—Buckaroo Banzai

"Dali is a fake paradise, but we love it anyway."

—Gong Jiaju

□   □   □

IN CHINA'S DYNASTIC PERIOD, the emperor would necessarily consolidate his power in a capital city. The day-to-day life of areas close to the capital could be directly overseen by the emperor and his cabinet, and was therefore tightly controlled.

As the Chinese territory expanded, envoys from the capital would travel to the outer fringes of the empire and set up vassal states. These more distant regions operated with a greater degree of autonomy, simply because they were further away from the emperor and his minions and thus more difficult to manage.

By the eighth century AD, six different clans of the Bai people had settled around a mountainous lake in what is today Yunnan Province. Pileguo, the leader of one of these clans, brokered an alliance with the other groups, and these lake people established the Kingdom of Nanzhao, with Taihe, a few miles south of Dali, as its capital.

For its first thirteen years of existence, the Kingdom of Nanzhao was aligned with the Tang Dynasty, but, in 750, the Nanzhao leaders rebelled against the Tang authorities. The emperor's government sent an army from the Tang Dynasty capital of Chang'an in an attempt to bring the rogue province in line, but the Nanzhao warriors were too powerful, and they emerged victorious.

Afterwards, the Nanzhao leaders, with Dali as their capital, expanded as far south as present-day Burma, Laos and Thailand and as far east as present-day Sichuan, eventually posing a serious threat to the Tang Dynasty. For several hundred years, Dali was the power center of a flourishing kingdom until, in 1253, it collapsed under attack from Kublai Khan's rampaging Mongol army.

□   □   □

UNLESS YOU'RE A MASOCHIST who pays no mind whatsoever to physical comfort, Beijing is not a pleasant place to be in the summer. The city's heat and humidity join forces with its polluted air to form an unholy trinity of oppressiveness.

I spent the summer of 2000 at Beijing's Qinghua University. My fellow foreign students and I spent our mornings in an ostensibly air-conditioned classroom that smelled like wet socks and old green tea, our afternoons out in the humid weather chowing dumplings at street stalls and making hundreds of flash cards to study vocabulary, and our evenings writing the same complex characters over and over again before decamping to a local restaurant for dinner, beer, and conversation.

This routine, shared with my new friends, was quite fun, and my Chinese was improving tremendously. But as the days went by, the cumulative effects of the less-than-ideal weather conditions began to chafe. It became hard to remember so many characters, and even harder to sleep restfully at night. Once, I got in the shower, turned the metal strip that served as a faucet to the coldest setting and actually nodded off, waking up spluttering when my head knocked against the bathroom wall.

In the middle of the semester, we had ten days' vacation in which we were free to travel, and a group of us decided to head southwest, to Yunnan Province. We were looking for temperate weather, clean air, and breathtaking scenery.

Yunnan has long been one of China's top travel destinations, due to its dizzying array of natural wonders and its *shaoshu minzu*, "ethnic minorities," as the Chinese refer to indigenous peoples. The vast majority of Chinese citizens—over 90 percent—are Han Chinese, who use this somewhat derogatory and condescending term to refer to the non-Han. These same citizens, ironically, are somewhat obsessed with "ethnic minorities," perhaps because they're both similar (in their Chineseness) and different (in their customs, etc.) than the Han Chinese.

In China's "ethnically diverse" areas, the minorities are generally homogenous. For example, Tibet is full of Tibetans and Xinjiang is packed with Uighurs. Yunnan, however, is home to more than twenty different ethnic groups. There are the Naxi in Lijiang; an offshoot of the Naxi, the Mosuo, live on the shores of Lugu Lake, where they have the only practicing matriarchal society in the world. The Dai people inhabit the tropical south, where they build wooden houses on stilts and practice Hinayana Buddhism.

There are Tibetans living on the snow-capped peaks of North Yunnan, and the mountains in the south play host to the Bulang people, who tattoo their whole bodies and chew betel nut, and so their teeth are permanently stained ink-black.

The Hui walk unnoticed among other Chinese; they are ethnically identical to the Han but are classified as a minority because of their Islamic faith. In Dali, the blue-clothed, ostensibly Buddhist Bai people are known for their friendliness.

These indigenous groups have been existing side by side with each other and with the Han Chinese for thousands of years. During this time, there have been all kinds of wars and conflict over territory, some more deadly than others. While the Han Chinese are now firmly "in charge" of Yunnan, the province remains tremendously ethnically diverse.

□ □ □

EVERY DAY ON the week prior to our departure, after we had eaten dinner, we returned to our sticky, stinky dormitory and crammed into a single room to share beer swigged from large green bottles as we discussed our upcoming travel plans. Mellowed from the beer and the camaraderie, we eagerly discussed the different places we would visit: The capital city of Kunming. The Old Town of Lijiang, a picturesque, perfectly preserved ancient Chinese city. The collection of karst peaks known collectively as the Stone Forest.

But most of all, we talked about Dali, the mountain town that had earned a reputation among Westerners in China as an oasis for the weary traveler. Dali, it was said, was a place where you could be happy sitting around all day doing absolutely nothing: an idle idyll. It sounded like paradise, nirvana, and the Garden of Eden all rolled into one.

□ □ □

THE FIVE OF US—Anna, a college classmate of mine from Michigan, her boyfriend Stefano, a slick ethnically Chinese guy born and raised in Rome, Helen, a tiny, headstrong Chinese girl from New Jersey, a guy we called Gebader, a tall, handsome but equally square goofball from Georgetown University, and I—arrived in Kunming, the capital of Yunnan, and spent a couple of days bumming around, visiting temples and walking around town during the day, bowling and bar-hopping by night.

After a couple days of relaxation, we boarded a bus for an overnight ride through the mountains to Lijiang. The sleeping arrangements on Chinese overnight buses resemble the pens that are used to house factory-raised chickens. There are two levels of seating on either side of the cabin: upper and lower horizontal berths, each designed for two people with a lumpy rectangular mass of fabric and padding surrounded by metal bars. It's like being in a cage without any sides.

Our group occupied the "back of the bus," a five-person bunk that takes up the rear. In order to chase away the smells of cigarette smoke and unwashed feet that combined to form the aroma of the bus, we had to open the little windows on each side of the bunk. Unfortunately, when the windows were open we could look past the side of the road, hundreds of feet down the mountain to the ground. The bus driver was blank-faced and driving way too fast. There were no guardrails to protect us from a potential fall. In three days, I was to turn twenty-one; the thought occurred to me that I might not make it.

Nevertheless, we arrived safely in Lijiang, where we hung out for a couple more days, eating and drinking and walking around the beautiful Old City alongside tens of thousands of Chinese tourists. On the day of our departure, we woke up early, still a bit sore, mentally and physically, from the rigors of the overnight bus. We left Lijiang in the late morning. After a comparatively luxurious and uneventful three-hour bus ride through stunning mountains, our group arrived in Dali in the late afternoon

We eagerly snatched up our backpacks from the belly of the bus and pushed our way through the crush of barking touts crowding the station, hawking food, rides, and hotel rooms. Once we had broken free from the throng, we clomped through the cobblestone streets of the Old City, burdened by our backpacks, searching for our destination: the Golden Sun Hotel.

□   □   □

AS EVERYONE WHO has visited Dali—and many Chinese cab drivers who haven't—can tell you, the place is beautiful, so beautiful that it doesn't seem real.

To the west of town, the Cangshan Mountains, a range of nineteen consecutive peaks, rise up majestically towards the heavens. From the cobblestone streets of the ancient city, the mountains look almost otherworldly, jutting thousands of feet into the sky like enormous statues guarding the city. The sky up here is bright and blue, completely free from pollution, and the mountains are constantly shrouded in enormous white clouds that change shape and direction seemingly at random.

Dali is bordered to the east by the shores of Erhai Lake, the second largest in the province. Indeed, Erhai is massive: it has a circumference of two hundred and fifty kilometers and, at its widest point, is thirty-seven kilometers across. The shores of the lake are studded with Bai villages; the Bai people are famed for their fishing method, which involves training cormorants—a kind of large black bird—to catch fish in their beaks then bring them back to the fisherman.

There's an old Chinese idiom to describe naturally harmonic beauty: "It has mountains, it has water, it has everything."

Chinese people are deeply enamored of this concept of *shanshui*—"mountains and water." They are also, more than any other nation of people I've ever encountered, seriously into their own history. Finally, as I mentioned, the Han Chinese have a powerful and somewhat disturbing fascination with ethnic minorities.

Since Dali's attributes include:

a) Natural beauty, specifically in the form of mountains and water.
b) A long and rich history.

c) Many ethnic minorities walking around in their brightly-colored, almost costume-like attire.

It has long been one of the most popular tourist destinations for Chinese people traveling in China.

□　□　□

DALI'S NOT A big place, but all the cobblestone streets look the same, so it's easy for the first-time visitor to get disoriented. We had been slogging around for half an hour, weighed down by our backpacks, when we finally admitted to ourselves that we had no idea where we were going. A couple of my classmates sat on a cement bench, yanked out our travel guide, and squinted at its low-quality map, trying to figure out our coordinates.

I set my pack down on the ground and stopped for a second to survey the scene, glancing up the hill towards the cloud-blanket hovering over the green Cangshan Mountains. In the distance, I heard the lazy clink of horse-cart bells.

After a few seconds spent sitting around and looking clueless, we were spotted by the inevitable array of touts, who began to gravitate towards us, no doubt preparing their sales pitches in their heads.

One friendly-looking, dark-skinned woman approached us and carefully pulled out a little notebook filled with photographs. She pointed to a picture of a shoddy-looking boat.

"Boat?" she asked, and we shook our heads, and sat there, trying to ignore her, until she left.

Another dark woman, who could have been the sister

of the first, sauntered over shyly and handed us a card for a guesthouse.

"Hotel?" she asked.

We explained that we already had a place to stay and tried to look away as she produced a photo of a dingy-looking room.

Someone figured out where we were, and we lumbered off towards the Golden Sun. The touts fell in behind us, but we walked purposefully, and they slipped away, one by one, in search of other prey.

We turned yet another corner, and with relief, spotted the sign for the Golden Sun. We checked into the place, which turned out to be the kind of faux-classy joint that is geared towards Chinese package tourists: marble lobby, marble bathrooms, an array of clocks on the wall behind the desk showing the time in world capitals.

My classmates decided to shower and rest up before dinner; as dusk spread over Dali, I went for a walk. As I strolled around the streets of the old city, I was approached by a stooped old lady, dressed in the traditional garb of the Bai ethnic minority: blue headdress, blue and black shawl, ornate silver earrings. She tottered up to me, nodding her head and exposing a toothless grin.

She reached into her pocket, pulled out a silver bracelet, and held it out in front of her, smiling and nodding her head, as if to say, "Buy this! Come on, buy it!"

I moved past her, walking up towards the mountains, away from the Golden Sun and the town of Dali. Suddenly, from behind me, I heard a sharp intake of breath and then a quick hiss: "Smoking the ganja?"

I turned around, incredulous. It's an open secret that Dali is the marijuana capital of China: the Bai chew cannabis seeds as a digestive tonic. The plant grows wild by the side of the road and up in the Cangshan Mountains.[11]

The old lady opened her shawl to reveal, cradled in her left hand, a plastic bag of dark green buds. For a split second, I thought about buying some—years later I'd be able to tell the tale of how I bought weed from an eighty-year-old woman on the street in China—but then I realized I was about to buy weed, from an elderly woman, on a crowded street in China.

I returned her smile, shrugged my shoulders, and continued to walk away from the Golden Sun and towards the mountains and the sound of horse bells. I made my way uphill along a narrow, cobblestone street. After a few minutes of climbing, I came to the north gate of the old city. I stopped to survey the scene: a group of scruffy men were sitting around next to a row of tired-looking horses attached to impromptu horse carts, smoking cigarettes and talking. These carts were fashioned from wooden benches atop a haphazardly assembled metal frame and looked none too sturdy.

They spotted me, and a couple of the men gestured towards the horses. I declined their invitation for a ride and leaned against the stone that surrounds the old city, looking up at the expanse of mountain rising up before me, so vast that it seemed to take up my entire frame of vision. The late afternoon sky darkened. It had rained earlier in the day, and each breath I took felt smooth and clean.

One of the horsemen decided to leave, presumably going

---

11 See "The Slacker" for more details.

home to his village for dinner. He boarded his cart, struck the horse with a whip, and made his way up the mountain. I closed my eyes, breathed deeply, and listened to the resonant clink of the horse bells as they slowly faded away into the distance.

When I opened my eyes again, all the horsemen had vanished. The mountains stood before me, a growing, dark shadow slipped over me. It felt comforting, like a long-forgotten promise that had finally been kept. Even though I had never been to Dali before, I felt like I had returned home after an extended exile.

Happy Birthday, I told myself; for a moment, I sat motionless, drinking in the sense of peace that hung over Dali like a gentle fog. It was almost dark, and so I headed back down the hill to meet up with my classmates for my birthday dinner.

□ □ □

THREE DAYS LATER, we left Dali and headed back to Beijing to resume classes; two years after that, I finished college and moved to Yunnan's capital city of Kunming, which I used as a base to explore the rest of the province. Dali was only a four-hour bus ride away, and I began heading up there whenever I had the chance.

When you spend an extended period of time in Yunnan, its distance from Beijing and "the rest of China" becomes more pronounced day by day. Everything in this part of China seems to move slower, people seem freer, somehow, and the pace of life is generally more relaxed.

The air is clean. Most of the time, the sky is blue. Instead of the pollution that sits stagnant over all Eastern Chinese cities, a mood of pleasantness, a feeling of well-being prevails in Yunnan.

This general air of contentedness often serves as a philosophical conduit to justify certain of life's problems; sure, there's traffic and dirty streets, but the traffic's not *that* bad and the streets aren't *that* dirty. Sure, there are certain parts of the province that are among the poorest in China, but at least they're poor and picturesque instead of poor and unsightly.

There are certain things that Yunnan lacks from a tourism standpoint, like good service, clean toilets, and effective airport security. It does not, however, have a shortage of places which possess astounding natural beauty: the cascading rice terraces of Yuanyang, the massive Tiger Leaping Gorge outside of Lijiang, the soaring Himalayan peaks of Zhongdian (now officially renamed Shangri-La.)

Dali is not the primary tourist destination in Yunnan; that honor belongs to the ancient city of Lijiang. The area surrounding Lijiang was classified as a UNESCO World Heritage Site; subsequently, the provincial government began an investment drive. Rich Chinese from coastal cities, Hong Kong, and Taiwan began to build massive tourist hotels around the walls of the old city.

The once-tranquil environment of Lijiang has largely been spoiled by poor municipal planning. The tourist infrastructure is built directly around the ancient city, which predictably results in constant chaos.

Thankfully, the massive hotels that serve tourists to Dali are located thirteen kilometers down the road from the Old City, in the town of Xiaguan, which is confusingly also referred to as "Dali City." Chinese tourists, who travel almost exclusively in large packs known as "tour groups," swarm the old city during the day to check out the pagodas and the mountain and gawk at the foreigners hanging out drinking coffee. (For many Chinese who live in places without a substantial Western population, white people are still a curiosity.) At night, however, the tour groups decamp to tourist restaurants in Xiaguan, and the ancient city becomes quiet, again.

◻   ◻   ◻

ONE OF MY closest friends in Kunming, Lao Wu, the chubby, loquacious owner of a successful travel company, is a native of neighboring Sichuan. He has made his home in Yunnan for many years and greatly enjoys poking fun at the province's *xiaoshu minzu wenhua*, or "ethnic minority culture."

One of his favorite sayings is that Yunnan natives are so lazy and "out of it" that you can tell them only to do two things at once; if you ask them to do three things, they will invariably forget one of the things you asked them to do. This is, of course, a ridiculous prejudice, and I told him so.

From then on, whenever he started on one of his "ethnic minority culture" tangents I would scowl at him but my chastisement never changed his mind.

One night in Dali when I was doing the research for this book, we were out having dinner at a local restaurant with a large group of people from Beijing and Guangzhou. Lao Wu loves to eat; however, he also loves to talk. So he'll spend a few minutes shoveling an enormous amount of meat and rice into his mouth; then, while everyone else is still preoccupied with the food, he'll start lecturing the table on the topic of his choice. That night in Dali, for the benefit of our out-of-town guests, he started in again about the whole "ethnic minority culture" thing.

I opened my mouth to rebut his statement and he quickly stopped me by thrusting the palm of his hand towards me in a "say no more" gesture. He arched his eyebrows and informed me that his travel company and, therefore, he himself, employed nearly one hundred natives of Yunnan and if anyone knows what they can and cannot do it should be him.

"Three things. Remember!" he said, ostensibly to me but really for the benefit of everyone at the table; he kept us hanging as he signaled for the waitress.

She hurried over to the table and he asked her to bring him a new set of chopsticks, a fresh bowl, and six more bottles of cold beer.

Sure enough, when she returned to the table, she had forgotten the beer.

Lao Wu looked at her expectantly, and she looked back at him with this blank kind of I-know-I-messed-up-but-I'm-not-sure-how face.

"Beer?" he asked.

She gave a little nod and hurried off to fetch the beer.

When she came back with the beer, she set the bottles down on the table. When she tried to open them, she realized she had forgotten the bottle opener. Quickly she returned with the opener, and once the bottles were open and our glasses filled, Lao Wu looked at me with a grin so enormous that it threatened to transcend the boundaries of his face. He laughed so hard the table shook.

□ □ □

IN 1984, THE CHINESE government officially classified Dali as a zone that was "open to foreigners" (as opposed to most of the rest of the country, which was off-limits.)

Half a decade later, as it became easier for foreigners to secure tourist visas for China, a trickle of Western travelers began to stream into Dali. Some of the more seasoned backpackers, who had been bumming around Southeast Asia for years, recognized an unspoiled paradise. They told their friends, and soon enough there were a bunch of Europeans, Australians, and Americans, many of them smelly and unkempt, hanging around in the old city of Dali for more than just a couple days at a time.

One young native entrepreneur noticed the foreigners and opened up a café selling the food they craved but couldn't get in China: coffee, pizza, and that eternal backpacker staple, granola with fruit and yogurt. He took the English name "Jack" and called his place, fittingly, "Café de Jack."

One of Jack's friends saw that Jack was doing gangbusters business and sensed that the market could stand a little bit of healthy competition. He began calling himself Jim, and opened "Jim's Peace Café" just down the street from "Café de Jack."

Once Lonely Planet and other travel guides lionized Dali as an idyllic getaway from the rigors of traveling in China, the backpacker population increased at an exponential rate. This led to even more entrepreneurial activity from local residents, and a veritable slew of Western-style cafés opened on and around one of the town's narrow streets. Eventually, Huguo

Lu—"Protecting Our Country Street"—earned the nickname *Yangren Jie,* or "Foreigners Street."

During the Reform and Opening period of the early nineties, a large middle class with disposable income emerged in many of China's eastern cities. For the first time, a significant group of Chinese had a chance to travel around the country for leisure. Many of the Chinese tour groups coming through Dali had never seen foreigners up close and in person before, or if they had, they hadn't seen a lot of them in the same place at the same time.

Oddly enough, the foreigners in Dali became a tourist attraction for the Chinese: to this day, the tour guides (clad in fake ethnic minority costumes) lead their way, waddling along in a line up Foreigners Street. The tourists can be distinguished by their identical brightly colored baseball caps with the travel company logo stenciled on the front.

The tour guide will then identify the varying types of foreigners who are hanging around, minding their own business, as if these strange creatures were species of animals in a zoo. (Example: a tour guide points at me and some Western friends and says, unaware that I understand her, "These are Englishmen. They like to come to Dali to enjoy the beautiful surroundings.")

□ □ □

AT THE SAME TIME, a few groups of Chinese artists and artsy types, disillusioned with the booming eastern cities, got wind of a bohemian community in Dali, pulled up their roots, and headed west.

This migration provided an escape from the smog-choked city life, away from shiny skyscrapers and two-hour commutes, away from the constant din of construction and the audible churning of money being made and spent.

It didn't hurt, of course, that living in Dali was cheaper than almost anywhere else in China.

So these messengers from the fringes of contemporary culture rented out cheap storefronts and opened up even more cafés. Some of them went into business for themselves or with friends; others pooled their money with Westerners who found themselves in Dali and didn't want to leave.

These migrants called their friends back east and told them to come to Dali. When those friends got there, they called up *their* friends.

They opened bookstores and CD shops. They opened home-style Cantonese restaurants. They opened bars in old houses, stores selling fashionable T-shirts and hippie garb, small hotels and guesthouses, all on and around Foreigners Street.

In the early 2000s, as Chinese art became a hot commodity on the world market, many of China's preeminent modern artists, like the Beijing painter Fang Lijun, the Taiwanese ex-New Yorker H. N. Han, and the sculptor Xue Jiye purchased second homes in Dali.

The sculptor Zhao Qing, a Dali native, built his own modern glass-and-steel house on the shore of Erhai Lake, near Shuanglang Village, which rises incongruously over the ramshackle village buildings like an unreal vision of the future.

Fueled by a sense of peace instilled by the idyllic setting, and aided by the effects of the local plum wine and the schwaggy grass from Cangshan Mountain, these two communities—Western backpackers/short-term residents and Chinese counterculture types/hangers-on—united to form a veritable international New Bohemia. They rode bicycles and old motorcycles, crammed into ramshackle houses, and spent their days creating art, hiking in the mountains, and swimming in the lake.

The cost of living in Dali has since risen considerably, of course, but you can still rent a house that would comfortably sleep four people for 400 yuan ($48) a month. An affordable meal of rice noodles costs one or two yuan (12–25¢).

In 2000, a few months before I arrived in Dali for the first time with my group of fellow students, two visual artists from the eastern province of Shandong, married couple Zhao Rongjie and Liu Xinmin, opened a small bar in an old stone structure at the top of Renmin Lu—"Street of the People"— one block north of Foreigners Street.

They called the place the Bird Bar and hired a rotating cast of scruffy Western youngsters to help run the joint. Their caring, den-mother-and-father attitude and party-hearty-slash-Zen approach to living made the Bird Bar Dali's de facto bohemian clubhouse. They played all kinds of hip music, collecting CDs from customers to eventually amass an enormous music library, and stayed open basically as long as people were still there, often into the early morning.

□ □ □

I MET RONGJIE and Xinmin, as everyone calls them, on my first night in Dali, when my classmates and I celebrated my twenty-first birthday in the Bird Bar. Almost immediately, we became fast friends: Rongjie, studious and sober, serves as the yin to Xinmin's boisterous yang, and they are both well-spoken and intelligent people.

Like its owners, the Bird Bar is tasteful. The bar itself is just a small, waist-high counter that occupies one corner of a large stone room. Behind the counter is a small, horizontal cooler to keep beer cold. Bottles of liquor are stacked on shelves that have been attached to the stone wall behind the bar.

The rest of the room is taken up by cushioned, futon-style benches; customers sit on the benches or on the stone floor. The nooks and crannies of the room are packed with old books and magazines, maps, board games, and toys.

Behind the stone room is a small courtyard; in the summer, customers hang out back there playing guitars and bongo drums, and in the winter, they sit in a circle around a fire pit to keep warm and swap stories.

In the countless nights I've spent hanging around the place, I've met hundreds of fascinating people. On any given night, the Bird Bar scene might include: famous artists from Beijing, pop stars from Taiwan, a *nouveau riche* businessman who has swapped his ill-fitting suit for a hippie shirt and a Buddha necklace, a foreign correspondent from a major American newspaper, a group of Swedish girls on a trip around the world, Chinese college students on spring break, all or some of the people who own the other businesses in town, which all shut earlier, and, of course, Rongjie, Xinmin, and their two enormous German shepherds, who roam around the bar as if they themselves were the owners.

◻ ◻ ◻

OVER THE PAST seven years, even more hip Chinese have set up shop in Dali; Westerners, Japanese, and Koreans have joined the party as well by moving to Dali in increasingly large numbers and opening their own small businesses.

The Bird Bar has since added a cozy little guesthouse behind the original structure, which they christened the Bird's Nest.

The artist Fang Lijun, known for his paintings of ghostly bald-headed figures (which look uncannily like Fang himself) opened a hotel down the street from the Bird Bar. It's certainly one of the more modern structures in Dali, tastefully constructed from steel and glass: the rooms feature floor-to-ceiling windows.

("You can take a shit while looking at the lake! It's amazing!" one of my Chinese friends exclaimed after his first time staying at the hotel.)

Once-quiet Renmin Lu has become a de facto "Second Foreigners Street," where the Phoenix Café, owned by a twenty-something kid from Sichuan, sits across the street from the Bad Monkey Bar, started by two English punters tired of their life back home.

Walking down a hill towards the lake, there are rows of new cafés with names like Fifty Bowls Music House and Toxic Electro Club.

CD shops sell the newest titles by Sonic Youth, the Eels, and Brian Eno, while several DVD stores have the complete works of Fassbinder, Godard, Cassavetes, Tarantino and Wong Kar-Wai.

The local officials, too, are doing their part for development: the Dali government knocked down a number of old and charming structures in the middle of the old city and replaced them with very tacky, new-seeming replicas of what they think those same old buildings should theoretically have originally looked like.

□ □ □

DURING THE 1960s, hippies and hipsters fled Europe and America, toting huge backpacks, to establish new countercultural capitals in exotic locales like Istanbul, Tehran, Marrakesh, Goa, and Kathmandu.

In the late seventies, as the geopolitical situation in Afghanistan and Iran shifted, it became impossible to travel overland to these cities. However, airplane travel became newly affordable, and intrepid souls set up new backpacker capitals all over India, Thailand, and South America. The idea of backpacking—or "budget travel"—slipped into the mainstream.

Thirty years later, many of these backpacker oases have changed dramatically. I've been to a few of them: Koh Phangan in Thailand. Vang Vieng in Laos. Essaouera in Morocco. These are wild, once-placid little towns, now whipped into dens of drug-and-alcohol-fueled hedonism by a steady tide of punters fresh out of university in Sydney or Manchester or out of the Israeli army.

What Dali has that these other places don't is a sense of local bohemianism. In Dali, unlike in Southeast Asia, the Chinese artists, writers, and slackers mingle and coexist with the Western artists, writers, and slackers. The longer you stay in Dali, the more peaceful and contented you become. Is it paradise? No, says, my longtime friend, the interpreter-cum-hustler Gong Jiaju: it's a fake paradise. But we love it, anyway.

10

The Screenwriter

"HAVE YOU EVER seen *Cinema Paradiso*?" asks Shao Xiaoli, sipping his glass of Yanjing beer. "Well, that's what my life was like. My father was the projectionist in the movie theater, and our family lived in the back of the place. Every day, starting when I was four and five years old, I would just watch movies, over and over again. I didn't want to go to school, and when I went, I didn't study hard. My dad would take me out to the mining districts, to the countryside, where they didn't have any movies, and we'd bring along our sixteen millimeter projector, and show them movies on the walls of their villages."

Like many successful artists, Xiaoli's got the sexy-ugly thing down pat. His face is made up of a ragtag bunch of not-entirely-harmonious features: wide cheeks, small eyes, crooked teeth, and an uneven mouth. Thrown together, these features form a brooding, yet compelling kind of mien. When I showed up at his place, a young college graduate from

Chongqing, the Chinese capital of *meinu,* or beautiful girls, was on her way out.

"She's twelve years younger than me." Xiaoli breaks into his crooked smile. "One wheel (Chinese zodiac cycle) younger. That's not bad, right?" Xiaoli asks with a playful smile on his face.

Xiaoli lives near Chaoyang Park, in the northeastern quadrant of inner Beijing, in a quaint Chinese apartment compound that's bisected by a tree-lined cement driveway. The place has a mellow feel that seems another world from the skyscrapers a kilometer or so to the east; the compound has its own row of shops: convenience store, hairdresser, laundry, long-distance call booth. Most of the people living in the compound have been here for thirty-odd years, and every night these old-school Beijingers come home toting bags of fresh vegetables and beer. After dinner, the men take off their shirts and sit around small tables playing Go and Chinese checkers while the women fan themselves and indulge in local gossip. The whole place is like a leftover fragment of China circa the Deng Xiaoping era. These days, though, many of the residents have cars, and so a former playground next door has become an impromptu parking lot.

There are eight massive concrete buildings in the compound, each made up of sixteen apartment blocks, each block with twelve apartments. About thirty of Xiaoli's friends have moved into the compound over the past two years: lawyers, ad agency executives, rock-and-roll musicians, painters, set designers—a concentrated version of hipster Beijing.

At night, after all the old Beijingers have gone to sleep, Xiaoli and his friends, male and female, sit in the compound's small concrete gazebo playing Chinese poker and drinking two-yuan (25¢) beer purchased from the surly man in the undershirt with the cigarette clamped between his teeth who runs the compound store. A small security booth separates the compound from the road; the security guard goes to sleep around 10 PM with his head on the desk, uniform cap resting by his side. The little garden is eerily calm: a single streetlight illuminates the gazebo and Xiaoli's crew slap cards down on the table, gossip, and sip their beers until the wee hours of the morning. A few times an hour, the silence will be broken by the furtive whispers of a young couple returning home or the bleat of a distant car horn.

□   □   □

XIAOLI IS A screenwriter; he's co-written the scripts for two major Chinese films in the past six years: *Piaoliang Mama* and *Zhou Yu's Train*. He's an accomplished young man.

Now, in order to pay the rent on his apartment and make some cash to finance his directorial debut, he's working on a TV series. The plot, he says, might remind me of *She'erma he Louyishi*.

After a few minutes, I figure out that he means *Thelma and Louise*.

He takes a sip of beer and starts rambling: "A woman in her late forties, still beautiful, takes a younger woman under her wing. The woman is the hot, sassy kind that might be a dancer at a nightclub, and they go take care of three guys . . ."

Xiaoli interrupts his plot description with a pointed non sequitur.

"Why in American movies do the good guys always use Apple computers and the bad guys use PCs?"

I look at my Apple, and his PC, and venture a guess that it has something to do with Apple shelling out a bunch of money for product placement, although, really, I have not noticed this phenomenon.

" . . . the hot, sexy kind that might be a dancer at a nightclub, and they go take care of three guys. One is an artist, and another one is a businessman, and the next guy, he's a writer . . ."

Xiaoli pours me another cup of tea. He doesn't have a refrigerator, and I can't stomach lukewarm Chinese beer.

He loses his train of thought. He gets up and strolls over to the corner of his apartment where there is a shelf piled high with thousands of pirated DVDs. He selects a bizarre title— *Lemonade Joe, or A Horse Opera*, an obscure Czech surrealist cowboy movie.

"Have you seen this one?" he asks, grinning. "It's amazing!"

□　□　□

XIAOLI'S FROM YIBIN, in Sichuan, a provincial city best known worldwide as the headquarters of Wu Liang Ye, China's most famous rice wine. (As Nixon said when he came to China: Going back to America, my airplane won't need any fuel, we can just throw some of this stuff in the gas tank.)

He spent his childhood in the family theater, watching movies whenever he wasn't studying, which was most of the time. In high school, he started reading whatever novels he could get his hands on, and he thought that maybe someday he could become a writer. But first there was one massive obstacle to overcome: the dreaded *gaokao*, China's infamous college entrance examination.

In the mid-eighties when Xiaoli was growing up, Sichuan was China's most populous province. Since there are college entrance quotas for each province, the Sichuan examination required the highest score in order to ensure a place at university.

It's hard to explain the sheer magnitude of the *gaokao's* importance: it makes the American SATs and British A-levels look like little more than third-grade spelling tests. Achieving a good *gaokao* score requires a comprehensive knowledge of all academic subjects.

In China in the late eighties and early nineties, college entrance ensured a relatively comfortable life and manifold opportunities. Failure to pass the exam would almost certainly result in a peasant existence for the rest of Xiaoli's life. He would spend the next sixty years working sixteen-hour days slaving away at a menial job for pennies, as a janitor or a taxi driver or putting together goods for export on an assembly line.

"My mother said: if you don't pass this test, the next day you will be out on the street and you can find your own food," remembers Xiaoli with a shiver.

While Xiaoli was preparing for the *gaokao*, he saw a notice posted on the bulletin board of his high school. Teachers from the Shanghai Playwriting Institute were traveling to Chengdu, the capital of Sichuan, to look for prospective students.

During the fall of his senior year in high school Xiaoli took the train up to Chengdu to meet with the teachers from the playwriting institute. He had never seen a Western-style play in his entire life, but he was a movie buff, and he figured that Western plays were like motion picture screenplays. His meeting with the teachers proved his theory correct; when he got back to Yibin, he bought a few books of Western plays and started to research.

A few weeks later, back in Yibin, Xiaoli took a special playwriting examination that had been sent over to his school from the Institute in Shanghai. He passed the playwriting exam with flying colors. Now, all he had to do to be accepted to the Shanghai Playwriting Institute was to achieve a passing score on the *gaokao*.

However, Xiaoli had spent too much of his time reading Western plays and dreaming about his future career as a playwright, and he did not adequately prepare for the *gaokao*. Xiaoli failed the test. In fact, he didn't even come close to passing.

□   □   □

TO HIS GREAT RELIEF, his parents decided that since he'd done so well on the playwriting test, Xiaoli should spend another year studying for the *gaokao* and that he should take the exam one more time. They weren't going to kick him out on the street. Xiaoli agreed, though he was having a hard time getting into the textbooks.

And then, just after he finished high school, everything changed. His father had a massive heart attack and died instantly on the floor of the family movie theater.

Xiaoli's mother was a primary school teacher with a modest income, and his older sister was away, studying at university. Without his father around to help support the family, Xiaoli would have to take his place as the primary breadwinner.

He bought all the books that he hadn't studied, as far back as middle school, and re-educated himself in every subject: math, chemistry, physics, geography, English. He was determined: it was time to ace the *gaokao*.

And this year, he decided to forgo the Shanghai Playwriting Institute and take the special examination at the only film school in China, the vaunted Beijing Movie Academy. It was a three-day train ride to Beijing, and Xiaoli slept only intermittently. He got off the train in Beijing and took a bus to the Beijing Movie Academy.

"As soon as I walked into the main gate of the school to take the test," recalls Xiaoli, "I knew I would pass. I felt a terribly powerful feeling, and I looked down at the black armband I was wearing (to indicate mourning for the loss of a parent). I knew my father was at my back helping me."

Xiaoli had to pass an oral examination, then watch a movie and write a critical report, and then take a three-hour written examination.

When he boarded the hard-seat train carriage for the long journey back to Yibin, he was sure that he'd passed the test. The hard-seat is the third class of Chinese trains; there is no sleeping berth, just an uncomfortable metal seat with others crowded in beside you. Often, the seats are sold out so there will be people sitting atop their luggage on the floor, sleeping in the aisles, smoking and spitting, talking and eating instant noodles to while away the long, uncomfortable hours. Xiaoli stayed awake for two days, head buried deep in his books, studying for the test that would likely determine the course of the rest of his life.

A few weeks after he got back to Yibin, he took the *gaokao* for the second time. This time, he got the highest score in the entire city. And as he suspected, he also passed the Beijing Movie Academy test. The scrawny kid from Sichuan was going to Beijing to be a filmmaker.

□ □ □

"AT THAT TIME," remembers Xiaoli, "I'm talking 1991, 1992, the only way to get into film was to go to Beijing Movie Academy. That's why all the Chinese filmmakers everyone knows, they all went there."

Like most of the students at the Beijing Movie Academy, Xiaoli wanted to enroll in the directing department. However, there were less than ten students who were selected for this area of study, and they all had family connections. So Xiaoli instead entered the next most prestigious field of study: screenwriting.

There were only twelve students in his class, and all except for a few of them were the sons and daughters of wealthy filmmakers and government officials. Xiaoli felt like a rank outsider; he'd just entered college, and already he was feeling the pressure of being unconnected, unknown, and certainly not wealthy. All the other students didn't need to study hard. They already knew that upon graduating, they would be able to rely upon their family connections to get filmmaking opportunities. Xiaoli had no such luck. One of his classmates was so audacious as to tell Xiaoli, "I'm definitely going to be a better filmmaker than you."

"Why?" asked Xiaoli.

"Because," said the arrogant prick, "I've got relatives that will set me up. I've got nothing to worry about."

This incident left an indelible mark on Xiaoli. "I will remember it until I die," Xiaoli says, in one of his rare serious moments. Then he smiles. "That kid went to America and started studying computers, you know, IT. He never made a film. When he saw my movie in his American video store he called me on the phone. I brought up this incident, and he didn't remember it. I was nice to him, though, we're friends now."

□ □ □

AT THE BEIJING Movie Academy Xiaoli was studying like a machine—his old days of procrastination and idleness long behind him. He knew that he'd have to work many times harder than the other kids in order to achieve the same degree of success they took for granted. And then, one day, he showed up for class and their teacher wasn't there; in his place stood several of the school's top officials.

They were taking each student aside into an empty classroom and talking to him for an hour or so. Something serious was going down, for sure, but Xiaoli wasn't sure what.

When it was Xiaoli's turn, the officials walked him down the hall into the adjacent room, where the school's headmaster sat behind a large desk.

"What do you think of your teacher, Lao Xing?" asked the headmaster.

"He's a good teacher," responded Xiaoli.

"Have you ever had sexual relations with him?"

"No way!" Xiaoli sputtered, "no way!"

"Are you sure?" asked the headmaster.

"Of course I'm sure!" said Xiaoli.

Satisfied, they led him back into the classroom and took the next student aside. "The teacher had been fucking half the boys in the class," remembers Xiaoli. "That was basically the end of my time at the Beijing Film Academy—our class had a black mark for the rest of our time there. No teachers wanted to be responsible for us, and no one required anything from us. It was quite an easy road." China's shame-based culture ensured that none of the other teachers at the Beijing Movie Academy wanted to be associated with Xiaoli's class—it had been besmirched by the molestation scandal. So, in effect, there was no adviser responsible for their studies, and the students were free to do as they liked.

"You know," Xiaoli recalls, lighting a Red Pagoda Mountain cigarette, "there are only two of us from that class still making movies. The rest have all changed their profession—advertising, IT, businesspeople."

"Oh yeah," he adds, "there are actually three of us. The teacher makes these crazy underground gay movies. He's one of the most famous homosexuals in all of China."

□ □ □

AFTER GRADUATING FROM the Academy, most of the students tried to stay in Beijing, as it has always been and still is the cultural capital of all China. But, at the time, it was easier said than done, because the *hukou* system was still in place.

The Chinese government designed the *hukou* system in order to control internal migration. Basically, it granted a citizen the right to live and work only in the place of his birth.

If he wanted to move to a different city, he had to first find a *danwei,* or work unit, the Communist equivalent of a company, to take him in.

When Xiaoli graduated, his affiliation with the Film Academy would likewise come to an end, and unless he could find a *danwei* to take him in, he would have to go back to Yibin. All the other students in his class were competing amongst themselves, exploiting family connections and giving out expensive gifts to *danwei* leaders, jockeying for positions in film-related *danwei.* Xiaoli decided not to enter the fray. As graduation approached, every other student in his class had a job secured, except for Xiaoli. He felt just like he felt after he failed the *gaokao* the first time around. Fucked.

A short time later, the headmaster of the Beijing Film Academy came back from a visit to the Shanghai Film Factory, where his colleagues had asked him for a screenwriting graduate student to start working down there. Since Xiaoli was the only one without a job lined up, he was offered the position. Xiaoli took the twenty-four-hour train trip down to Shanghai, but he decided that the job wasn't cool enough; besides, he didn't know anyone in Shanghai. "It was a completely alien city," he recalls. "How could I develop there?"

The officials at the Beijing Film Academy were dismayed: they felt that Xiaoli had wasted a valuable opportunity.

□ □ □

XIAOLI PREPARED FOR GRADUATION, unsure of his future. He spent his spare time hanging around with his best friend, a directing student two years his junior named Wang Haixing. Wang, a virgin, was terribly and hopelessly in love with a beautiful American exchange student, a girl from New York, but he didn't know what to do about it. Xiaoli helped Wang practice his pickup lines, and even went so far as to accompany Wang to the girl's house and wait at the door for him.

Xiaoli was a good teacher, and it worked; Wang and the American girl fell in love. But the American girl was going to a Hong Kong filmmaking university, and so their romance was in jeopardy. Wang asked the Beijing Film Academy officials if he could go to Hong Kong to study. Alas, he recalls, they simply "laughed in his face."

Jokingly Xiaoli said, "Maybe I'll go down there and keep her safe for you"; then he thought about it and realized that maybe going to Hong Kong wasn't such a bad idea after all. After all, Hong Kong was the capital of Asian cinema, and he had been watching Hong Kong movies since he was a kid. The Beijing Film Academy officials thought it was a fine idea—where else was this undistinguished student from the "black" class going to go when he graduated?—and so they wrote him a letter of recommendation.

There was only one problem. In Hong Kong, people speak Cantonese, which is completely different than the Mandarin spoken in Beijing. So Xiaoli decided that first going to Guangzhou—formerly called Canton, on the Chinese mainland directly across from Hong Kong—would be a good idea. There, he could learn the language, get some job, and prepare for his life as a graduate student in Hong Kong. He had just finished college and he wanted to live a little, anyway. Go out on the town, have a few drinks, maybe meet some pretty girls.

One or two months, maximum. Then he'd get serious with his studies.

He never made it to Hong Kong.

□   □   □

"I CAME FOR one or two months," Xiaoli recalls fondly, "and I stayed for five years."

Guangzhou is China's third "international city," after Beijing and Shanghai. Due to its location across the Pearl River from Hong Kong, it's traditionally been China's wealthiest region; most Chinese immigrants in the West are from the Guangzhou area.

Xiaoli didn't know anyone in Guangzhou, was struggling with the language, and needed a job. He was quickly running out of money. Every major Chinese city has a massive, state-owned film company, so Xiaoli showed up at the Guangzhou Film Factory, presented his degree from the Beijing Film Academy (far and away the best film school in China) and was hired on the spot as a script reader.

"I was reading these terrible scripts every day," he says, "writing critical reports, and they were so, so bad. You couldn't believe it. I got bored after a month and took off. But most importantly, I knew I could do better."

Through some new friends, he secured a job at an ad agency, and started directing and writing scripts for China's new at-home shopping network. "Selling silver bracelets, and stuff like that."

One humid Guangzhou evening, out at dinner with some

friends and colleagues, he met the well-known film director Sun Zhou. They got to know each other well, regularly staying up all night drinking and talking about movies. After they had known each other for a few months, Sun Zhou made his proposition. "Why don't you come work for me?" he asked. "We'll make movies together."

It was then that Xiaoli knew that he would never get to Hong Kong. Why go to graduate school with the hopes of making movies later, he reasoned, if I can just make movies now? In Guangzhou, they were in the epicenter of China's economic revolution. It seemed that everyone was busy with work all day, able to pursue fortune for the first time in their lives. Everyone, that is, except for Zhou and Xiaoli, who hung out at Zhou's home, talking about movies, sipping tea, and generally enjoying a quiet and relaxed life in this bustling city jam-packed with upwardly mobile hustlers. At night, they'd go out and party with the moneymakers, never picking up the check, living off the famous generosity of Guangzhou's *nouveau riche.*

Even though each major Chinese city hosts a state-owned film company, making films in China is a difficult proposition. As in the West, a major obstacle to filmmaking is securing financing. A major difference between East and West, though, is that all films in China must be approved by the government before one frame of film is shot. This approval process is both long and arduous. Permissions to film can be denied, the script can be censored or rejected, the film quotas can be exceeded. In order to make an "aboveground film" (officially sanctioned, unlike the work of China's aforementioned most famous homosexual), one that can be shown in a movie theater, the filmmaker needs to secure both financial and political backing and apply for literally hundreds of licenses, varied and obscure.

In China, for every ten movies that have gone through the requisite stages of pre-production—a finished script, actors, a director, and crew all lined up—only one of these movies will get made. Either the script won't be approved by the Ministry of Culture or the financing will fall through.

Zhou and Xiaoli collaborated on three scripts. Each time they presented their scripts to the government and to the investors, they came close to actually being able to begin shooting. But ultimately, they could not secure the necessary approval. "I wasn't frustrated, though," remembers Xiaoli. "At that time, every day, I felt like there would be beautiful things waiting for me the next day."

With their fourth finished screenplay—*Piaoliang Mama*—the pair finally happened upon the correct combination of an approved-by-the-government script and good luck with their investors. They made the film, a highly stylized tale of a single mother caring for her deaf child. Thanks to a powerful performance by the famous actress Gong Li, the film secured an international release. It was retitled *Breaking the Silence* and won awards in Canada and Hong Kong.

Their next project, *Zhou Yu's Train*, was a success in China, too. (I remember taking a date to see the film in the theater when I was living in Yunnan Province. She cried; I had a hard time understanding the plot. There were no subtitles, and a lot of flashbacks.) Gong Li returned to play the title character, Zhou Yu, and the film was once again released internationally.

□ □ □

"I WAS VERY LONELY in Guangzhou," says Xiaoli, "but I didn't realize it until I saw that movie by Tsai Ming-Liang, *What Time is it There?*"

This film, released in 2001, tells the story of a man in Taipei who pines for a girl in Paris. The lonely man resets all of the clocks in Taipei to Paris time as a symbolic gesture of his love.

"I cried," he remembers, "the girl in Paris, it reminded me so much of my life. Slowly, I realized that there was nothing more I could do in Guangzhou. I didn't want to make advertisements, and I didn't want to get rich. I'd been there for five years. That's a long time. I wanted to go back to Beijing."

□ □ □

WORKING ON MOVIES with Zhou left Xiaoli with a little bit of cash; when he returned to Beijing, in order to save money, he rented a cheap room in a bathhouse. A friend got him a gig directing some episodes of a TV series, and he was looking for a permanent apartment when the SARS panic hit Beijing. Suddenly, everyone was wearing white masks, and many people were dying. Text messages were flying back and forth among Beijingers, circulating rumors of a government cover-up of the epidemic. (This later turned out to be true: a Beijing doctor, Jiang Yanyong, blew the whistle on the government's secret "SARS hospitals.") Along with a good deal of Beijing artists, Xiaoli fled west, to Yunnan Province.

After the threat of SARS vanished, he returned to Beijing,

and took a job writing a TV series. In China there are literally hundreds of free TV stations, all with original programming. Therefore, there are a lot of opportunities to write for television, and it's a far more lucrative endeavor than writing for film. While Chinese TV stations can depend on advertising revenue to pay their employees, most Chinese people do not see movies in the theater, choosing instead in this digital age to buy pirated DVDs for a fraction of the cost of a theater ticket. At the turn of the twenty-first century, theaters are a luxury entertainment reserved for those urbanites with a lot of spending money. Back in Xiaoli's father's day, peasants didn't have access to TV and so the theater was necessary.

Also, when working on a TV series, the scriptwriter is effectively the boss. Unlike with film scripts, which are vulnerable to the director's interpretation, in TV writing, the scriptwriter's status is higher than the director's.

"All the things I've been writing for the past couple years," Xiaoli grins, "are basically to make some money and to get my name out there. But I don't want to make money, just to have money, like most other writers."

◻ ◻ ◻

OVER THE COURSE of my hanging out with Xiaoli, I met several other scriptwriters. One drove a new silver BMW; one owned three apartments and was preparing for vacation in Frankfurt; yet another had just lost tens of thousands of US dollars betting on World Cup football.

Xiaoli, consciously, lives a more modest life: the rent on his apartment is incredibly cheap, by Beijing standards, and he doesn't have any interest in buying a house or a car. He doesn't want to write eight or nine scripts a day, like his successful friends; he'd rather write one a day, make it a little bit better, and therefore make less money than they, as they churn out script after script, but at least have more fun and retain some artistic integrity.

"Chinese television is really shitty," explains Xiaoli, "and we can't make it good, even if we want to. The censors are not only for content, but also for complexity; if something's too confusing, then we can't have it on TV. The average people won't understand. The actors have to cry here, laugh here, the whole thing is so fake. It's really not a very good job."

In Chinese visual media—movies and television—challenging and provocative subject matter is basically off-limits. Not only the old Hollywood standbys, violence and nudity (Chinese films must be approved for all audiences), but also anything vaguely political in nature is prohibited by the Party's Ministry of Culture. In 2006, Hollywood flicks such as *Brokeback Mountain* and *Pirates of the Caribbean* were banned from Chinese theaters: for homosexuality in the first; too many ghosts—their sexual preference unknown—in the second. *The Da Vinci Code* was pulled from theaters after just a couple weeks for . . . mysterious reasons. *Mission: Impossible III*, which was partially filmed in Shanghai, had to be "edited" in order to secure approval for screening in China: the censors felt that scenes that showed laundry hanging on lines were insulting to their country. (Of course, in almost all of China, including Shanghai, people dry their clothes by hanging them on lines.)

Domestic Chinese films, commercial and art-house alike,

are subject to even stricter regulations, and it's difficult to work within the rules, especially considering that most of these budding filmmakers have seen all kinds of films from other countries. They are influenced by Japanese horror flicks, the French New Wave, Hollywood, Bollywood, and the American indie auteurs of the nineties. To make a comparable movie in China, however, would be impossible.

First of all, the films would be too provocative to be approved by the censors. Secondly, the films would be deemed too convoluted for the average Chinese person to understand. The Chinese educational system stresses learning by repetition; from a very young age, students are bombarded by thousands of Chinese characters, historical facts, and math equations that they are expected to memorize. Western educational staples like critical thinking are actively discouraged. Students are actually given poor grades for displaying active and fertile imaginations. Creative short stories are dismissed; students who question—let alone debate—their professors are rewarded with disdain instead of encouragement.

This is why China produces thousands of qualified engineers and scientists but so few top-grade scholars of the humanities. And this is why the Ministry of Culture—and many writers—might feel that their population is ill-equipped to understand and enjoy complexity, subtlety, and nuance in film and television.

◻   ◻   ◻

XIAOLI'S GOT A SOLUTION to this government-imposed creative blockade. Instead of pouring his creative energy into writing another lousy script, or working on a puerile television series, he has started work on his first feature-length documentary about the cultural aftershocks of the Third Indochina War.

A little history: in February 1979, after the Sino-Soviet split, 80,000 troops from China's People's Liberation Army invaded USSR-backed Vietnam as an act of defiance against the Soviets. (The official and absurd reason given for the war was alleged mistreatment of Vietnam's ethnic Chinese population.)

Drawing from his own modest savings, using digital video cameras borrowed from friends, and recruiting a pal of his to operate the cameras, Xiaoli traveled to Guangxi and Yunnan, the provinces of China that border Vietnam, and interviewed hundreds of villagers in order to explore the lingering effects of the war in these areas.

Xiaoli will make another trip down to the border region to finish the interviews for his film. He's manically excited about the project; indeed, he has unearthed some fascinating stories. He tells me about an old soldier, so damaged by the effects of the war that he couldn't get an erection unless there are war movies on television; his wife's solution was to buy the pirated DVD box set of *Band of Brothers*. He tells me about hundreds of mixed couples, intermarriages between Chinese and Vietnamese, who live near the border and were forced to watch their own families and friends be killed during the war. He tells me about the village in Guangxi Province that is still—twenty-seven years after the war—riddled with land mines; one-third of the village's residents, young and old, are missing limbs. He tells me about the farmer whose Vietnamese wife was abducted by her family and taken across the border;

he had to pay for her release in livestock. He tells me about the human smuggling, Vietnamese peasant women being sold to rich Chinese businessmen for a few hundred US dollars, and about the black market weapons pouring into China.

Xiaoli has over a hundred hours of footage thus far. "The effects of war on communities," he explains, "are fascinating, and many people outside of China don't even know that this war existed." His film, he hopes, will bring an often-over-looked part of history and a neglected slice of China to the attention of a domestic and international audience.

But it's going to be a long uphill battle to get this documentary to the attention of the elusive international audience. First, he has to get all the footage he needs—the story is only partially told, thus far. In order to bring a full camera crew into the remaining border villages in China, he'll need permission from both the central government's Ministry of Culture and the local government bureaus on location. His last trip was an undercover mission: no permits, no official permission. While it's possible that the permits will be granted as they have thus far, it's more likely that they won't. His luck has held, thus far, but it very well may run out. The Communist Party is understandably wary about their recent history, and they can't be sure of what kind of past atrocities Xiaoli might dredge up during his chats with the locals.

"We'll see," sighs Xiaoli; "hopefully, it will work out. But we're in China. So maybe not."

He lights another cigarette and sighs.

11

The Filmmaker

IN FEBRUARY 2003, I was in Kunming, the capital of Western China's Yunnan Province, running a nightclub. I was living across the street from the club in a grubby apartment that my business partner had rented. Our place was on the top floor of a six-story cinder-block building, conveniently located inside the gates of the provincial soccer stadium.

It was a mild February: usually, I'd get up around noon, take a shower if the sun was shining (we had solar-heated hot water, so on cloudy days, I would prefer to go unwashed rather than suffer a freezing cold shower) and, desperate for a cup of strong coffee and a breakfast that involved eggs and toast instead of noodles and chili oil, walk the two miles north to Kunming's university district.

On the way, I would stop at little carts where ethnic minority women sold fresh pineapple halves impaled on wooden sticks, straight from the tropics of southern Yunnan. The pineapple was delicious, though it was a bit tricky to eat, especially while walking. I played a game with myself, kind of like pineapple Jenga, trying to take even bites all around the fruit so the whole thing wouldn't fall off the stick. It was a glorious season in a magical place.

One cloudy morning, I was changing my underwear in lieu of a shower when I heard a sharp knock at the door. Since no one had ever knocked on our door before, and since I was living there illegally, without the proper permits necessary to reside in a Chinese compound, I wasn't really sure what to do. I went into my business partner's bedroom and tried to wake him, but he was passed out, sleeping off a wild night of carousing.

There was another knock. "*Gonganju!*" said the voice behind the door. Public Security Bureau. The cops. The fuzz. The heat. I was fucked. I didn't know exactly what kind of punishment I'd be in for. A question-and-answer session down at the police station? Certainly. Kicked out of my apartment? Probably. Kicked out of China? Probably not, but nothing is ever a sure thing in China, where the "rule of law" is flexible as rubber.

Reluctantly, I threw on a shirt and pants and opened the door. A district policeman was standing in our trash-strewn hallway. I didn't know the cop, but his higher-ups were regulars at my place across the street, eating and drinking more than their fill, for free, of course.

He pushed past me and strolled into our apartment, surveying the piles of clothes and English-language books and pirated DVDs all over the floor. We worked every night and came home just to sleep for a few hours before heading out again, and so we rarely (never) cleaned the place, which was therefore in a constant state of casual destruction.

"Who are you?" he asked.

I explained who I was, and that I ran the place across the street, where his bosses came all the time, and so on.

"Are you legally registered to live here?" he questioned.

"No, I usually stay at the hotel across the street," I lied, "but it was full because of the conference (there was no conference) so I'm staying with my friend for a few nights."

"Who is he?" the cop asked.

Luckily, my business partner had roused himself. He stepped into the living room wearing only his underwear, and took control of the situation.

"He's the other owner of the place across the street, we're friendly with all the cops . . ." He started naming all of the head police in the city, the district captain, even the mayor.

The cop had heard enough and decided not to fuck with us anymore. "Are you the only two in here?"

"Do you see anyone else?" my business partner asked.

"Well, I hope you won't mind if I take a look around," said the cop.

"Of course," replied my business partner.

The cop looked in both of our bedrooms and in the living room. He opened all the closets. We didn't have a refrigerator, but if we did, he probably would have looked in there, too.

"All right," the cop said. "Thank you." He pointed at me. "If your foreign guests wish to reside in residential compounds you need to register within forty-eight hours to the Public Security Bureau."

"Yes, of course I will," I responded.

"What's this whole thing about?" demanded my business

partner, still a little sore at having been woken up from his fitful slumber.

"We are investigating a crime," said the cop.

He closed the door. A few seconds later, we could hear him knocking on the door across the hall.

It wasn't until later that afternoon that we learned the police were knocking on *every single door,* and inspecting *every single apartment,* in a city of more than four million people.

That's how badly they wanted, no, *needed* to catch Ma Jiajue.

□   □   □

MA JIAJUE GREW up in abject poverty in a tiny, remote village in the Guangxi Zhuang Autonomous Region, one of China's poorest provinces. His parents ran a small laundry: they earned around 500 yuan ($60) a month on which to support themselves and their several children.

Ma Jiajue was the youngest child in the family and also the brightest. He was an introverted young man who devoted himself to his studies. Though he didn't have many close friends, he was an excellent student, placing second in a national physics competition during his middle school years.

After he entered high school, his grades began to slip, and he was no longer one of the top students in his class. Ma Jiajue realized that he probably wasn't going to pass the *gaokao,* China's extremely difficult college entrance examination. Since he was young, his parents had been counting on him to get a good job and support the family. The pressure must have been stifling. In November 1999, he ran away from home, only to be found and brought back a few days later.

The following year, his fortunes changed. He ascended once again to the top of his class; after taking the *gaokao* and achieving a good score, he was awarded a place at fairly prestigious Yunnan University, just one province away. His parents were tremendously proud, as he was the first in a long line of peasants to go to college. To help him through his studies, they gave him their entire life savings: 6,000 yuan ($725).

In September 2000, Ma enrolled at Yunnan University. According to those who knew him, he tried to be very sociable during his first year on campus; however, he was tremendously self-conscious about his impoverished background and, to those who knew him, he seemed a bit of a strange guy. He became a loner on campus. Not the well-known kind of eccentric loner to whom everyone gives tacit respect from afar, but the other, sadder kind of loner: the kind that nobody really notices.

Ma Jiajue continued his college career, broke, friendless, and girlfriendless in an environment full of couples holding hands, and groups of students hanging out till all hours at the kind of places college students can go if they have money: restaurants, bars, movies, bowling alleys. Sometimes, he'd play cards or mah-jongg with his roommates in his cramped dorm room; a few times, he went along on outings with his roommates, but he never had money to pay. They would foot the bill, but, in that way that only adolescents can be cruel, always give him a little grief about it later on.

◻ ◻ ◻

BY FEBRUARY 12, 2003, most students of Yunnan University had already headed home for the Chinese New Year holiday. In China, the lunar new year, or Spring Festival, is a time when the whole country shuts down for two weeks and everyone goes home to visit family. During the New Year, planes, buses, and especially trains are jammed with migrant workers, college students, anyone who works far away from their hometown. It is a torrent of humanity.

After scraping up the money for their fare, people queue up for days in order to purchase their train tickets home; once they've secured the tickets, they must ride in a packed-out carriage, pressed body-to-body with hundreds of other people, for up to two days as they make their way back towards their families. I've been to the train station just before New Year, and it's a frightening and unforgettable experience. There are people everywhere, most of them migrant workers who have been given a brief respite from their factories and construction sites and restaurants. Everyone is frenzied, and many are unwashed.

Ma Jiajue didn't have the necessary funds for a train ticket back to Guangxi. He had no choice but to remain on campus in the cramped confines of his dorm room.

That evening, he and some other students were playing cards in the dorm room. A classmate accused Ma of cheating. Ma denied it; the classmate mocked him as a social misfit.

The following day, Ma collected what money he had, went out to a nearby hardware store, and purchased a sledgehammer and a package of large plastic trash bags. That evening, he smashed one of his roommates to death. Ma smashed up the body and tied it up in a plastic bag, then placed the bag in the compartment underneath the victim's bed. (In order to maximize valuable storage space, bunks in Chinese university dorm rooms are hollow. The mattresses can be lifted up to place belongings underneath.)

The next day, Valentine's Day, he repeated the process with two more of his roommates.

On February 15, he killed a fourth roommate and disposed of the body in an identical manner.

Then, he disappeared.

No one noticed the bodies until eight days later, when a student alerted university officials to the stench coming from a certain dormitory room.

□　□　□

IN CCP-ERA CHINA, nothing like this had ever happened before. The country's university students are the chosen few, the elite, the princes and princesses of the new China. They were supposed to be leading China into a bountiful new era of "socialism with Chinese characteristics," and they were certainly not supposed to be killing and dismembering their roommates.

The scope of the ensuing manhunt was unbelievable. The eight-day lag between the final murder and the discovery of the bodies meant that Ma Jiajue could be anywhere by now.

First, black-and-white flyers stamped with the official seal of the police department appeared on every surface in Kunming and the surrounding area. The police were offering a reward of 150,000 yuan for information leading to the capture of the fugitive. The flyers featured a grainy, black-and-white portrait of Ma Jiajue, no doubt gleaned from the official copy of his Yunnan University identity card.

In the university enrollment photo, Ma sports a bushy flat-top haircut and an impassive look of expectation on his face. His eyes are a bit too far apart and his features seem a little bit off-center. He looks like an eager, impressionable country boy who has summoned up the courage to make something of himself in the big city.

When the flyers yielded no results, the police raised the reward to 200,000 yuan and proceeded to search every apartment in the city of four million. But they still couldn't find Ma Jiajue.

The police got hold of another picture of Ma. In it, he's wearing a white undershirt, flexing his biceps, with his fists raised; his mouth is curled into an exaggerated sneer. This new, seemingly more "incriminating" photo, was added to the wanted poster.

The black-and-white flyers spread from Kunming to all the other major cities in China: Beijing, Shanghai, Chengdu, Guangzhou. No city-dweller in China could walk down the street for ten minutes without being confronted by Ma Jiajue's grainy face staring at them from a flyer attached to a telephone pole or pasted onto a wall. The reward was up to 250,000 yuan, now, and Ma Jiajue had been declared "Public Enemy Number One."

Many of my Chinese friends found the picture hilarious and began flexing their biceps and sneering as a form of greeting to one another.

On the Internet, debate raged in chat rooms and online bulletin boards, with Chinese netizens discussing Ma Jiajue and the potential motive behind his crimes. He was condemned as a villain. He was lauded as a hero.

The Party, no doubt worried that this affair could bloom into an enormous controversy, issued a reporting ban on the Ma Jiajue case. Only a select few government-run papers could cover the story.

Scores of Ma Jiajue sightings from all around China poured into police hotlines. Each of these suspected Ma Jiajues was detained, interrogated, and released when he was found not to be the real Ma Jiajue.

In Fengcheng, a small city in Northeast China's Liaoning Province, two men from the south of the country checked into a hotel. The desk clerk thought one of them looked like Ma Jiajue.

The two men were corrupt bankers from the countryside of Yunnan Province. They had embezzled 1.9 million yuan from the government-run bank and split town. Neither, however, was Ma Jiajue. After trying to bribe the local policemen, they were rebuffed and consequently arrested. Ma Jiajue, of course, was still at large.

A few days later, on March 15, 2004, in the resort city of Sanya on China's tropical Hainan Island, Chen Xianzhuang, a pedicab driver, saw a suspicious character rooting through the garbage in a neighborhood market.

Chen followed the suspect in his pedicab for a couple hours and then called the Sanya police, who swarmed in and arrested the man. A confession and a DNA test later, it was official: Ma Jiajue was finally in police custody. The government papers trumpeted a victory for Chinese law enforcement.

Chen Xianzhuang pocketed the 250,000-yuan reward.

□ □ □

ON MARCH 17, 2004, a platoon of armed police officers escorted Ma Jiajue back to Kunming to stand trial.

On April 22, 2004, his trial began in the Kunming Intermediate Court.

On April 24, 2004, Ma Jiajue was sentenced to death. He was ordered to pay 20,000 yuan to the families of his victims as compensation.

On June 17, 2004, Ma Jiajue, twenty-four years old, was executed with a single bullet to the back of his head.

□ □ □

TWO YEARS LATER, when I returned to China to research this book, the Ma Jiajue case often came up in conversation. While his case was not covered extensively in the international press, it made serious headlines in China. Ma Jiajue was like the Columbine shooters, the Menendez Brothers, and O.J. Simpson all rolled into one. He had become the most famous twenty-first century criminal in China.

Most strangely, I heard young people talk about Ma Jiajue with a kind of awed respect. While people I spoke with pretty much agreed that what he had done was horrible, they also generally felt that they could understand why he committed his crime, and that the murders were justifiable. Posthumously, Ma Jiajue was transformed into a kind of folk hero for the younger set. He was the nerd, the runt, the kid who got picked on but finally had the guts to kill the bully that had made his life a living hell.

When I heard that a twenty-five-year-old Beijing college student had made a movie on digital video called "Ma Jiajue," I became immediately obsessed with meeting the guy and watching his film. I spent hours combing the Internet in both English and Chinese, searching for information about the movie and its creator.

Eventually, I learned that the filmmaker went by the name "Hongfeng," and that he was a student not in Beijing, but in Qingdao. I called all my connections in Qingdao and asked them to help me find him. Days passed and I was no closer to locating the mysterious "Hongfeng." I felt like the Kunming police must have when they were searching for Ma Jiajue: impatient and useless.

During a second round of Google searches a few days later, I found an article about Hongfeng in the online edition of an Australian newspaper. I sent out an e-mail or two and finally managed to get the contact information of the China-based journalist who had written the story. The Australian didn't have Hongfeng's information, but his Chinese colleague did. Eventually, I managed to locate the colleague, and, one phone call later, I had Hongfeng's mobile number.

□ □ □

I CALLED HONGFENG a few times in a row, but he never answered. I could not leave a message; due to a variety of technological circumstances and cultural differences, the Chinese have never gotten used to voice mail. Some pundits speculate that Chinese people don't like it because it takes too long to check; others think that China's emphasis on face-to-face interaction makes voice mail worthless. You can imagine how inconvenient this can be when trying to meet up with someone.

I texted Hongfeng: "I'm an American writer interested in seeing your movie. Are you currently in Qingdao?"

He responded via text a few hours later, saying that he didn't believe me. I called him again; this time he picked up, and I explained myself. He was in Beijing, and I was out west, in Dali, the mountain town outside of Kunming, where the Ma Jiajue murders had taken place. My American accent must have assured him I was genuine. We agreed to meet in Qingdao in one week's time.

□ □ □

THE NEWSPAPER ARTICLE I had found online described Hongfeng as a rail-thin, deadly serious artist-type, and so that's who I was expecting: the kind of hyper-affected kid who wears black glasses and black sweaters and who never cracks a smile because he's so weighed down by the unbearable heaviness of day-to-day existence, not least the more existential aspects of life. (There are a lot of young artists like this in China. Of course, there are a lot of young artists like this in every country.)

It came as quite a surprise, then, when Hongfeng stepped into my friend Lao Zhang's Parisian-style café. He's a thick, sturdy fellow who walks slowly, with what seems to be a slight limp. He's got heavy-lidded eyes that hide behind metal-rimmed glasses, and so he seems to be always a few seconds away from falling asleep.

He dresses in T-shirts, baggy shorts and sandals, the uniform of the aspiring Hollywood screenwriter. His chin is coated with a layer of stubble that comes together to form a patchy beard, which he likes to stroke affectionately when he's talking or thinking, like a teenaged, Chinese Fidel Castro.

Like most young people in China, Hongfeng chain-smokes, and he has a shiny silver Zippo lighter that he obviously cherishes. He's always pulling it out of his pocket, rubbing it between his fingers, flicking the top open and closed, filling it with fluid, etc. Whenever anyone in the room pulls out a cigarette (which is often) Hongfeng will always be there with his trusty Zippo.

He is twenty-two, but looks significantly older, possibly due to a combination of extreme stress, poor diet, and smoking five packs of cigarettes a day.

We ordered a couple cups of coffee. I told him that I would treat him to whatever he wanted off the menu; he scrutinized it for a while before deciding on a lamb pizza. When I suggested that he might want to change his order to, perhaps, pepperoni or sausage—after all, the reasons why they don't serve lamb pizza in the West seem like awful good ones—he brushed me off with a wave of his hand.

Well, if it's lamb pizza he wants, lamb pizza he shall receive, I thought, and I told him that I wanted to watch his movie before we talked about it, and he agreed: I plugged headphones into my laptop, brought along for the occasion, and he handed me the DVD.

□　□　□

MA JIAJUE, THE MOVIE, was created as Hongfeng's senior project at Qingdao University. It's shot on digital video, and the image quality, while not outstanding, is generally pretty good although the lighting, especially in the indoor scenes, could use some serious improvement. Hongfeng doesn't make any attempts to be realistic: the young classmate of Hongfeng's who plays Ma Jiajue doesn't even slightly resemble the murderer. Overall, the film comes off as what it is: a student film.

The movie, from Hongfeng's own screenplay, tells the fictionalized story of Ma Jiajue in the period leading up to and including the murders. We see Ma struggling to keep up his schoolwork, failing to find a girlfriend, and suffering from the pain of his roommates' ostracism.

From a dramatic standpoint, the movie largely falls flat. The dialogue tends towards the clichéd and over-dramatic, and the characters are painfully free of nuance, painted instead in the kind of broad strokes used by amateur authors.

From the start, Hongfeng views Ma Jiajue as a sympathetic character, as an earnest outcast who tries his best to gain acceptance by the community at large. As the film progresses, Ma is forced to do his roommate's laundry by hand, to give his roommates back massages, and even to surrender his food at the cafeteria.

We see Ma growing increasingly stressed, his behavior more frenzied, clearly haunted by his insecurities. He starts smoking. He rejects even the students who make cursory attempts to be nice to him. Playing cards with his roommates, he's accused of cheating. He snaps.

The murders are portrayed in slow-motion, with low-budget sound effects. Ma Jiajue takes off, and the film ends with scrolling text recounting the culmination of the story: the arrest, the trial, the execution.

□   □   □

AS I WATCHED the movie Hongfeng sat next to me, chomping on slices from his lamb pizza, his broad face ponderous, looking at me every so often to see if he could gauge my reaction. After it was done, he asked me what I thought.

And I told him: *Ma Jiajue*, the film, is quite effective, even haunting. (The script is so hackneyed as to be painful, but I left that out.) Watching poor Ma stumble, completely alone, through the torture of his everyday life is extremely unpleasant. Hongfeng clearly wants the viewer to identify with Ma, and in this sense he's succeeded: as I watched the film, I felt Ma's pain.

□   □   □

"WHEN I FIRST read about this case in the newspaper," explains Hongfeng, "I thought: Why? How could this happen? I couldn't sleep for months. I had nightmares. Ma Jiajue was running through my brain every night."

"At the time," Hongfeng says, "I really wanted a laptop computer. It took me two years, working odd jobs, a little money here and a little money there, to save up for a laptop. And then, when I had the money, I realized I needed to do something different."

Although Hongfeng had watched a lot of pirated movies on DVD, he had never made a movie himself and he wasn't quite sure where to start. "First, I took three months, and wrote this script," he explains.

He borrowed a DV camera from one of his classmates.

Next, it was time to cast the film. It was easy enough to find people for most of the parts—the friends, teachers, etc.—but Hongfeng was confronted with one massive problem: no one wanted to play Ma Jiajue.

"The first couple guys that I found to do it quit," said Hongfeng. "No one wanted to be the murderer on-screen."

Eventually, he cajoled one of his closest friends to play the part. "Is that why the actor doesn't really look like Ma Jiajue?" I asked.

Hongfeng grinned like a sheepdog. "Of course. The first guy looked like him, and that's why he really didn't want to do it in the end. He didn't want to go around school and have everyone call him Ma Jiajue!"

After the cast was secured, Hongfeng and a crew of two friends made the film over a period of weeks, using Qingdao University as a stand-in for Yunnan University. The classrooms, the cramped dorm rooms, and the basic cafeteria provide an interesting glimpse into the daily life of a student at an elite Chinese university.

Hongfeng edited the film on a computer, and added Chinese and (somewhat dubious) English subtitles. He also added a spooky soundtrack that he thought would really create the kind of horrific, hopeless atmosphere he was going for.

"My professor thought it was ridiculous," explains Hongfeng, more than a little sheepishly. "He yelled at me! [He] said that I couldn't put this kind of movie on at school! Definitely not!"

When the soundtrack was removed, and the film was screened at Qingdao University, it got several notices in the Chinese press. This hype led to Hongfeng being invited to several other universities to screen his film, and to lead a discussion afterwards.

"That made me very happy," Hongfeng muses. "I wanted to make an educational film. And this DV (movie) is an educational film." He pauses for a second, and then adds: "It should be shown at universities across China, and hopefully all over the world."

I couldn't help but smile: Hongfeng's minor celebrity had already gone to his head.

□ □ □

HONGFENG PLACED HIS PALM over his abdomen, and excused himself to the restroom; he said the lamb pizza had disagreed with his stomach.

As Hongfeng worked out his intestinal issues, I ordered another cup of coffee and stared out the window at the cars rushing down Hong Kong Road, Qingdao's main artery, contemplating the elephant in the room: how, and why, could Ma Jiajue—a misguided, deranged young man who killed four of his peers—be portrayed as an entirely sympathetic character and regarded with respect that bordered on reverence?

Hongfeng returned with an embarrassed smile on his face, looking somewhat ashen. I expressed to him these concerns, and he nodded gravely. I ordered a couple beers, and he lit a cigarette with his Zippo.

□ □ □

"FIRST, YOU HAVE to think about why he did it. He lived with these people for four years and then he killed them. Why? He was about to graduate! The thing you have to realize about Ma

Jiajue," Hongfeng continued, "is that he was a very, very sensitive person."

"When he entered college, he was full of hope. He could have a good life. He could have a good wife. He could have a good job. Four years later, his *lixiang* [a Chinese word roughly, but not quite, meaning 'ideals'] was gone."

"He had no *lixiang* anymore. That's why he did it. But why did he have no *lixiang?* We must answer this question. These cases happen all the time. Why?"

Hongfeng runs down a list of stories that have been in the news recently: college students at many elite universities committing suicide, a college student killing himself and his girlfriend, a pregnant college student poisoning herself. He's got a good point: In China, suicide has become the leading cause of death for people age twenty to thirty-five. An enormous percentage of these suicides are college students and young urbanites, unable to face the enormous pressure brought on by a rapidly changing society.

"First," he considers, "the problem is with the [Chinese] educational system. There are so many problems. No one is there to help these students. There is no communication. The Chinese educational system is scary. China is developed . . . but our communication is not developed."

□   □   □

HONGFENG HAS A POINT: the pressures faced by Chinese university students and young urbanites can easily become soul-destroying. They are almost all only children. The hopes of their entire family—crucial in China's Confucian value system—are riding on these young people. As the gap between rich and poor grows wider, they are consumed with uncertainty over getting good grades and finding a good job. They are paralyzed with fear of the uncertain future. And if that fear grows into hopelessness, they have no one to talk to. And if that hopelessness becomes a depression that festers and metastasizes until it's consumed their whole lives, they live in abject misery.

"Okay," I reply, "there are some reasons why he might have done it. But they don't justify his crimes, right? Or, according to you, do they?"

"On the Internet," Hongfeng says, "people worship Ma Jiajue. They call him a hero. But the Internet is a public toilet. It's a place for everyone to piss and shit. I'd say, from what I've found, maybe sixty or seventy percent of people support Ma Jiajue. A majority. Why? Because he made a statement about the system. Ma Jiajue was a poor student, and he was tormented by the other, wealthy students. He is a symbol of a spiritual problem."

And so, instead of condemning Ma Jiajue for his crimes, they identify with him. He is one of their own.

口 口 口

THE DAY AFTER our meeting in the café, I woke up late and gave Hongfeng a call. My old business partner from Kunming now runs a nightclub in Qingdao, and I asked if Hongfeng would want to screen his film there in a few days. He agreed.

I called several friends to come check out the film.

Hongfeng gave a little speech about Ma Jiajue and about the making of the movie, and then the lights went down and a group of friends and colleagues settled in to watch.

Surprisingly to me, my Chinese friends (mostly in their thirties or forties and college-educated) hated it and were more than happy to tell me so. They thought the film was vaguely humorous, but they are already (mostly) successful and proud of it. They could not identify.

Hongfeng didn't seem to notice any dissatisfaction: everyone had clapped at the end, after all, and he was basking in the afterglow of being the center of attention. We went outside to the club's patio, drank a beer, and talked some more about the future of his film.

"A couple distributors in Guangzhou are interested," Hongfeng told me. "They've come here for two rounds of talks, which have both failed."

"My style is very psychological," he continued, "so I can't find investors."

He sipped his beer and stroked his scraggly beard.

"I've been talking to Jia Zhangke [arguably the most famous art film director in China]. We are going to have a meeting. I want to do a trilogy. Three movies. Like *Star Wars*. If I can't get any investors, I'll pay (to make the films) myself. The difference between a little DV movie, and a proper film, the difference is so big . . ."

"*Manmanrdelai*,"—things will come slowly but surely—I reassure him.

"Well, this film has allowed me to go to a lot of places," he says. "And I think it was useful. That's what movies should be about—not making money, but being useful. I want to be old and look back and say, what I did was useful."

A frenzied game of liar's dice started up at a table behind us.

"Of course," Hongfeng blurted out of nowhere, "I cannot

claim to understand Ma Jiajue. I am very humble." I smiled and patted him on the back. Hongfeng's anything but humble; in fact, his fatal flaw may prove to be his casual arrogance, which seems to be way out of proportion with his artistic ability. But he's young, and he's hungry, and he's right: he is doing something useful.

His movie forces its viewers to really consider a number of problems that are too often swept under the rug in Chinese society: the lack of interpersonal communication and the psychological effects of the growing gap between the rich and the poor.

12

The Killers

LAO ZHANG IS HUNGRY for blood. He hasn't killed in four days, and he feels like there are wires shorting out in his brain. He feels like an addict in serious need of a fix. He has been keeping odd hours. Sometimes, he won't sleep for three days, and then he'll crash and pass out for two days in a row.

A heavy shade covers the window in his bedroom, and when he wakes up, he can no longer tell if it is day or night. In the darkness, he reaches over to his nightstand, feeling around for his Mount Tai premium cigarettes.

He finds the pack, lights a smoke, and inhales deeply. He fumbles for his glasses, puts them on, and squints at the clock on his cellular phone. It is eleven o' clock. Morning? Nope. Evening. He smiles broadly and sucks on his cigarette. He swings his legs over the bed and stubs out the cigarette, the smile never leaving his face. First, he will take a shower and brush his hair.

Then, it will be time to kill.

□   □   □

SIXTEEN MEN ARE SEATED around a long table in a small room. The table is cluttered with half-empty cups of tea, cans of Red Bull, sunflower-seed shells, and ashtrays overflowing with cigarette butts. Most of the men are smoking cigarettes, and the room has no ventilation. Most of this country's public places— restaurants, bars, even museums and hospitals—are unbearably smoky, but this room is even more smoky than most. It's ridiculous, really, but no one seems to mind or even to notice. The men have glassy eyes. They seem washed out and wired at the same time; hyper-weary, like they make a habit of going without sleep for days at a time. A small plexiglass window on the back wall contains four long fluorescent bulbs, calibrated to simulate artificial daylight.

Three of the men are police officers. Four more are killers. The rest are peasants. The task at hand is for the policemen to find out who the killers are and to apprehend them. The killers are trying to be mistaken for peasants so they will be able to leave freely.

Outside, morning has just broken, and the sun has risen over the ocean and cast its light on the eastern port city of Qingdao, famous for its idyllic beaches and excellent beer. The policemen have until noon to catch the killers, and they're not making much progress. They have large black bags under their eyes; as they suck on Red River and Peaceful Temple cigarettes, you feel like you can almost see the bags swelling, getting larger and darker.

◻   ◻   ◻

ONE OF THE men, number eight, according to the black card sitting in a plastic holder on the table in front of him, small and bespectacled, weaselly-looking, launches into a defensive salvo: He's just a peasant, not a killer. He's a peasant and to mistake him for a killer would be a crime. He's a peasant, just a simple peasant. He repeats this like a mantra. Behind his glasses, his eyes blink nervously, and there is desperation in his voice. He is just a simple peasant, not a killer.

It's time to vote. Lao Zhang, cigarette in hand, adjusts his glasses with his other hand and stares at the weasel. From the front of the room, the judge barks: "Number eight!"

Lao Zhang thrusts his right hand into the air. He looks around the room; his is the only hand up. Number eight has bought himself some more time.

The electronic scoreboard at the front of the room lets loose a loud beep, and techno music blasts out of speakers on the walls. Number eight has won. He's gotten away with murder.

As soon as the music starts playing, everyone in the room gets up and starts screaming at each other. The policemen are pissed off at the peasants, the peasants are pissed off at the policemen, and the killers are high-fiving in joy because they've won the game and scored thirty-five points. Lao Zhang's screaming at everyone else. He knew it was number eight! How could they be so stupid!

After a moment, the hubbub dies down. There's no clock in the room. By this time, everyone knows it's very late. Lao Zhang lights a smoke, and the players next to him follow suit.

"*Fa pai!*"—"distribute the cards"—someone says, and the next round begins.

❑ ❑ ❑

IT'S AN AVERAGE late night/early morning at the Qingdao branch of the Killing People Club. The killers aren't really killers, the policemen aren't really policemen, and the peasants aren't peasants: they are all urban, educated Chinese involved in a complicated role-playing game.

The lobby of the Killing People Club is sparsely decorated. It looks like a cross between a flophouse and a defunct bowling alley. In one corner, a few ratty couches bracket ashtrays the size of garbage cans. Across the room, a small shop sells water, Red Bull, tea, sunflower seeds, cigarettes, and other staples of the all-nighter.

Upstairs are six identical rooms. In each are sixteen marginally comfortable, Day-Glo orange chairs arranged in a U-shape around a yellow Formica table. Sixteen ashtrays, also Day-Glo orange, sit on the table, one in front of each chair.

In the mouth of the "U" stands the judge's podium. The judge, incongruously, is played by a young Chinese woman in some kind of perverse waitress uniform; pale pink apron and matching bow in her hair. Mounted on the wall behind her is an electronic scoreboard showing the code names of each player: "Western Wind," "Snake Head," "Little Black Fatty," "Hedgehog." Lao Zhang is "Barman Lao Zhang." (My Killing People name is "Dragon Head Stick #1," a sly nod to the popular Hong Kong film *Election*.)

Techno music begins to blare from the lousy speakers

mounted on the ceiling, signaling the start of the game. Like most amplified music in China, the volume has been set way too high, the speakers are cheap, and so the music consequently becomes crackly and distorted.

The waitress-judge passes around a tray with metal squares, which are about the size and shape of a Zippo lighter. Each player flicks open the square to reveal a picture underneath: killer (man in a black mask and ninja-style robe) policeman (man in a blue US-style police uniform) or peasant (farmer wearing a coolie hat and baggy Mao-era clothing.)

The judge pushes a button on her console. "Everyone close your eyes!" barks a distorted electronic voice. She watches to makes sure everyone's eyes are closed and presses another button. The expectation of the new game hangs pregnantly over the room like the cloud of smoke that's making me hack up a lung.

"Killers, open your eyes!"

□ □ □

LAO ZHANG IS six feet tall and whippet-thin. He co-owns two successful French restaurants in Qingdao's central business district. He's got a long, raggedy ponytail that hangs down to his waistline. He wears a pair of tiny spectacles, a scraggly beard, and, generally, a huge smile that reveals a gap on the left side of his mouth where the incisor should be.

His hippie-like appearance and emaciated torso lend him the general air of a junkie; however, he doesn't drink or do any drugs, save for the Mount Tai or Nanjing cigarettes that he chain-smokes. A few years ago, he liked to stay out all night taking Ecstasy and chasing women, but he's had his fill of carousing and claims that those days are behind him. He stays thin by eating only one meal a day, usually a plate piled high with fried noodles.

This year he turned thirty-five, but he looks at least a decade older. When he went to see the Rolling Stones in Shanghai, an elderly security guard referred to him as "Grandfather," and it really pissed him off.

□   □   □

I ARRIVED IN QINGDAO with Lao Wei, a former classmate from my undergraduate days in Beijing. We were planning to stay at a local friend's apartment, but our host was out of town on business. He had, however, left the keys to his place with Lao Zhang. I tried to get in touch with Lao Zhang, but his cellular phone was "*guan ji*"—powered off.

Lao Wei and I made our way over to La Villa, one of Lao Zhang's restaurants, but the manager on duty told us that he wasn't around. We took a seat at a table and ordered coffee, strong and straight, from an imported espresso machine, and called Lao Zhang again, but his phone was still off.

An hour later, he returned my call (he had seen my number on his call log) and said that he'd be coming by to get us. The better part of another hour passed and we had a couple more cups of coffee. Outside of the major cities, which now boast both Starbucks and independent cafés, good coffee is hard to come by in China. Ten years ago, it was borderline impossible to find.

Eventually, Lao Zhang's short, pretty wife, Doudou— "Little Black Fatty" in the Killing People Game—came in and handed me a set of keys to a spare apartment behind La Villa.

"I thought Lao Zhang would be coming," I said.

"He's not around," she said.

I didn't want to press the issue. Last time I visited Qingdao, their relationship had been in trouble; Lao Zhang had found a much younger girlfriend and was spending his afternoons shacked up in a love nest somewhere.

So I thanked Doudou; she left, and I ordered a cold Qingdao beer. A few minutes later, I noticed a familiar face across the room. Wang Gang is a bespectacled, attractive kid in his mid-twenties. He serves as the general manager and de facto DJ for both of Lao Zhang's restaurants. He came over, and we exchanged pleasantries. Wang Gang bought me another beer, and I asked after Lao Zhang.

"He's out playing this Killing People Game," said Wang Gang. "He's crazy. Plays all night, every night. Doesn't go to work anymore."

He wasn't lying: for the next several days, my friend and I hung out in Lao Zhang's restaurant, drinking coffee and enjoying one of the few wireless Internet hotspots in Qingdao. The last time I was in Qingdao, Lao Zhang was always around, fixing things, puttering around the place, or sitting in the corner drinking tea. This time, he was nowhere to be seen.

He had discovered the Killing People Game. At first, he would play for a few hours once a week. Then, he'd stay out all night playing, once or twice a week. Finally, it had gotten to the point when Lao Zhang developed a daily routine around the game: he woke up in the late afternoon, ate a plate of noodles, went to the Killing People Club, and stayed there until the sun came up the next morning. His wife took care of the day-to-day operations of his business, and all of his friends—except the ones who were also members of the Killing People Club—wondered where he'd gone and why his phone was always powered off.

□   □   □

AT FIRST I THOUGHT Lao Zhang was an isolated case, a guy who was, for whatever reason, addicted to the Killing People Game. Certain people, after all, have addictive personalities: junkies, gaming nerds, compulsive eaters. But then, I started to play the game in Qingdao, spending most evenings at the Club, and I saw the same familiar faces night after night. As I made my way around the country and continued to stop in at Killing People Clubs all across China, I met many people who, like Lao Zhang, were basically spending their entire waking lives within the confines of the Club. I realized that the Killing People Game had reached critical mass. It was no longer a fad but a full-blown epidemic.

There are sixteen players. The objective of the game is simple: killers want to avoid detection. They also want to ferret out the policemen and kill them. The policemen, conversely, want to identify and catch the killers. And the peasants, who, like Chinese peasants, don't have much real power, but still could be killed, want to aid the policemen in catching the killers.

It's a team game: the four killers are on one team and the policemen and peasants are on the opposing team, which we'll call the "Society" team. If the policemen and the peasants can identify and vote out all the killers before the policemen are killed, then the "Society" wins: the policemen receive forty points and the peasants ten points each. If the killers can avoid detection long enough to kill all the policemen, then the Killers each get fifty points. Since players typically play upwards of five rounds a night, usually everyone will get a chance to be a killer or policeman (it's much more fun than being a "passive" peasant.)

After each player has taken a card to establish his identity, the judge barks through a loudspeaker for everyone to close his eyes and bow his head. The techno music starts playing.

Then, the four killers open their eyes and look around the circle to identify each other. Using hand signals, they attempt to agree upon which player to kill. After they've reached a consensus—signified by nodding all around—the wild techno music stops and they are treated to a cheesy, eighties-style sound effect: a "thunk" that's supposed to symbolize someone getting killed.

The killers, having sated their hunger for blood, close their eyes and bow their heads. The computerized voice returns, instructing the four policemen to open their eyes. Using hand signals, the policemen motion to the judge which other one player they want to "investigate": each round, the judge will tell the policemen whether one of the people in the room is or is not a killer. A massive red thumbs-up or thumbs-down will appear on the electronic scoreboard in the front of the room.

At the judge's instruction, all the players open their eyes. (The peasants have kept their eyes closed the whole time and therefore have no idea what's going on.)

The judge reads out the name of the player whom the killers have agreed to kill ("The victim is number seven: Black

Cloud" and suchlike.) The person who has been killed receives a chance to eulogize himself and muse on whom he suspects is responsible for his murder.

Then, the other players each get a chance to speak for thirty seconds and accuse their chosen suspects of being killers. If the policemen have identified a killer, they attempt to impress this fact upon the other players, without revealing their identity as policemen. The killers attempt to deflect suspicion to other players. This roundtable culminates in an election, à la the US television show *Survivor*: someone gets voted out of the game.

After the first round, the player who has been killed and the player who has been voted out are now "eliminated." Fourteen players remain.

The game continues, with the policemen trying to get the killers voted out of the game and the killers trying to kill the policemen.

An average round with sixteen people usually takes a little less than an hour to play through. The game ends when all the killers have been discovered by the policemen and peasants and voted out, or when the killers identify and kill all the policemen. Points are awarded and displayed on a large LCD screen in the front of the room.

□ □ □

THE KILLING PEOPLE Game is actually an American invention, created by a group of computer programmers in Silicon Valley who played it as an exercise in procrastination to blow off steam while working on challenging projects.

A group of students from Shanghai who were studying at Stanford in the mid-nineties learned the game and brought it back to China. For a while, among Chinese engineering circles, the game became a pleasant way to pass the time on long train rides and stuffy summer nights in overcrowded college dormitories.

In late 2005, the first dedicated Killing People Club opened in an average-looking office building in central Beijing. The game's popularity blossomed among the city's fashionable elite, and soon the building's parking lot was full of Mercedes-Benzes and BMWs. "It caught fire very quickly," said Xiao Li, who has been working at the Killing People Club since its inception. "All kinds of people—big bosses, policemen—wearing fancy clothes."

Soon, the Killing People Club expanded to neighboring Tianjin, and by 2006, the craze had expanded to fifteen other cities. All over China, people are turning on to the Killing People Club. Membership has risen exponentially. As of this writing, there are over ten thousand members of the Club, and hundreds of new members register every day.

The Club charges a one-time registration fee of 100 yuan ($12.50) and hourly fees that hover around ten yuan ($1.20).

□   □   □

LAO ZHANG'S HAPPY. In the past week, his point total reached the number-one position in all of Qingdao. The Killing People Club has a website[12] which is updated daily and members of the

---

12 www.xclub.com.cn

Club use a password to log in and check the previous night's rankings. In Beijing, "The Literary Animal" led the field with 775 points; in Chengdu, it was "Fish-O," with 260 points.

The ultimate goal of the game, as in all games where points are accrued over a long period of time, is to attain the maximum amount of points. Of course, the more hours spent at the Club, the more points one can achieve. However, since even a marginal player will still score a couple hundred points over the course of a long night, it's not necessarily the best players who have the most points: instead, it's the players who have spent the longest time within the confines of the Club.

"Right now, there are a couple people who are superstars in the Killing People Club world," Lao Zhang comments, referring to two old hands in Beijing who play the game so much that they have, far and away, the highest point totals in the nation.

Across the entire country, thousands of people are staying up all night, every night, playing the Killing People Game, paying ten yuan an hour, even quitting or neglecting their jobs to play.

Why has this phenomenon taken over so many people's lives? Why are people so obsessed with the Killing People Game?

"We all need a little escape sometimes," says Lao Zhang, stroking his beard.

He laughs. "Also, it's really fun."

Lao Zhang's not lying; the first time I popped open the metal lid of my card to reveal a picture of the killer underneath, I felt a sharp rush of exhilaration; a jolt of adrenaline later, I was trying to transform my face into an expressionless mask. When I opened my eyes to greet my fellow killers and choose who we would be eliminating from the game, I felt a real sense of camaraderie. When nothing of value's at stake, it's always fun to lie, to deceive other people: it's even more fun if a few others are in on the scheme.

◻   ◻   ◻

ON THE WALLS of the lobby in the Chengdu Killing People Club are photographs of a gaming session, where the people playing the game have their faces covered by grey, shapeless plastic masks that resemble cartoon robot heads, with lighter, square areas of plastic in the approximate locations of the eyes and mouth.

Because they're unwieldy and uncomfortable, most outlets of the Club have stopped using the masks, trusting the players to close their eyes and not peek at the other people in the room. Some very serious players, however, insist that the masks are an integral part of the game. They offer insurance against cheating.

I was sitting in the lobby of the Chengdu Killing People Club, which is more upscale than most of its counterparts, in that it has decently upholstered furniture and several computers so that dedicated players of the Game can check their e-mail between binges. The Chengdu Club also boasts a few vending machines dispensing caffeinated beverages and instant noodles which supply refreshments to late-night gamers. I was drinking a cup of muddy-tasting instant coffee and looking at these masked faces in the photographs, and then it struck me what the images reminded me of: the photographs that came out of Abu Ghraib of people being tortured—helpless captives bending down, their heads covered by hoods, blind and scared.

In the Cultural Revolution of the 1960s, millions of Chinese were systematically identified as "rightist enemies of the state." Under the leadership of Mao Zedong, these ordinary people were rooted out and killed: teachers, intellectuals, people who wore glasses, people with good handwriting, people who owned land, and everyone else who might have been deemed a threat to the anti-intellectual, anti-capitalist regime.

The government encouraged its "patriotic citizens" to be wary of their fellow men and women; informing on one's neighbors, one's friends, even one's spouse, was seen as an obligation to the Supreme Leader.

It was hell. The Cultural Revolution shattered Confucian family ties that formed the backbone of the Chinese cultural and moral system. In the name of the Chinese Communist Party, children were forced to turn against their parents. Wives publicly denounced their husbands. It was a society of paranoia, public humiliation, and private torture. It was psychological warfare: every citizen for himself.

□   □   □

WHILE LAO ZHANG told me that he enjoyed playing the Killing People Game, there was something about the Killing Club that seemed off—based on my first experience, it didn't seem like anyone was having very much fun. The faces of the players ranged from grim to angry. No one smiled or laughed. Everyone seemed nervous at all times, as evidenced by the players' compulsive chain-smoking and sunflower-seed-eating.

At times when I played I enjoyed myself, because I had somehow stumbled onto an interesting phenomenon. But I was viewing the game as an outsider, as an observer. The more I tried to understand why people would spend their entire waking life at the Killing People Club, the more baffling the whole thing became. On several occasions, I stayed at the Club for six and seven hours at a time, well into the morning hours: by that time, playing the game had become quite unpleasant. It isn't—and it shouldn't be—very fun to sit in an uncomfortable, brightly lit room for prolonged periods of time. If you're eliminated in the early stages of each round, the amount of "dead time" can be almost unbearable.

On one occasion, I decided to play a few rounds of the game with a group who were wearing the masks. They are made from thick silver plastic; when my head was bowed, face flush against the plastic, covered in sweat, with awful music blaring in the background, it reminded me of a torture method that was used by the Germans in World War II where the enemy prisoner was blindfolded and forced to listen to the same song being played on repeat for hours at a time.

It wasn't fun, in the slightest, and as the game progressed when I took my mask off and looked at the other players, it seemed like they weren't having fun, either.

□ □ □

IN TODAY'S CHINESE SOCIETY, the echoes of the Cultural Revolution are keenly felt but never discussed. The central government decided to mark the recent fortieth anniversary of those terrible years by doing . . . absolutely nothing to remind people that the Cultural Revolution ever happened at all. In government-issued history textbooks, the period from 1966 to 1976 is *kong-bai*—a blank slate. Those years are literally not discussed. The government is attempting to erase them from history. After all, to acknowledge the atrocities committed when the Communist Party was founded would be to implicitly question the Party's legitimacy.

Many of the players at the Killing People Club are old enough to have lived through the Cultural Revolution; others are too young to understand the depth and scale of the atrocities that the government inflicted upon its people.

The passion of the members of the Killing People Club often becomes brutally intense: they scream at each other and even threaten physical violence when their teammates make mistakes. The Club members are part of the white-collar class of Chinese urbanites. Yet here they are, playing unfairly victimized peasants and sinister policemen. They are paying money to engage in psychological warfare against each other, just as they, or their parents, were forced by the government to do.

Is the popularity of the Killing People Club, then, an exercise in masochism? Is it a way to acknowledge a terrible slice of history without actually acknowledging it, in the traditional Chinese manner of deflecting blame to avoid shame, just like Chairman Mao's atrocities were explained away by the government when it announced that he was "70 percent right and 30 percent wrong?" Is the Killing People Club a way for educated Chinese citizens to subvert their history as victims and to become, briefly and metaphorically, the oppressor?

Or is the game just a fad that happens to be addictive, like gambling or computer games, both of which are hugely popular in China?

□   □   □

WHEN I ASK Lao Zhang what he thinks of my theory, he laughs, and says that the Cultural Revolution and the Killing People Game have nothing to do with each other. He says that the game is just fun, just a way to pass the time with other intelligent people. It's an escape, he repeats again and again, people need an escape. In China, regular people can't get involved in politics, there's no forum for the open discussion of ideas, and this is where the people go that would be shooting the breeze about their government in some coffee shop if they were from New York or Amsterdam. It's just an escape, he says. There is no metaphorical meaning to it; no socially cathartic release, no cultural psychosis.

A couple months later, I returned to Qingdao. Lao Zhang was back together with his wife, and with another of his girlfriends. He still wasn't coming to work on a regular basis, but he'd stopped playing the Killing People Game, he told me. No more killing people. He wasn't going there anymore. "Really?" I asked, somewhat incredulously.

He grinned sheepishly. "Well, only once or twice a week . . ."

13

The Real Hustler

JIMMY BOY IS getting really tired of all these little trips around Shanghai, delivering all these one-gram bags of cocaine. Just this afternoon, he had to go all the way out to Pudong, like twenty kilometers away, just to drop off one bag.

He's working too hard. This is bullshit. Small-time bullshit. Slave bullshit.

It's the summertime now: June has already come and gone, and Jimmy Boy has got July and August to make the kind of money he doesn't have: the big money. The big money that'll allow him to pay for his sister's university tuition, the kind of money that'll keep his mother's rent paid, the kind of money that'll buy his girlfriends luxury makeup and designer clothes, the kind of money that maybe, just maybe, will allow him to get out of this business forever. He's got two more months of busy season to set up a big score. Then winter will descend on Shanghai, and the big-money buyers will stay in the comfort of their own homes instead of going out every night and getting fucked up.

A couple kilos of impure, flaky coke and maybe a couple kilos of black hash from Afghanistan. A big Western Union payment back home, a big chance to change his phone number and get out of this slave lifestyle.

But with each passing day and no solid leads that might bring him closer to the big score, with the polluted haze that hangs over the city like a permanent brown blanket growing more and more oppressive, Jimmy Boy's chafing at the bit with frustration.

I met Jimmy Boy through a friend in Shanghai, a friend with good connections and a penchant for pharmaceuticals. After talking to Jimmy Boy a couple times out at nightclubs, I persuaded him to meet me for a meal and conversation.

We're eating lunch at a small, modern, brightly lit Cantonese café on Hengshan Road, in Shanghai's French Concession. Jimmy Boy ordered a whole fish and finished it in a matter of minutes, even picking up the bones and sucking on them to get at the last bits of remaining flesh.

His Nokia cell phone beeps: it's a customer who lives in Gubei, all the way out by the old airport.

"One bag," he says, "one lousy bag . . ." He sighs. "That's still a lot of money to me right now." Jimmy Boy hails a taxi and hops into the backseat, enjoying the cool rush of air-conditioning. He dials the customer.

"Hey. Tell the taxi driver where to go," says Jimmy Boy, in his sing-songy patois. He hands the phone to the driver, who receives the coordinates: Jimmy Boy can't speak Chinese. I wave goodbye as they zoom off towards Gubei, a thirty-minute trip through mid-afternoon, stop-and-go traffic. Taxis in China are cheap and plentiful; while Shanghai's cabs are the most expensive, they're still relatively affordable, and, unlike in other cities, the AC in these taxis almost always works.

□   □   □

HE WON'T TELL me his age, though I'd guess him to be somewhere around thirty. His wardrobe varies tremendously. Most of the time he favors T-shirts, shorts, and flip-flops, though occasionally he'll get decked out in full hip-hop-gangsta regalia: oversized athletic jersey, matching baggy pants, a gold chain or two around his neck.

Sometimes, if he's going to work a classy affair, a restaurant opening or a party at the Ritz or Bar Rouge, a high-end nightspot on the Bund, overlooking the river, he'll put on his newly purchased three-piece suit.

Jimmy Boy grew up in a slum outside of Abuja, the capital of Nigeria. His childhood, as he tells it, was marked by the typical problems that plague the poor of sub-Saharan Africa: hunger, disease, the constant threat of violence, and a sense of complete hopelessness. When his father disappeared to parts unknown, Jimmy Boy's mother and sister were facing an even grimmer form of poverty.

"There are no job opportunities in Nigeria," says Jimmy Boy. "The government is too corrupt, man, motherfucking corrupt." His words are simple but true. Although Nigeria has been blessed with abundant natural resources—it is one of the world's largest petroleum producers and has one of the biggest natural gas reserves on Earth—decades of poor governance have left the country's economy in a shambles. Nigeria is a founding member of OPEC and should have passed some of its oil wealth down to its population, but instead the country is saddled with a massive foreign debt. In 2005 figures, GDP was only $692 per capita.

The Nigerians have a reputation for being exceptionally resourceful. They also have a reputation for being some of the world's most skillful and vicious con artists. So-called "419 scams," which involve sending out spam e-mails, attempting to bait Westerners into parting with a few thousand dollars up-front with the promise from the Nigerian party of sharing with the mark millions of dollars hidden in international banks, employ an estimated 250,000 Nigerians. These e-mails, from aliases like Joseph Ukegwo and Barrister Buba Moha, usually start off something like this:

> Dear Friend,
> My name is Barrister Buba Moha a Solicitor and the Personal Attorney to John Steiner an American who worked with an Oil Company in Nigeria.

If the scam didn't work, there wouldn't be the population equivalent of a medium-size city working on it. According to the popular website Snopes.com, James Caldwell of the US Secret Service said in 1997 that "We have confirmed losses, just in the United States, of $150 million in the last fifteen months." This figure is dated, but the most recent available; most likely, the actual losses are far greater.

In China, especially the international cities like Beijing, Shanghai, and Guangzhou, Nigerians are everywhere. Some of them are legitimate businessmen, working for multinational mining and technology companies. With one eye firmly trained on Nigeria's natural resources, the "nouveau mandarins" in Beijing have made a concerted effort to foster ties between the most populous nation in the world and the most populous nation in Africa. They're doing a successful job: Nigerian students, engineers, and executives are flocking to China in record numbers.

Other Nigerians in China, however, are hustlers. They've grown up in a life of poverty and have come to China for one reason: to make money to send home. Legitimate work options normally available to foreigners, such as teaching English, are hard to find. Though English is the official language in Nigeria, most Nigerians speak English in a sing-songy patois, and Chinese parents would much rather have Americans or British (or even Israelis or Italians) teaching their kids than a Nigerian: there's nothing prestigious about a black English teacher who can't even speak English "the right way." Young Nigerians in China are faced with the same dilemma they faced back home: lack of suitable employment. So they turn to illegal activity to make their money.

□   □   □

JIMMY BOY REMEMBERS when he first decided to come to China. All he knew were the kung-fu movies they showed on Nigerian TV: wizened hermits living on remote mountain peaks, ninjas skulking around in the dead of night, trying to kill their enemy, or whomever.

But his friends who returned from China all said that it was great over there: good food, cute little women, and easy money. The economy was booming, they said, and looking at the front pages of the Nigerian newspapers, it seemed to be true: it seemed every other day there was an announcement about "China-Nigeria friendship."

In Abuja, Nigeria's capital, or Lagos, its largest city, a one-year China business visa costs $3,500—a formidable price for many Nigerians. However, Jimmy Boy's isn't an ordinary visa. It has already been stamped in someone else's Nigerian passport, which bears the name of a quasi-legitimate Nigerian businessman. In the eyes of the Chinese immigration officials, Jimmy Boy's name is Emeka Okereke, a junior-level manager of a petroleum concern. The real Okereke, of course, didn't want to come to China and he's back home in Lagos spending his $3,500 on god knows what.

Some Nigerians travel to China using other people's passports without bothering to change the picture; they figure that most Chinese immigration agents can't tell the difference between one black face and another. However, it's still generally safer to use one's own photograph. Thankfully for would-be Nigerian émigrés, there are plenty of underground print shops that, for the comparatively low price of $300, will remove the original passport holder's photo and insert the buyer's photo. The end result is almost always good enough to fool foreign immigration officials. The passport itself is "real," after all, and will scan through the machine with no problem at all.

▫ ▫ ▫

BEIJING IS THE ARRIVAL point for Nigerians when they first fly into in China. Here, there's a sizeable expatriate community, and there are blocks of flats where you can hear Yoruba and Ebro spoken in addition to English and Chinese. If you ask most young Nigerians what they're doing in China, they'll undoubtedly reply, "teaching English." In China, a great deal of foreigners from all over the world have come to teach English.

Most are ambitious young college graduates who are, at least at first, associated with a school; however, the market for private lessons is vast, and bright college graduates from the West and wastrel long-term expats alike get their beer and rent money by teaching private English lessons.

Of course, since these lessons are private and conducted in the homes of the students, it's very difficult for the Chinese government to ascertain who is actually teaching English and who is just using the guise of "English teacher" for other, more illicit enterprises.

The main nightlife strip in Beijing, Sanlitun, or, as it's known by locals, "Jiubajie" (Bar Street) sits squarely in the center of the embassy district. One side of the street has, like so much of Beijing, recently been demolished to make way for a modern high-rise to be completed before the 2008 Olympics. The other side of the street houses a row of pretty much nondescript Western-style bars and cafés. Chalkboards on the walls outside advertise the specials: Tsingtao Beer, Happy Hour, Gin and Tonic, Club Sandwich.

Up until early 2005 when it was demolished, the main Beijing hub for seedy nightlife of all sorts could be found just around the corner on Sanlitun Nanjie (South Street). While Sanlitun proper is a wide street, with lots of traffic, Sanlitun South was little more than a glorified alley, an offshoot of the main drag that ran for a hundred yards into a dead end.

The drink prices were decidedly cheaper in Sanlitun South than on the main strip—ten yuan ($1.20) got you a bottle of China's most popular, most exported beer, Tsingtao—and the wild atmosphere contrasted starkly with the more antiseptic Sanlitun of today. On little tables set up in front of a little shack called Rainbow's Time, hooligans of all nationalities puffed strawberry tobacco from massive hookahs before heading down the street to try to get laid at the New-Orleans-themed Durty Nellie's. Uighurs from Xinjiang, wearing their Muslim skullcaps, lined the sidewalk barbecuing mutton kebabs on portable charcoal grills. Drunk Western exchange students sipped cans of beer on the street and screamed out into the night. Chinese urbanites, blotto on rice wine, stumbled red-faced out of the bars. This was where the Nigerians plied their wares.

After Sanlitun Nanjie was demolished, many of its bars and seedy characters relocated to another narrow street, this time just east of the main Sanlitun strip. While this "New Sanlitun South" can't quite match the glorious seediness of the old, it's still plenty sketchy.

When you enter this narrow street, Nigerians stand in the shadows like sentries guarding some unbelievably screwed-up imperial city. If you've got white skin, they'll assume you've got more money and more of a jones than anyone else hanging around, and get up in your face, pitching their wares. I got the Ecstasy, the good shit, man. Coke. Black hash. Weed.

Heroin. Speed. A head-shake or a "no thanks" doesn't turn them off. They're persistent and aggressive to the point of being completely unpleasant. They're hustlers, and you're their mark. Most of the time, they'll take you for a ride, charging exorbitant prices for a small ball of hash or an Ecstasy tablet. If you get ripped off, it's not the worst that can happen: there are countless tales of Beijing neophytes handing over hundreds of yuan in exchange for Ecstasy that turned out to be aspirin, grass that turned out to be oregano, or coke that was nothing more than ground-up baby laxative. According to some Chinese friends, a couple expats even overdosed on some strange Nigerian mystery pills, turning up dead in their apartments after drug-fueled nights out at the clubs.

□　□　□

WHEN JIMMY BOY first arrived in China, it was only natural that he went straight to Beijing and hooked up with the Nigerian community there. After only a few weeks, he realized that the best way for him to make money would be to start selling drugs.

But there were already too many pushers for the Beijing marketplace, and he didn't like their aggressive behavior. Most of the Beijing Nigerians were from Lagos, to the south of his hometown, and Jimmy Boy felt like they were harassing foreigners and Chinese alike, giving their country a bad name. "Often," he says, "I feel afraid to tell people I am from Nigeria. I tell people I am from other African countries instead because I know of the bad reputation of the Nigerian people."

A couple weeks, a little bit of wrangling, and a few thousand yuan later (spent taking influential men in the business out to dinner), Jimmy Boy finally achieved his goal. He scored a meeting with a captain of the Nigerian drug syndicate. In a clean, five-star hotel room, he made the connection that would allow him to purchase kilograms of black hash from Afghanistan and twenty-five-gram "bullets" of Colombian cocaine at a fair price.

After he got the product, Jimmy Boy knew he needed to get out of Beijing. There was too much competition, he didn't care for the aggressiveness of his fellow pushers, and he didn't really like the city very much. When the wind blew in from the Gobi Desert to the north, he could barely breathe because the air was so dusty. From other sources in the African community, he had heard about opportunities down south in Shanghai. China's economic center was also caught in the throes of a new kind of cultural revolution. It seemed like every company in the world was racing to set up an office in Shanghai.

Shanghai has a history of foreign occupation. Over the past two hundred years, areas of the city have been controlled by the English, the French, the Americans, and the Japanese. Today, Shanghai remains the only internationally diverse city in China. It's a city of migrants: bankers from London and Wall Street, restaurateurs from Paris, consultants from Germany, designers from Singapore, hustlers from everywhere else in China. The Chinese economy has continued its record-setting growth, and Shanghai is rich with foreign investment and domestic capital. Much has been made of the emergence of a Chinese "middle class"; Shanghai, ever one step ahead, has already developed an "overclass." This overclass consists of foreigners on expatriate salaries, overseas Chinese business-men, government officials, Shanghainese business owners, and anyone with the good fortune to own one of the old-style downtown apartments that can fetch $10,000 in monthly rent.

Shanghai's the biggest city in a country that's perpetually under construction. At night, seen from a car driving along any of the elevated roads that intersect the city, the place spread out before your eyes seems almost impossibly large. Thousands of high-rises jut up into the sky, phallic symbols of prosperity and of progress. Fifteen years ago, these same spaces were occupied by squat socialist six-story houses. Now they're being replaced by glossy office buildings for multi-national corporations, top-of-the-line, serviced apartments for these corporations' overpaid executives, and posh luxury hotels for the visiting bosses of the executives, and, of course, condominium apartments.

Multinational companies and their well-paid executives, manufacturers, venture capitalists, restaurateurs, nightlife impresarios from all over the world: they were all heading to Shanghai, a city awash in capital, a city more "Westernized" than the rest of China.

Armed with a duffel full of drugs, Jimmy Boy took a taxi to Beijing Railway Station, made his way through the small army of migrant workers that were camped on the ground outside, and caught the overnight train heading south.

□   □   □

AND THAT'S HOW Jimmy Boy found himself in Shanghai. At first, it was hard for him to do business. He didn't know very many people, and so he went out to Shanghai's swankiest nightspots, places where everyone's dressed in the newest fashions from Milan and Paris and drinks cost upwards of 100 yuan—a year's cash income for many of China's 800 million subsistence farmers. He would strike up conversations with Westerners, posing as an English teacher, looking sharp in his only suit. He'd slip into the conversation that he had a "friend" that could obtain cocaine or hashish. In Shanghai, there is a preponderance of bored Westerners with money to burn, and Jimmy Boy soon found himself doing a brisk business.

He took each twenty-five-gram "bullet" and broke it up into twenty-five individual baggies. (I would venture a guess that he "cut" the product with other white, powdery substances—baking powder or ground-up pills—thereby increasing his yield, but he didn't cop to it.) Each gram baggie sells for 1,200 renminbi, or $150. The stuff's not cheap when you're this far away from South America.

Sometimes, he found himself in uncomfortable situations. One of his best customers, whom he considered a friend, delivered a harsh rebuke when Jimmy Boy said hello to him at a swish party. "Listen here, Jimmy Boy," said the American financier. "If I'm talking to a bunch of guys in suits, and you're wearing hip-hop gear, do not come up to me and say hello. Who the fuck am I supposed to say you are? My English teacher?"

A few days later, Jimmy Boy bought his first three-piece suit. As time passed, he built up his client base like any successful drug dealer: his customers told their friends, who told their friends, and so on. Soon enough, his cell phone was ringing constantly, and he was taking taxicabs all around the massive city, all afternoon and all night, dropping off packets of cocaine.

□   □   □

HOW DOES THE stuff get here? That's the million-yuan question. Other drugs, like heroin and hashish, are produced locally—in Afghanistan and the Golden Triangle—and are therefore readily available in China. But cocaine? The climate necessary for the coca leaf to grow is only present in South America, which is about as far from China as you can possibly get.

There are several syndicates that deal drugs around the world. The South Americans, the Middle Easterners, and the Hong Kong Triads have been actively (and publicly) involved in moving drugs for several decades. In the past ten years, however, whenever these groups have faltered due to increased pressure from law enforcement agencies, the Nigerian drug rings step in.

The cocaine is smuggled, by plane or ship, from South America to Nigeria. Once in Nigeria, it is packed into the false soles of shoes, into stuffed animals carried on by children, into condoms to be swallowed. The "mule" is then flown to a certain city in the Middle East, where security checks are lenient and customs officials can, if necessary, be bribed to look the other way. From there, the mules board connecting flights into Beijing, via Hong Kong if necessary.

After each visit from his mules, the Nigerian kingpin in Beijing has a kilogram or so of dope. Jimmy Boy buys his twenty-five-gram "bullets" from the kingpin in Beijing for roughly 10,000 yuan ($1,200), brings them down to Shanghai by train, and sells each gram for 1,200 yuan, neatly tripling his initial investment. The ultimate street value of a kilo of coke in China? 1,200 yuan x 1,000 = 1.2

million yuan, or $150,000. Not exactly chump change down in Lagos.

Jimmy Boy is proud of the quality of his hash—he offers me a sample and seems upset when I tell him that I don't smoke. He finds that most of the hash and marijuana in China is "shit, man, absolute shit." He sells only the best "black hash," produced in the mountainous region in Afghanistan near Pakistan, the same area where Osama bin Laden's purportedly been hanging out for the past few years.

How does the hash get into China? "Afghanistan people," says Jimmy Boy. "They have diplomatic passports." He buys a kilogram of hashish from the Beijing kingpin for 14,000 yuan ($1,750). By the turn of the twenty-first century, smoking marijuana has become commonplace among all classes of people in the Western world, and Shanghai's got a lot of hash-hungry Westerners. Jimmy Boy exploits this opportunity, selling 500-yuan bags to Canadian English teachers and German engineers at a tremendous 3,000-percent markup.

□   □   □

JIMMY BOY DOESN'T have any local customers. "The Chinese people, man—I don't fuck with them. Too dangerous. I need to find people I can trust, and I don't know any." His client base is composed exclusively of Shanghai's massive expatriate population, whose demand for coke and hash is seemingly insatiable, especially because there aren't too many dealers in town.

When he's on the job, Jimmy Boy gets to visit Shanghai's most expensive nightspots, and he never has to pay for a drink. There are always customers ready to buy him $10 gin-and-tonics, to offer him Marlboro cigarettes, to ply him with small talk, which makes him feel good for a while. He's the guy with the shit, and, sometimes, especially when he's dressed up in his three-piece suit, the attention he gets at such swanky places makes him feel important.

But sometimes, like any drug dealer, he's gotta wonder: do these people really like me, or do they just like the drugs I have? It's hard to tell. Some of the customers get rough with him when they're drunk or coked up, like the guy who gave him shit about his clothes that time, but some of them seem to really care, giving him hints on getting by in Shanghai, telling him about the newest hotspots. Some customers try to introduce him to girls, but that's not a problem for him: plenty of Chinese women have an affinity for black men, and he's taken advantage of the opportunities afforded him. The only time he spends money is when he's out with one girl or another, taking them to a nice dinner before going back to his pad.

□ □ □

JIMMY BOY LIKES the good-time girls, but his attitude towards the Chinese people in general is considerably cooler. The Chinese, reared on a diet of television and movies where Africans are consistently portrayed as villains, are tremendously prejudiced. Many educated Chinese people I have spoken with have expressed rather matter-of-factly their belief that Africans are more similar to apes than other races, and that is why they make the best dancers and athletes.

It's hard being black in China. Shanghai is not so bad, though—the locals there are used to foreigners, both black and white. But Jimmy Boy's got quite a few customers in nearby cities, mostly English teachers and foreign students who buy kilograms of hash every month and divvy it up amongst their friends. Life in places like Wuxi can get pretty boring for a Westerner, and so when Jimmy Boy hits these smaller towns, he's treated like a doctor arriving in a faraway land with the antidote to some deadly disease.

But the Chinese are another story. He feels they look at him as if, at best, he is a creature arrived from some other planet. They point at him, stare and gawk, and while their reaction to him is more annoying than threatening, it's still uncomfortable when men look at him and shout "*hei ren*"— "black man"—as if he might be a villain bent on raping their women and eating their children.

It gets Jimmy Boy down sometimes, this second-class treatment by the Chinese, constantly being stared at everywhere he goes. He can't let it affect him too much, though: he's got to keep his head straight, keep looking for that big score.

□　□　□

ACCORDING TO THE Xinhua News Agency, in the period from January 2005 to April 2006, the Chinese police cracked 52,500 drug trafficking cases. In this time, they seized 7.2 tons of heroin, 2.994 tons of opium, 6.3 tons of methamphetamine hydrochloride, 2.74 tons of ketamine and 2.48 million Ecstasy pills.

Of course, the Chinese police haven't done a particularly good job of eradicating the drug problem. Drugs are readily available almost everywhere in this huge country. The numbers above look impressive only because there are so many people selling drugs—many more, of course, are consuming them.

A few days before I met with Jimmy Boy, on June 26, China celebrated the United Nations' Anti-Drug Day, by summarily executing at least twenty-seven drug traffickers from around the country and sentencing at least twelve more to death. This has become an eerie kind of ritual; every year, in the days leading up to Anti-Drug Day, the Chinese government will select a few of the more notorious drug dealers that have been apprehended in the last year and send them before the firing squad. This serves as both the obvious deterrent to would-be smugglers and dealers, and the government's attempt to show solidarity with the global drug-fighting community.

Jimmy Boy is unaware of the annual executions, and when I mention them, his eyes go so wide that they're almost popping out of his face. He drops the fish bone back onto his plate where it lands with a splat in a pool of soy sauce. "They would kill me?" he asks. "You think? You think they would kill me? How do they do it?"

"Firing squad," I say. "Bullet to the back of the head." (They actually use a single bullet to the back of the head rather than standing the victim against a wall before a number of executors.) Seeing the alarmed expression on his face, I try to be reassuring: "But they usually don't execute foreign nationals in China," I tell him. "Just life in prison."

It's a strange feeling: normally, when I think about China executing people, it is as an abstract and enormous number. But sitting across the table from me is a man who every day risks getting killed, or, more likely, spending the rest of his life in a squalid foreign jail, just to make a little bit of money.

My thoughts had drifted. I'm silent for a few minutes. Jimmy Boy is obsessed with the executions, and he asks again how they execute drug traffickers.

□   □   □

IT'S NOT LIKE in America, where there's a trial, sentencing, and potentially one or more appeals, stretched out over a number of years. In China, the criminal can be arrested, tried, sentenced to death, and executed in a matter of weeks.

Until the mid-nineties, local governments would, several times a year, organize a twisted parade, where criminals were led around town on the back of pickup trucks, signs around their neck pronouncing their crimes. Public executions were held in local sports stadiums and broadcast on television. These public humiliations prior to execution have largely been eliminated during the economic boom of the last decade— such displays don't sit well with Westerners.

Now, the whole execution process takes place within the confines of the prison. The condemned kneels on the ground and bows his head. The executioner then fires a bullet into the back of the criminal's head. If the criminal continues to twitch, another bullet will be fired, to ensure that he's dead. The killings aren't broadcast on TV anymore, but everyone still knows about them through newspaper reports and the nightly news.

Jimmy Boy's freaked out. He hasn't really pictured himself kneeling before the executioner until now. But he figures his chances of getting caught are pretty low, and in a classic act of neurotic self-denial, he figures that even if they do catch someone in his territory, it's not going to be him. He's careful, doing all his transactions in code: "g" for gram, "bh" for black hash. He should be okay, and anyway, all he needs is a couple big scores and he can quit this racket for good.

Nervously, he shakes my hand and asks me directions to an address in Shanghai's business district. He slips on a pair of sunglasses and hails a cab, and I watch his vehicle slip seamlessly into the afternoon traffic, just like Jimmy Boy has slipped seamlessly into the world of Shanghai's high rollers.

The next time I see Jimmy Boy around, out at a posh nightclub on the banks of Suzhou Creek, Israel has launched an attack on Lebanon, destabilizing the region and putting Jimmy Boy's drug connections out of commission. He's no closer to the big score than he was a couple months back, and he knows that time is running out. He's selling the last of his one-gram bags to the bankers and the models, hoping that his higher-ups will work out some kind of alternate plan. Maybe he'll move a couple kilos of black hash still readily available from his Beijing connection; that would be a big score.

Then he can wire some money home, maybe bring a friend from Nigeria over here to do the street hustling so he can move up one step on the pyramid, make more money for less work. Some of his friends live down in Guangzhou and Shenzhen, and he's thinking about heading south for a little while, but a few Nigerians were recently arrested for trafficking there and it's a risky scene. He doesn't know, yet, what's happened to them.

He tells me he thinks again about what I told him at lunch that day, how the Chinese government executes traffickers. He lights a cigarette and flicks the ash nervously. He looks out into the crowd at the club, lost in thought, perhaps conjuring the vision in his head of kneeling down on the ground, closing his eyes, waiting for the executioner's bullet in the back of the neck—and then he fingers the roll of bills in his pocket. His cell rings. He nods goodbye to me, and hails a cab to make yet another delivery.

14

The Punks

"Our band could be your life. Real names will be the proof. Me and Mike Watt, we played for years. Punk rock changed our life."

—D. Boon, the Minutemen,
"History Lesson, Part 2"

"Scream for the life, scream for the right, scream for the truth and faith! Don't stop! When you start screaming for the silent masses!"

—SMZB

□   □   □

IT'S MID-JUNE AND the city of Wuhan is already blistering hot. It's the kind of dry, dusty heat that makes you want to take a shower every time you step outside, even if you're stepping outside directly after taking a shower. In the summer, the temperature hovers around forty degrees Celsius (104 degrees Fahrenheit).

In Eastern and Central China, the weather is across-the-board awful; most major cities are freezing cold in winter and blistering hot in summer. Wuhan, however, is the hottest of the legendary "Three Furnaces," the three hottest cities in China. (The other two are Nanjing and Chongqing, though most Chinese will give you a different answer. For example, everyone in Shandong insists that their capital, Jinan, is one of the furnaces; people from Hebei will tell you that Changsha is one of the furnaces.)

As the hottest furnace, Wuhan has earned a reputation as the most unpleasant city in a country full of unpleasant cities. The air in Wuhan is not only hot; it's dirty. Wuhan is one of the largest production centers in China for iron and steel, and for automobile manufacturing.

Going to Wuhan in the summer feels like walking into a sauna where a vagrant has started an industrial fire in an oil drum. "The pollution problem has gotten much better in the last few years," says Lao Wang, the proprietor of a small shop near the river.

This is an oppressive city, a boiling cauldron of industry and sheer humanity. According to the government's official 2006 estimates, the city's population numbers 9.1 million, not counting migrant workers and other unregistered citizens. Wuhan is a massive, sprawling beast, bisected by the Yangtze River. Massive new shopping malls (Gucci, Wal-Mart, Pizza Hut) exist side-by-side with pockets of old China: grimy food stalls, stores selling piles of what appears to be garbage but is actually recycled clothing, cooking tools and other miscellaneous flotsam and jetsam. Businessmen babble into their cell phones while migrant construction workers take naps in their wheelbarrows.

Three enormous, mile-long bridges span the river. The first bridge (named, in true Communist fashion, "#1 Bridge") was regarded as one of the first great feats of Communist architecture; the third, and largest, was completed in 2000 to handle the heavy traffic of the New Economy. Gorgeous colonial buildings from the 1920s that once housed the City Bank of New York and the Bank of Hong Kong have been taken over by the Chinese-run Everbright Banking Corporation and the Agricultural Bank of China.

I'm staying in a run-down, state-owned guesthouse in the center of town. Cigarette burns dot the carpet like flea bites on a stray dog. I've been in the room for ten minutes, just long enough to wash my hands, brush my teeth with bottled water, and take a watery shit, when the phone rings.

It's a sprightly female voice on the other end.

"Massage?"

I decline and flop down on the bed. I feel like the lead actor in a bad horror movie; something bad is about to happen to me, but I can't be sure what, or how. I ate a suspect plate of egg fried rice in a street stall about an hour ago, and the bacteria in my stomach have seemingly organized an army and begun their slow march down towards my colon. My eyes sting from the pollution. I open a liter bottle of warm Snow beer and take a swig.

Welcome to Wuhan: imperial capital, number-one furnace, jewel of the Yangtze River, and the epicenter of Chinese underground punk rock.

◻   ◻   ◻

UNLESS YOU KNEW exactly where to look, finding the Vox Bar would be impossible. I had the bar's business card, and it still took me half an hour of walking up and down Lumo Road to spot the place. The Vox Bar occupies the second story of a five-story pay-by-the-hour hotel in the university district. The whole street is lined with these pay-by-the-hour hotels; interspersed with the hotels are Chinese college dormitories that redefine the word "cramped." Six or eight students will live in a two-hundred-square-foot room. If any of these undergraduates are lucky enough to find a girlfriend or boyfriend, making love in the dormitory is not a viable option. With a couple hundred thousand college students in the immediate vicinity, the pay-by-the hour market is a gold mine for entrepreneurial property owners.

The hotel above Vox doesn't even have a name, and its only inhabitants are embarrassed, postcoital college students and a ragtag bunch of Uighurs, Turkic people from the Chinese autonomous region of Xinjiang.

On Saturdays, when Vox hosts punk rock shows, the skull-capped Uighurs move little chairs out onto the sidewalk in order to stare at the punk rock crowd. This is especially funny because the punks are also staring at the Uighurs, in a curious way, not a menacing way. "Those guys are cool," says one of the punks. "They smoke hash every day. They have the good stuff."

◻   ◻   ◻

WU WEI'S STANDING by the door, tapping his foot nervously. In a couple hours, his veteran band SMZB (or *shengming zhibing*,

The Cake of Life) will take the stage to perform at the release party of their most recent record, "Scream for Life: Tribute." The bar is practically empty. The girl selling tickets is taking a nap next to a pile of punk rock magazines. The concert is scheduled to start in ten minutes.

□ □ □

ZHU NING IS the godfather of Wuhan punk rock, original drummer for SMZB, and the co-owner of the Vox Bar. (Disclosure: his business partner is an American friend of mine.) The show's about to begin, but he's not apprehensive, he's busy. While most Chinese bar owners are content to kick back with a cold Tsingtao while a crew of underpaid, underappreciated staff does all the work, Zhu has the work ethic of ten men. Instead of spending money on a team of construction workers, Zhu built the entire inside of the club himself, ripping out the old interiors and putting in little booths, building a bar, throwing together a ramshackle stage, and patching together the sound system.

□ □ □

THE SHOW'S MINUTES from starting and there's work to be done: they need enough domestic beer, enough Bud and Heineken, Jack Daniels and Stolichnaya, Zhongnanhai and Triple 5 cigarettes, enough ice cubes, clean glasses, enough small bills at the door, enough toilet paper . . .

CBGB, the former New York City centerpiece of the American punk rock movement, was said to have the dirtiest, most unusable bathrooms of all time. If a dirty bathroom is somehow a measure of a club's "punk rockness," then the Vox Bar must be the most punk rock bar in the world. In order to get to the bathroom, you must first pass through a concrete hallway strewn with uncollected trash. The toilet itself consists of the standard Chinese two squat-style holes-in-the-ground, but at Vox, a dim blue light illuminates the bathroom and makes the whole experience more bizarre, and the ground is slick with wastewater and piss.

□   □   □

FOUR BANDS ARE SCHEDULED to perform tonight, and the concert is supposed to start at 8:30, but like rock concerts everywhere from Marseilles to Tahiti to Dakar, the show will start late. At nine o'clock, only a few people are sitting around the club drinking Wuhan Snow beer and playing dice. "No Milk Today" by Herman's Hermits blares incongruously from the stereo. An African guy wearing an oversize FUBU jersey sits on a couch in the back, his Chinese girlfriend nestled asleep against his chest.

Slowly, the audience begins to trickle in. The Chinese teenagers are pierced, tattooed, and dressed in their best rock-and-roll clothes; they sport T-shirts with images of the Doors, Nirvana, Green Day, the Clash. Spiked bracelets. Dyed hair. One chubby kid with a Buddha-like grin under his bowl haircut wears a Casualties T-shirt and tight, punk-style plaid pants.

Finally, at half past nine, the first band, Ten Bottle Hearts, takes the stage and plays an energetic set that wins the small crowd over despite some pretty glaring rhythmic difficulties.

For the finale, they butcher "Should I Stay or Should I Go," missing notes and screaming in unintelligible English. When they finish, the DJ throws on the Clash version. This is not meant to be ironic.

Throughout the next two supporting bands, the crowd swells exponentially. After the third band finishes their set, the room has become packed, barely enough room to make your way through without spilling your beer as you squeeze your way between good-looking young people in varying degrees of punkitude. Most of the men and some of the women are smoking, and the familiar nicotine haze that hangs in every Chinese establishment forms a slow, swirling cloud.

Like any quality rock band, SMZB is making the audience wait. Everyone is growing antsy. The DJ flips a switch, and a video screen crawls down from the ceiling.

SMZB's new video, for their song "No Friend, No Life," appears on the screen. The crowd cheers at the opening lines: "In your heart, you cannot just have yourself/Because this world is a killer."

Wu Wei and his band stroll on stage. He grins at the crowd and tunes up his guitar. It is going to be a good show. On the stage behind him, a massive banner hangs from the ceiling. It proclaims: "SMZB: Punk Revellers of China."

□ □ □

IN THE MID-NINETIES, Zhu Ning and Wu Wei met each other while they were both studying at the Beijing MIDI School, China's most prestigious music institute. They discovered a mutual love of Nirvana, the Red Hot Chili Peppers, punk rock and hardcore music; however, at the time (as now) finding legitimate compact discs was basically impossible.

Luckily for Zhu, Wu, and their generation of aspiring musicians, European wholesalers and distributors often sent their unused promotional copies and the titles that didn't sell over to China in shipping containers; enterprising Cantonese set up a distribution network to ship these otherwise-unattainable discs all over China. These "cut-out" CDs are how the nascent Chinese punkers and indie-rockers learned about rock and roll. Zhu and Wu, as early "heads," knew all the best CD shops in Beijing to find these discs, and they would spend hours scouring the selection, trying to figure out whether a CD was any good by looking at the cover art and pictures of the musicians in the liner notes.

After graduation, Zhu Ning and Wu Wei decided to form a band. The two were good friends but polar opposites: while Zhu is retiring and polite to a fault, Wu Wei is chatty and charismatic. They packed up their instruments and their CD collections and headed to Zhu's hometown of Panzhihua, a city in Sichuan Province known for its steel mills and toxic air. Zhu played the drums, and Wu handled the guitar duties; they wrote the lyrics together, as a team. They named the band *shengming zhibing* and saw modest success playing in small clubs, here and there. After a few months, Wu Wei, a Wuhan boy by birth, decided to return to his hometown. After he had been there a couple months, he called Zhu Ning and told him that there might be more opportunities for their band to develop in the much bigger city of Wuhan. Zhu thought about it for a second, then decided, why the hell not? He hopped on the night train and was there the next evening.

This combination of soft-spoken Zhu Ning and effusive Wu Wei, this blend of yin and yang, became the progenitor of the entire Wuhan punk rock scene.

❑   ❑   ❑

THOUGH THE TERM "punk music" was first used in reference to American garage-rock bands in the 1960s, the movement that has become generally known as punk rock began in Europe and America in the mid-seventies. Its founding fathers—the Sex Pistols, the Clash, the Ramones—are revered as musical gods by Chinese punk rockers. "Most Chinese punk bands," says Xiao Chen, an aspiring guitar player, "when they first get together they just play songs by the Sex Pistols and the Ramones, because they are so good and so simple."

When these bands sing covers of English-language punk songs, their words, sung in English by people that don't really speak that language, are often confused and almost always unintelligible. "Twenty-twenty-twenty-four-hours-ago, I want to be sedated" becomes "Twenanennnafo how does it go? I want to be slake-id." However, they most certainly understand the most general message of punk rock: the world is fucked up, the *system* is fucked up, and while we may not be able to change anything, no one can stop us from screaming as loud as we want to.

This freedom of expression is a rarity in today's China, where journalists, scholars, members of the Falun Gong, Tibetan separatists, and anyone else who dares to criticize the government in print are routinely thrown in jail without trial and subjected to torture.

In the West, punk has already become somewhat of a cliché; ostensible "punk bands" like Green Day, Good Charlotte, and Fall Out Boy sign contracts with monolith record labels and play in the Pepsi Center, the PNC Bank Arts Center, the Continental Airlines Arena. Any vestige of actual rebellion that was once expressed in underground clubs has long since been swallowed up by the juggernaut of consumerism.

But in China, the government, in some respects, *is* fascist. There is no freedom of expression, and no place for criticism of the leadership. Also, too-rapid development has led to massive income disparity, creating a social rift that threatens to tear apart the whole society. SMZB and other political punks take these problems and give them a voice; they unite a youth community behind an age-old and vitally important message: as a society, as a culture, we have lost our way.

□ □ □

"YOU SUFFERING MOTHERS! No one knows your feeling! In 1989, your sons do not come back again. When they meet the army, when they are facing the guns, your sons feel fear, but still they go forward!"

Wu Wei is jumping up and down, feet spread apart, banging out the chords to "Bullets over Tiananmen" on his cherry-red Gibson SG.

In front of the stage, a crowd of fifty or so punkers pogo like fanatics, singing along to all the words even though the CD hasn't come out yet. The atmosphere is electric; something special is taking place tonight, and the crowd seems to sense it, becoming more and more frenzied with each chorus, smashing into each other, occasionally stumbling out of the pit to take sips from bottles of lukewarm Wuhan Snow beer.

Wu Wei strips down to a black undershirt, revealing a lean, lanky frame covered in tattoos. To his left and right are Pu Gu and Zhang Hua, on bass and guitar. They are both seasoned musicians with the energy of speed freaks. Wu's wife, Hu Juan, sits behind the drums, bashing away with amazing precision, sexy in a tight GBH T-shirt that's soaked through with sweat.

The band's music is not particularly original, though they've recently added a flute player who often doubles the lead guitar line in an attempt to be "more creative." Except for a few flute solos that serve as melodic introductions to the songs, the flute can barely be heard over the wailing guitars and booming bass. Even though the flute is ineffective and the chord changes are rote, the band's energy and presence are undeniable. Wu Wei has the crowd just where he wants them as they burst into their new single, "No Friend, No Life."

The crowd sings along: "You cannot have only yourself in your heart/Because this world is a killer."

From the side of the stage, Zhu Ning watches his old band perform with a pleased expression on his face.

□ □ □

IN 1997, AFTER Zhu Ning and Wu Wei met up once more, this time in Wuhan, a group of young Wuhanese caught on to punk music after meeting Zhu and Wu and attending SMZB shows. Before long, a lot of these kids wanted to start bands of their own. They bought cheap electric guitars, basses and amps, learned a few simple chords, and formed groups with names like Big Buns and Shitdog. One major problem presented itself: Zhu was the only drummer in all of Wuhan. "I was playing in five bands at once," he recalls. "It was crazy."

Like almost all aspiring Chinese rockers do at some point, Zhu Ning and Wu Wei left Wuhan for Beijing. All of China's most famous rock bands are either from Beijing or live there. In addition to being the capital of China, Beijing is most certainly China's cultural center. "Bands go up to Beijing," says Zhu Ning, "because they think that's how they can succeed. They have an idea that once you get to Beijing, you'll get signed to a record company, and become popular right away. They arrive in the city and are amazed at all the bars, all the performance spaces, but they don't know anything. They don't know how hard it is."

When they arrived in Beijing, Zhu and Wu moved back into one of the compounds near the university district that was populated entirely by rock-and-roll musicians, the kind of place that has served as the training ground for several of the figures in this book. They thought this would be a positive environment for creativity and for SMZB; they were wrong. "It was terrible," remembers Zhu. "All of these musicians in one place, constantly talking shit and criticizing the playing of others. Half of them weren't even playing for real! They were just slacking, sitting around doing nothing, taking money from their families."

Also, Zhu soon came face-to-face with an old nemesis from his college days: the terrible snobbery of Beijingers towards *waidiren*, people from other places in China. Beijing rock musicians are an opinionated and arrogant bunch, and they were constantly reminding Zhu and Wei of their provincial roots. Club owners and recording studios give bands from Beijing preferential treatment, thanks to the bands' network of local friends and connections. It was tough. They could rarely get a gig, and when they did, they only got support slots for other small bands. After a couple years, Zhu wanted to go back to Wuhan; Wu, and the rest of the band, wanted to stay. Zhu wanted to experiment musically, to break out of the simple constructs of verse-chorus-verse major-key punk rock, where Wu wanted to employ more pop elements in his songs. They split up, and SMZB started auditioning for a new drummer.

◻ ◻ ◻

SMZB ARE IN the groove: every open chord, every drum fill, every little bassline, every backing vocal. Even the flute player is playing one of the best shows of his life. The audience hasn't calmed down one bit. The music blares out loud and clear onto the sidewalk outside, and a group of middle-aged neighbors, many of them in slippers and underclothes, stand on the pavement listening to the band, smoking cigarettes and drinking from thermoses of tea.

Wu Wei leads the band through most of the songs from the new album and a lot of the old hits: "PRC," "Wuhan Prison," "God Save the Punk." Most of the songs are sung in English; remarkably, the lyrics are incendiary, offering a brutal, honest critique of the Communist Party's shortcomings. SMZB finishes the set with a performance of "China Dream":

This Oriental empire is just like a big tomb.
It buries conscience, morality and truth.
It is just like a big prison.
It prisons freedom and dream.
People are living in a nightmare like this.
When will they wake up?

Perhaps it's obvious why SMZB's songs are sung mostly in English. One reason, presumably, is an attempt to appeal to a foreign audience, another, most certainly, is to let the lyrics fly under the watchful eye of the Communist Party's Ministry of Culture.

The drummer's hair hangs down into her face and she's banging on her kit like she's trying to break it. The guitar player's rocking back and forth, covered in sweat, eyes focused on the ground. And Wu Wei's controlling the mike like a rebel leader rallying his troops for one final charge into battle. The sweaty crowd screams in ecstasy, high-fiving each other. The chubby kid in the Casualties T-shirt lifts his hands in the air and screams. The song comes crashing to an abrupt end; the band, even more sweaty than the crowd, takes a bow in all their tattooed glory. Wu Wei smiles and thanks his hometown crowd. They've succeeded. The show is over. The kids make a dash to the back of the room to buy the new SMZB CD for twenty yuan: $2.50.

□   □   □

WITH SMZB HAVING left the stage, the crowd has moved outside to get some (comparably) fresh air. I notice that Wu Wei's got a Dead Milkmen tattoo on his right pectoral. I tell him that the bass player of the Dead Milkmen killed himself last year. A grim look comes onto his face, then disappears. "You know, I had two friends that died this past year. This show and our new CD are dedicated to them. One of them killed himself, and the other crashed his motorcycle into the back of a truck. I wish they could be here tonight."

The sweat on Wu Wei's face is reflected in the streetlight. His thin black shirt clings damply to his slender frame. In spite of his somber tone, he's got a huge smile on his face. This is as good as it gets: playing a hometown show to a packed crowd. While the life of an up-and-coming rock and roller is tough anywhere in the world, it's especially difficult in China. While many aspiring musicians in America or Europe often hold down mind-numbing service industry jobs to pay the rent, in China this is impossible: the fifteen-hour-a-day, seven-day-a-week work schedule that these jobs require would leave no time for practicing or performing.

SMZB are lucky: they've got a sponsorship from Gibson Guitars, which provides their instruments and amps. But, successful as they are, the members live a spartan life. They make their homes in small, old-school apartments in decaying Communist-style projects. They eat instant noodles and ten-cent fried rice. The ubiquity of pirated CDs in China means that there's no market for legitimate product, and the few thousand yuan the band earns from performing must be stretched out for as long as possible.

It's around midnight; the scene on the sidewalk now resembles a Chinese punk-rock version of the parking lot at a Grateful Dead show. There are over a hundred kids on the sidewalk in front of the club, starting up their motorcycles, drinking cans of cold beer purchased from a little shop next door, sitting on the curb smoking cigarettes and talking shit. People from the neighborhood are strolling around in their underclothes, wondering where all these kids came from.

I walk over to Wu Wei and start a chat about his lyrics when suddenly, the sound of shattering glass stops us mid-conversation. It's tremendously loud, like an explosion. In a few minutes, we'll realize that a fifth-floor window has come loose from its frame and crashed to the ground. By some miracle, none of the kids standing below are hit directly, but a number of them are cut from the flying glass. Only one kid is hurt badly; he stands a few feet from us, shock registered on his face. We can see large pieces of glass in his arms and a huge shard sticking out of the back of his neck. He is bleeding profusely.

Another kid takes a pack of tissues out of his pocket and tries to wipe the blood off his stricken comrade. He throws the blood-soaked tissues on the ground, and soon wads of bloody tissues join the cigarette butts and empty beer cans that litter the sidewalk and gutter.

An older punk decides to take charge. He yells out, asking for the location of the nearest hospital. A neighbor rushes up with directions and a group of punks spirit their injured brother off to get stitches. Zhu Ning sprints down the stairs and starts sweeping up the glass in case the police pass by. No one will report the incident. The window will be quietly repaired. Wu Wei looks on with approval. The young people's collective response to this crisis seems both remarkably efficient and oddly touching. This is community at its finest.

The crisis has passed, and a sense of calm infuses the scene. I walk up to a group of kids in skateboarding gear who are sitting on small chairs in a circle near the bloody tissues. They're involved in a youthful, enthusiastic, blow-by-blow recap of the events of five minutes ago: "The glass fell down!" "The guy poked his head out the window!" One of them lights a joint and offers it to me, but I decline.

"Is that the black stuff or the green stuff?" I ask, using the Chinese terms for hash and marijuana.

"It's the yellow stuff," says the ringleader, and he shows me a small cellophane-wrapped packet. Another of the kids flashes a toothy smile. "Oh man, I am so messed up," he says, and lets his head loll back, a tired smile on his face.

These Wuhan punks may be hip compared to the average Chinese teenager, but they're smoking incense, and they don't know it. For a second, I consider telling them, but instead, I say "Yeah, that's the good stuff." They smile and exchange tired high-fives.

□ □ □

THE NEXT DAY, I show up at the Vox Bar in the early evening to meet Zhu Ning. He's late, out eating dinner, and I'm sitting at a table going over my notes about the show the night before, drinking a beer, and watching a couple kids play pool.

Zhu rushes in, apologizes for being late, and sits down at my table. He sighs and, though he rarely drinks, takes a sip of Wuhan Snow beer. While Wu Wei makes a statement through his powerful lyrics, Zhu is undeniably the linchpin of the Wuhan punk scene. He's a small, compact man with a buzzcut, a ready smile on his face, and boundless reserves of enthusiasm.

In the late nineties, after Zhu returned to Wuhan while the rest of SMZB stayed in Beijing, he started the first Vox Bar in an abandoned church (there are a fair number of still-standing Christian churches scattered around China) and it soon became the stuff of legend among mainland rockers, housing national acts like Brain Failure and Hang on the Box as well as local Wuhan bands.

Around the same time, he started a new, more experimental band of his own. Eventually, though, the Culture Bureau found out about the Vox Bar and shut the place down, citing an arcane law that no bars could be within 800 meters of a school. Zhu didn't bother to point out that there are many bars right outside the gates of Wuhan University; in China, the government makes the rules. If they want to shut you down, they shut you down, and there's nothing you can do about it . . . unless you happen to have a high-level connection in the government or military.

With the assistance of a couple of American ESL teachers, Zhu opened the new Vox Bar in 2005. "The place was terrible," he recalls, "just another lousy Chinese bar." The concept of a "dive bar" doesn't exist in China, with the exception of Vox and a few little places in the Beijing university district. Though there are certainly hip, casually fancy Western nightspots in many cities, the typical Chinese bar consists of a series of private rooms where groups of friends can congregate to play dice, get shitfaced, and carouse with girlfriends or prostitutes. This blatant hedonism is condemned by younger, hip Chinese. "I tore out the private rooms," says Zhu, "and built the place with my own two hands."

"The most important thing in life," says Zhu, "is to do what you want to do. Sure, this is a business, and I have to break even. But what I want is an opportunity to play music, and a place for bands to come play their music. Bands can't get a following without performing; in Wuhan, this is the only good place to perform. So of course I have to help them. It's tiring, working every day, but it's what I want to do, so I'm happy."

In the past year and a half, Zhu has brought more than one hundred bands to Wuhan: Beijing punk superstars Brain Failure, garage-rock icons SUBS, Chengdu psych band Proximity Butterfly, and a number of European punk and hardcore bands. Revered Swedish punks The (International) Noise Conspiracy were scheduled to play a few months back, but the Chinese government found out about their officially unapproved tour. In China, all foreign musical acts (films, books, etc.) must be approved by the censors before they are allowed to perform. Most smaller performers fly under the Ministry's radar, but The (International) Noise Conspiracy got discovered by the censors and sent back to Stockholm.

On the side, Zhu teaches drums to kids with rock–and-roll aspirations. He says that he's not a good teacher, but this is just his humble nature. Everyone else I spoke with in Wuhan agrees that Zhu is a terrific drummer.

"Music is all I want to do," says Zhu. "And I am doing it. I am going to start a new band soon." China's economic boom has given the culture a serious injection of materialism and consumerism. By providing Wuhan's punks and rockers with a home base, with a variety of musical performances, with musical equipment, and with well-thought-out advice,

Zhu effectively counters this spiritual pollution with his own blend of compassion and his mantra: above all, be true to oneself.

□ □ □

DURING THE LATE 1990s and early 2000s, the Western media published many articles about the Beijing punk scene. Western freelancers living in Beijing profiled an array of punk groups; the German filmmakers Susanne Mesmer and George Lindt made a film entitled "Beijing Bubbles" that chronicled the life and hard times of six Beijing bands.

Though many of these bands have performed in Vox, the scene in Wuhan is much more supportive than the scene in Beijing. In Beijing, bands have to clamor to get attention and to get gigs in order to achieve recognition and, hopefully, secure a recording contract or sponsorship; this commercial drive is reflected in these bands' accessible music and inoffensive lyrical content. In Beijing, the punks have blue hair and massive, spiky Mohawks, but rarely do they dare to take on the giant beast lurking in the corner: the CCP and its corrupt, backward policies.

A scene like the one that Zhu Ning has created, with the emphasis placed squarely on music and personal expression rather than posturing and commercial success, has understandably fostered a wider range of lyrical expression. SMZB's lyrics, though they are often made up of broken English, are remarkably astute and terrifically biting. On their new record, they take on such themes as: the Tiananmen Square massacre, the need for unity in the face of an oppressive government, the Chinese government's spending money on a space program instead of feeding their starving people, the Chinese government's reluctance to inform the public about current events, and the social problems caused by the development of a consumer society. Few other bands are saying this stuff on the mainland; aside from SMZB, almost no one will discuss these issues in a public forum. People are either scared of the government, brainwashed by nationalism, or too busy enjoying their relative freedom to stand up for their principles.

◻ ◻ ◻

IN SHANGHAI, A FEW weeks later, I catch up with Wu Wei again. The band's gone on a very short tour—two stops, the other in Nanjing—to support "Scream for Life." Wu Wei's tired, and a bit nervous. He stands beside the ticket booth, resplendent in a black leather jacket and tight plaid pants, chain-smoking and tapping his foot on the concrete at 140 beats per minute. The crowd in Wuhan eats up his antics, and all his friends are there, but Shanghai's a different story altogether.

"Do you like Shanghai?" I ask him.

He shakes his head and smiles nervously. Shanghai crowds are notoriously standoffish and removed: It is a bourgeois town. The kids are more likely to be listening to the latest house DJs from Japan or Ibiza on their genuine iPods than listening to copied CDs of obscure punk bands on generic-brand stereos.

It's 10 PM and just about time for SMZB to play. I wish Wu Wei well, we shake hands, and I walk into the venue, clutching a cold Tsingtao. It's a dilapidated warehouse on the edge of town, half-full of bored-looking kids who are wearing a more expensive version of the punk outfits favored in Wuhan.

Tonight, SMZB hits the stage and they kick into their first number, "Friend for Life." The crowd remains motionless. After thirty seconds of thunderous guitar chords, the band stops abruptly; there's a problem with the drum microphones. Wu Wei apologizes, and the grumbling soundman climbs onto the stage.

In order to get to this gig, Wu Wei and his bandmates have taken the long overnight train from Wuhan. Eighteen hours on a hard platform the size of a massage table, his guitar next to him. He's been playing in a popular punk band for thirteen years, and this is as far as he has gotten: hours in an uncomfortable train compartment choked with the pungent odors of sweat and smoke.

The soundman finishes swapping out the microphones. Wu Wei steps up to the microphone and screams "SMZB!" By the first chorus, he's won the small crowd over. The cooler scene in Shanghai cannot compare to the frenzied mosh pit in Wuhan, but at least he's getting the standoffish Shanghai crowd to jump up and down. After the show, Wu Wei will be getting back on the train home, another eighteen hours in cramped quarters. But when you're in the front row, looking up at his face as he's up there on stage, screaming for his life, you know that this is what he was born to do.

15

The Journalist

ZHOU XINGPING CAN'T remember how many times he's been detained by the police. Seven, or eight, or something like that.

But he has enjoyed good fortune. Each time they have gotten to him, he has been with a foreigner, so the detention is more funny than anything else. The police just hold him for a few hours, deliver a stern lecture accompanied by a warning to "never do this again," and then let him go.

Yes, he's been one of the lucky ones; some of his colleagues have not enjoyed his good fortune. They've disappeared from their offices, from shopping malls, from villages and from fancy restaurants. When they fail to come home at night, their loved ones phone the authorities in an attempt to find out their whereabouts, but are met with stony bureaucratic evasion.

In the end, some get off relatively easy: they return days, weeks, or months later, skinny, bearded, and hollow. The less fortunate ones don't come back at all: they languish in jail, detained on charges of "fraud," of "treason," of "spreading classified information," of "divulging state secrets."

"You want to do something good," laments Zhou, "but you feel like a criminal." And, indeed, Zhou has lived the life of a criminal: constantly evading the authorities, finding safe places to hide out for a while, using pay phones and constantly switching SIM cards to avoid phone taps.

But he's not a conventional criminal. His weapons are not guns and knives—his weapons are words, and his only crime is exposing, through these words, some unsavory business the Chinese government doesn't want anyone to know about. Zhou Xingping is a journalist.

□ □ □

I MET ZHOU for the first time several years ago in Yunnan Province, although I don't remember much about our first brief encounter. We were introduced one night by a common friend, at a bar, over beers, and it was late; there was a big crowd assembled, and we had all drunk a little bit too much.

That same friend suggested I interview Zhou for this book, and I racked my brain trying to recall what we had talked about that first night we met. I remembered a friend saying that Zhou was on the run from someone for doing something. It wasn't an unusual situation, though; down in Yunnan, it seemed like half the people I met were on the run, or pretending to be. The more I tried to recall what Zhou looked like, the more shadowy and indistinct my mental picture became.

I called Zhou on his cell phone, and he told me that he was out of town, but would be back in a few days. The next time I called, he apologized and said that he had returned to Beijing but left again and to try calling him next week. I did as he requested; on the phone, he told me that he was very busy—I had already figured that one out—but he would be glad to spend some time with me.

We agreed to meet in a coffee shop in Jianwai SOHO, a monolith of the New Beijing. China's capital, in the days leading up to the 2008 Olympics, was an incongruous blend of the traditional and the modern, like a mash-up of ancient Chinese music and a booming techno beat, or perhaps a throbbing industrial pulse: the whole place was under construction. Twenty-four hours a day, migrant workers from the countryside were building more and more gigantic skyscrapers in a relentless drive towards modernity.

SOHO, one of China's leading real estate developers, has, in the past ten years, been creating the most cutting-edge building compounds in China. Jianwai SOHO, its newest project, was designed by the Japanese architect Riken Yamamoto.

Ten enormous white steel-and-glass buildings are arranged around a courtyard with patches of perfectly manicured grass bisected by concrete walkways. It looks like some strange late-eighties ideal of a sanitized, healthy future; while most of Beijing gives new meaning to the words grubby and grimy, Jianwai SOHO is eerily spotless. Stooped old women in blue uniform jackets endlessly walk around with little brushes and metal shovels, bending down to collect each discarded soda can and cigarette butt.

It was early evening when I went to rendezvous with Zhou. In the middle of the Jianwai SOHO complex, I arrived early to eat at a restaurant I had heard served excellent specialties from Guizhou Province. I began strolling around, checking out the buildings and looking for the restaurant. I had underestimated the size of the complex, and I quickly became lost, wandering aimlessly through a maze made up of gigantic office blocks.

In China, there are a lot of people around, all the time. Deep in the countryside, each little patch of land is attended to by somebody. Except for the truly uninhabitable areas, there's no real vacant space, nowhere that's free of a human presence.

The population-dense cities are, of course, even more crammed with people than the countryside. Rush hour in Beijing makes Manhattan look like Appalachia as commuters on trains, busses, bicycles and foot squeeze past one another, going every which way. Even in the middle of the night, the streets are comparatively crowded with revelers, migrant workers, and senior citizens taking evening constitutionals.

But as I wandered around Jianwai SOHO, looking for the Guizhou restaurant, I began to feel uneasy, spooked: there were almost no other people around. Sure, there were a few others strolling along the concrete pathways that bisected neatly manicured lawns, but the complex was largely empty, especially compared to bustling Jianguomen Avenue, the street I had been walking on just minutes before. It was beginning to get dark. The grounds nearly sparkled, almost impossibly free of litter. For a moment, I felt like I'd stepped through a wormhole into an alternate reality: a very un-China-like China.

□ □ □

INSIDE, THE RESTAURANT was *renao:* hot, crowded, and noisy, just like China should be. Everything seemed normal again. As I finished up my hot and sour fish stew, Zhou called my cell phone; he came into the restaurant to meet me. I paid the check and we walked to an adjacent coffee shop.

□ □ □

ZHOU IS A NEAT, compact man in a slightly quirky version of the typical freelancer's uniform: pink Dunlop golf shirt, blue jeans, dirty white sneakers. He is thirty-seven, but it's hard to tell that by looking at him; the cumulative effect of his flattop haircut and his bright, intelligent eyes combine to create a veneer of agelessness: he could be either an old twenty-five or a young forty.

He chain-smokes low-tar Zhongnanhai cigarettes nervously, and fiddles with each cigarette butt in the ashtray once he has put it out. He's perpetually jittery, on edge, wired, with a quiet intensity. Every few minutes, his cell phone goes off, and he often glances around nervously, as if thinking about something else.

The café is comfortable. We choose a table at the back and sit on pillowed benches, facing each other. Zhou orders a pot of green tea—he apologizes with a little smile, saying that coffee's too strong for his stomach. He pours the tea, and as the steam curls up from our glasses, we look out the window at the austere SOHO complex, drinking in the sense of affluence, the space of emptiness, and the sheer *newness* of it all.

"Three hours away from here," says Zhou Xingping, dragging on his cigarette, lines forming around the corners of his eyes, nodding his head slightly, as if to point towards the countryside between Beijing and Tianjin, "there are people that don't have any food."

□ □ □

IT WAS IN an equally impoverished part of China, a few hundred miles east, and nearly a decade ago, when the fledgling journalist Zhou Xingping caught his first big scoop. The story wasn't his alone—there were several other diligent Chinese reporters researching the issue. But it was the defining moment of his career. Zhou shares the responsibility for breaking one of the most important China-related stories in recent history.

Here's how it went down. In the early nineties, a group of well-connected businessmen in Central China's Henan Province secured the government contract to supply blood to the province's hospitals.

In the dirt-poor villages of Henan, these businessmen, in cahoots with provincial officials, set up blood collection centers where they could buy the peasants' blood for a fraction of what they would pay from urban dwellers.

On village walls throughout the countryside, authorities painted a slogan in enormous red characters: "Selling your blood is glorious." Some peasants seized on this opportunity to supplement their meager income, and made repeated trips to the collection centers.

In some of the centers, the people doing the collecting used centrifuges to extract the valuable plasma from the blood.

Then, they reinjected the donors with red blood cells from the communal, plasma-free blood. Since the donors were only losing plasma and not red blood cells, they could give blood more often. While this system of collection and cultivation no doubt maximized profits for everyone, it was also the perfect environment for the spread of disease.

In order to save money in other centers, the collectors decided to reuse the needles; in addition, donors were not screened for hepatitis B, hepatitis C or HIV.

After a couple years, a lot of people in the villages of Henan began to get sick. The largely uneducated peasants didn't know what was wrong with them; they referred to the mysterious disease that was ravaging their community as "fever," or "the strange sickness."

Soon enough, local doctors expressed alarm at the number of deathly ill patients that were coming into their offices for examination. At first, the doctors couldn't identify the disease; eventually, some of them figured out that a huge fraction of their patients were infected with HIV.

When they reported their findings to the provincial government, the doctors were told to keep quiet. Anyone who defied this edict was harassed and threatened. The provincial government, of course, knew that if the story was made public that bad things would happen; instead of trying to solve the problem, they decided to cover it up.

A female doctor who was then in her sixties, Gao Yaojie, figured out what had happened, and she refused to heed the gag order. Using her own money, she printed up hundreds of thousands of leaflets and pamphlets which volunteers distributed throughout Henan, informing the populace about AIDS;

what it was, how it was transmitted, and where they could go for help.

Despite the government's attempts at information control, they couldn't stop the rumor mill of rural China: people called their relatives to warn them of the strange new disease, and rumors of entire villages afflicted with this illness began to circulate throughout the country.

◻ ◻ ◻

ZHOU HEARD THE RUMORS and chased them from Beijing to Henan, where he met Gao Yaojie and found out first-hand the gory details. There were several villages where the HIV infection rate was over fifty percent. People were sick, people were dying, and there wasn't any medicine to help them because the government wouldn't admit that there was a problem.

"It was a risky time," he remembers. "[In Henan], if the police thought you were a journalist, they would try to detain and arrest you."

Eventually, Zhou published a few articles about the tragedy and the implied cover-up. Through his web of contacts, he managed to tip off the international media to the scandal. The fallout was incredible. By this time, the central government in Beijing was no doubt aware of the crisis. However, the government continued to deny that there was an AIDS epidemic in Henan, while the world reacted with outrage and demanded that the Party address the issue.

Foreign journalists flocked to Henan to cover the story, and Zhou acted as a fixer and on-the-ground correspondent; later, he became a de facto AIDS activist, traveling to Europe with Gao Yaojie to speak about the growing problem of AIDS in China.

"It took *two years*," he remembers, "for them [the government] to admit there was a problem."

Zhou refills his cup of tea leaves with steaming hot water. "They thought: there is no AIDS in socialism!"

He cracks an uncomfortable smile that, for just a moment, turns into a leer before he sticks another cigarette into his mouth.

□   □   □

ZHOU DEVOTED SEVERAL YEARS of his life to the story of the Henan AIDS scandal. Now, looking back, he feels he accomplished nothing. To illustrate his point, Zhou tells me a story that took place a year before our conversation, in the summer of 2005, when he was invited to a gala at Beijing University "celebrating" International AIDS Day.

First, he recounts, there was an introduction to International AIDS Day by a Beijing University professor.

Then, a little girl read a poem about AIDS. "She's never even seen anyone with AIDS!" scoffs Zhou.

Another professor presented a book about AIDS featuring a number of Tang Dynasty poems.

Finally, they showed a series of pictures of people in Africa.

"What do they think—read these poems, then you won't get AIDS? These people have never even been [to the AIDS villages in Henan Province]."

Exasperated, Zhou shakes his head, mutters in frustration, and takes a slurp of his tea.

□ □ □

THREE DAYS BEFORE our meeting, the Chinese government enacted a new statute prohibiting media outlets from reporting on "sudden incidents" without prior approval from the Communist Party's Ministry of Information. The law's phrasing is purposely oblique: basically any current event that would qualify as news could be called "sudden."

Therefore, reporting the news without express permission is, effectively, a crime.

"Do you know this Chinese expression," Zhou asks me, arching his eyebrows, "*yumin zhengce?*" (It means "to keep the masses ignorant.") "In the past, the emperors, now, the government, they encourage people to be stupid . . . modern people, they should not do things like this."

I ask Zhou what articles he's working on these days, and he gives a surprising answer: "I'm still a freelance journalist, but I stopped writing in 2003."

I ask him what he means. "I'm doing other kind[s] of journalism work," he says—instead of writing himself, he's acting as a fixer, helping Western journalists get the stories they need.

When I ask him why he stopped writing himself, a tired, distant look creeps over his face. "I was writing for a long time. 1999 to 2001, that's all I did . . . then I slowed down, then I stopped . . . I got too frustrated."

"The media in China," notes Zhou, "is all controlled by

the government. Every newspaper and magazine is owned by the government. Some (media outlets) like *Nanfangdushibao* (Southern Weekend) and *Caijing* Magazine, they are saying some different things, they are trying, you know? But they are still owned by the government, so there is no solution."

"It's been like this for fifty years," says Zhou, "newspapers are just a piece of paper for the government to talk about how good they are. This is a habit. Imagine if one day they picked up the newspaper and it was criticizing them. This would be impossible, you know?"

"There was no future for me," he remarks, matter-of-factly and somewhat bitterly, "so I stopped."

□   □   □

IT IS OFTEN and duly noted by pundits around the world that China's economic growth has not led to corresponding social reforms. It's generally assumed by a large number of liberal Westerners that an economically flourishing society will automatically give rise to an open and flourishing free marketplace for the exchange of ideas.

China's not a completely totalitarian state like North Korea, Burma, or Turkmenistan, where citizens exist in a total media lockdown, where the only reading material available is a poorly produced broadsheet printed in some dusty government office trumpeting the achievements of the country's leaders and the glory of its people. In these countries, the only thing to watch on television is a single station replaying black-and-white movies and the weather forecast from two months ago.

In fact, contrary to Zhou's observations that the media is entirely government-owned, China's media sector is semi-privatized and flourishing. There are more than 2,000 newspapers throughout the country, publishing a shocking 100 million copies daily. There are at least 8,000 magazines: news magazines, sports magazines, magazines for history buffs, magazines for pet lovers. There are more than 700 television stations. On the newsstands, you can buy Chinese editions of *National Geographic, Cosmopolitan, GQ,* and scads of other Western titles.

However, just because there's competition in the media sector and a healthy number of periodicals available for purchase doesn't mean that citizens can enjoy access to even remotely unbiased reportage; that is, journalism that doesn't toe the party line.

Here's why. In China, any printed publication—newspapers, magazines, and so on—must have a six-digit *kanhao,* or publication number. The first two digits indicate the province in which the periodical is printed, and the second four digits are a registration number that can only be obtained with governmental approval.

Consequently, these publication numbers are tremendously difficult to obtain, especially for anyone who might want to publish anything "edgy": i.e., critical of the government.

Chinese citizens are free to read about beauty products, about nature, about the NBA and world soccer leagues. Thanks to a few of the more daring newspaper editors, they can now occasionally enjoy a very mildly critical editorial dialogue that touches on social problems and policy concerns.

Ten years ago, even this would have been unthinkable.

Optimists point to these minor changes as signs of progress; realists like Zhou Xingping think these minor concessions are meaningless because any kind of news or editorial reporting that questions the legitimacy of the government and its leaders is strictly forbidden.

□   □   □

THOSE WHO COMPLAIN about media bias in the West should pick up an English-language copy of a *China Daily* sometime; all the headlines discuss the good works of the Communist Party and the effectiveness of their economic policies.

It's gotten to the point that intelligent people who dare to question the official line on certain issues—keep in mind, those who dare question amount to only a small percentage of the Chinese population—can actually obtain real news by understanding that the *opposite* of the stated facts is actually the truth.

For example, if an article proclaimed "Police in Gansu Province to crack down on human smuggling" the wily observer would understand that human smuggling in Gansu had reached epidemic proportions.

To illustrate just how amazing this reverse-truth phenomenon is, I'll offer a quick examination of the top headlines released by Xinhua, the Chinese government's news agency, for July 9, 2006.

▶ "State Council vows rural laborers to be paid on time" (Real meaning: rural laborers are not getting paid on time)

- ▶ "Year of Russia injects new vigor into Sino-Russian ties" (Real Meaning: we need your oil, and your support in the U.N.)
- ▶ "Party watchdogs call for well [sic] implementation of central policies" (Real Meaning: provincial leaders are breaking the rules frequently and flagrantly).

▢ ▢ ▢

THE PENALTIES FOR VIOLATING media taboos are intimidating. According to Reporters Without Borders, a journalist watchdog organization, China had thirty-one journalists in jail as of January 1, 2007—more than any country in the world.

In 2006 alone, Zhao Yan, a researcher for the *New York Times*, was convicted of "fraud" after the *Times* published an article correctly reporting the impending retirement of President Jiang Zemin. Ching Cheong, a Hong Kong resident and reporter for the Singapore-based *Straits Times*, got slapped with charges of "espionage" while researching former Communist Party leader Zhao Ziyang. In March 2007, Zhang Jianhong, an online journalist who published an exposé about the Chinese government's procurement of organs from living prisoners, was sentenced to six years in jail for "inciting subversion of state's authority."

▢ ▢ ▢

IF A CHINESE JOURNALIST writes and reports a groundbreaking but sensitive article, his editor and the bosses of the media company will most likely refuse to print it. On the slim chance it gets published, if the piece catches the eye of the government censors, the journalist will be fired at best and imprisoned at worst. What's a journalist to do when it is difficult or impossible for him to write about the facts he's uncovered?

For a large portion of contemporary Chinese journalists, the answer is to sit in their apartments all day, copying their stories verbatim from the Internet, only venturing outside to accept bribes from corporations in exchange for favorable coverage of their products or to accept payoffs in exchange for burying critical stories. According to Zhou, all these shady practices are so widespread that they've come to be accepted as standard journalistic methodology.

Other journalists dig for sensational, tabloid-style dirt, the more lurid, the better. Indeed, this kind of "journalism" thrives nearly unchecked in every culture. In China, though, facts are relative.

Zhou tells me that once he and a colleague went to the North Korean border to do a story about women who sneak over into China in order to find a husband and assimilate into society. These women are so desperate to get out of North Korea that they'll marry absolutely anyone. Zhou and his colleague met one such couple—an old, disabled man and a young, attractive North Korean woman—and spent time at their house, drinking and talking. They returned to Beijing, where the colleague was to write the article.

"Then the story came out," recalls Zhou, "and it was all lies!" Instead of writing a factual, thoughtful story, his colleague had spun their visit into a twisted tabloid story of sexual abuse and forced imprisonment.

□ □ □

ZHOU XINGPING IS a true journalist, in the classic muckraking sense. He loves writing, loves reporting, loves spinning a story into a work of art. He loves being out on the front lines and digging for information. But he's getting older, and it's too dangerous, and there's no money in it, and he can't even publish anything worthwhile anyway. So he's stopped writing.

"So if you're not working as a journalist for Chinese publications anymore," I ask Zhou, "what are you doing?"

His eyes gleam as he exclaims: "China's a crazy country, and Beijing's a crazy city . . . and so I have to be crazy too."

Zhou's idea of "crazy"? Going freelance and making money from the people who have the most money to spend: the Western corporate media.

Using the vast store of connections he accumulated during and after the Henan AIDS scandal days, Zhou spends his days as a freelance fixer, researcher, and correspondent, mostly for the BBC and sometimes for *Time* and *National Geographic*, finding sources and getting stories. While we were talking in the coffee shop, he got a call on his cell phone, and explained that he was attempting to procure train tickets to Tibet for staff from the *New York Times.*

Western journalists value him for his on-the-ground experience and for his skill as a fixer: making Chinese people, farmers and peasants, feel comfortable enough to share their stories.

Working freelance for the BBC pays a hell of a lot better than selling articles to Chinese newspapers. The property market in Beijing is caught in the throes of a spectacular pre-Olympics boom, and Zhou's used his earnings to mortgage two apartments here, with an eye towards selling them in a few years for a hefty profit, to ensure that he'll have enough money to get by and support his parents in their old age. The evaporation of the state pension system—the "iron rice bowl"—has affected both subsistence farmers and white-collar workers. In today's China, it's every man for himself; Zhou knows he can't do this kind of running around for his entire life, so he's trying to make as much money in as little time as possible.

□   □   □

IN 2005, THE BBC came to China to film an ambitious four-part documentary series, "China from the Inside." Zhou finagled a spot on the staff in the way that most people get jobs in China's relationship-based culture: through a personal friend, an old colleague that lives in London.

The director of the series was famed filmmaker Jonathan Lewis, who has helmed more than eighty documentaries, earning himself a clutch of awards along the way. The Chinese government agreed to allow Lewis and his crew face-to-face meetings with Chinese officials and unprecedented access to previously restricted areas.

I ask Zhou why the government agreed to this.

Zhou smiles. "He [Lewis] made a miniseries about the rape of Nanjing and how badly the Japanese treated the Chinese."

When Zhou first met Jonathan Lewis, they talked for two hours, and didn't like each other much. Zhou found the filmmaker arrogant and his expectations unrealistic, a typical case of the foreigner coming to China and trying to do things in the Western way, not realizing that the cultural differences would prevent him from achieving a successful result.

"He didn't like me," Zhou says, "so I didn't get the job at first. He said I had too much sympathy for the poor people."

"Isn't that a noble thing, having sympathy for poor people?" I asked.

"You would think so," Zhou replied.

Later, in the usual fashion, the agreement between the BBC and the CCP broke down, and Lewis had to re-think his plan for filming the documentary. He needed Zhou's experience and insight, and agreed to bring Zhou on board for a trip to Tibet, but paid him only a meager salary.

"We [the BBC crew] had to pay 150,000 yuan ($19,000) just to get into Tibet and film," Zhou recalls, "and they were paying me nothing, they were paying me to sit around and smoke. But then when they got there, no one did anything! I had to do everything! When I got home, I said, listen, either you pay me many times what I'm getting paid now or I can't work for you anymore. If you pay, I will work."

Lewis agreed. Zhou became one of the researchers on the project, traveling with the BBC crew all over China to help bring a more nuanced, unbiased view of his country to the international community.

In the meantime, he made more than enough money to cover his mortgage payments for a while.

□　□　□

DESPITE HIS NEWFOUND relative financial security, Zhou radiates a weary loneliness. He converses like a manic depressive: each of his interesting stories, which he tells excitedly and passionately, is followed by a little crash where he becomes momentarily sad and silent. He's a kind and compassionate person who talks angrily about the government one moment and, the next, muses wistfully about how he enjoys helping people and how all he wants is a little bit of peace and quiet. He's proud of his work with the BBC—it's prestigious and provides a comfortable standard of living—but it's easy to intuit that he's desperate to somehow do *more*, to get to some essential truth, to help purge his world of the blackness of corruption and illegitimacy.

We meet twice more over the course of the summer for tea and conversation. Each time, Zhou's got something new to tell me about. Like any good journalist, he's a fabulous storyteller. When he's sounding off about cancer clusters from chemicals in the Huai River, about a village leader who poured acid on the face of his wife when she asked for a divorce, about a mysterious waterborne disease in the Dongting Lake in Hunan Province that has left hundreds of peasants sick and bloated, dying slow deaths, I can almost taste his sublimated nervous energy. Now, when I think of Zhou, the image comes to mind of a newsroom, completely empty save for an old-school news ticker, spitting out tape after tape of headline onto the floor for no one to read.

16

A Night Out in Beijing

"It's never too late for the next line. This is important to understand when you try to keep up with people still going very strong at seven in the morning. people are extremely fond of ketamine here, reflecting in the plates full of it on half the tables, but there's always room for anything else, and don't be surprised if you see someone smoking ice in a booth over there. lines can be snorted anywhere, and they are, people don't even bother going to the bathroom. and all the booze, oh my god, blue label or hennessy xo, all the same. you get out of there and move on to an after, at someones home, dj's and all, to continue the evening into the day, this time preferably one crushed on the table and solidarically shared by all. the new evening comes, let's go have a few drinks before we go out again . . . oh my god what crap is flowing out of me . . ."

–E-mail from my friend Ralf, August 2007

□   □   □

ON MY FIRST NIGHT back in China to do research for this book, an American colleague who I'll call Lao Wei and I took a cab over to Tango, a four-story dance club located across from the Lama Temple on the north end of central Beijing.

In 2000, Lao Wei and I were classmates here in an exchange program at Qinghua University, north of the city. We became fast friends, and spent almost the whole summer hanging around together, getting into trouble when we weren't busy memorizing hundreds of Chinese characters and polishing our tones.

We've been back to Beijing since, but never at the same time, and we're both amazed at how much it has changed in seven short years. The Olympic Games are a little more than two years away, and the Chinese government has been on a construction rampage. Whole sections of town have been razed and are being rebuilt from the ground up. Some parts of the city are almost unrecognizable. Thousands of buildings and houses have been demolished, displacing (by some estimates) over a million Beijing residents.

□   □   □

CONSTRUCTION ON THE Lama Temple was started in the late seventeenth century, and it was originally the residence for the imperial court's eunuchs. It then became the court of the emperor's son, Prince Yong, who himself became the Yongzheng Emperor. His successor, the emperor Qianglong, made the temple into a place for high-level Tibetan and Mongol lamas to reside and worship.

Across the street from the Lama Temple, the enormous building that houses Tango was built in the early 2000s by a crew of migrant workers from the countryside as a place for Beijing's well-heeled to party. The place is a monolith: the whole complex is almost one hundred thousand square feet. The basement features almost a hundred private karaoke rooms and a self-serve buffet-style restaurant, while the top three floors are taken up by gigantic dance clubs. While Tango won't be winning any international prizes for nightclub design, the place has swanky enough décor to make its patrons feel cool: stone floors, velvet curtains, wooden tables with designer lamps casting out light dark enough to make everyone look good.

□ □ □

LAO WEI AND I are here to meet another friend of ours, Ralf, a tall, blond Norwegian. We have known Ralf for years; he's an affable, purposeful kid, now in his mid-twenties. He bummed around Yunnan, in Western China, for a couple of years, living off money he'd saved back home, reading books in the daytime and causing trouble at night. Eventually, he met and married a beautiful girl from Beijing and set up shop in a flat owned by her parents on the outskirts of the city.

When we called him a few hours ago, Ralf was still at home, but he promised us that the party tonight was slamming, that the DJs were top quality, that he couldn't wait to see us, and that he'd be coming to Tango very soon.

Using a series of escalators, Lao Wei and I ascend to Tango's top floor, where we're supposed to meet Ralf. It's around 11 PM and the place is packed with scenesters: nouveau Chinese yuppies in designer jeans and expensive eyeglasses, teenagers dressed in baggy clothing and gold chains, sweaty Western expatriates in their twenties, impossibly young-looking Chinese girls with dyed hair and facial piercings.

On a stage in the front of this cavernous room, a Chinese DJ spins deep house, a slow, simple, and very popular style of ultra-repetitive electronic music. Tango boasts a top-flight sound system, on par with the best in the world. With a setup this expensive, you can feel the beat resonate through your body like little, rhythmic earthquakes.

Hundreds of sweaty kids are moving in unison to the beat; in the darkness, from fifty feet away, they look like a single, giant organism, pulsing in sync to an invisible heart. Most of them are Chinese, of course, but there are foreigners as well, Europeans, Americans, Russian girls with long legs and short skirts, a few renegade Nigerians.

Lao Wei and I sit down on one of the plush velvet couches that line the sides of the room and sip our Carlsberg beer, which cost us forty yuan, or $5. In upmarket places like this, they don't serve Chinese beer and liquor, only well-known Western brands. We scan the dance floor, looking for Ralf, although it's more of a time-killing activity than anything: a six-foot-five Norwegian isn't too hard to spot in a crowd full of Chinese. He's nowhere to be seen, so we buy a couple more overpriced beers and try to talk over the deafening music.

◻ ◻ ◻

SIX YEARS AGO, Lao Wei and I spent our weekends at Beijing's megaclubs: giant pleasure palaces with names like Orange, Banana, and Babyface, invariably packed full of hip, moneyed Chinese urbanites, nightlife-loving expatriates, and trendy exchange students.

Back then, if you kept your eyes open, you might have noticed that some of the party goers seemed more than a little off-kilter, but not the sloppy, slurring intoxication that comes from drinking alcohol to excess. Rumors of late-night, drug-fueled parties swirled around, but no one had ever actually been to one. At the clubs, pupils were dilated, jaws were grinding, some people always had a bottle of water in hand, and no one got tired from dancing long into the night. The shadowy presence of club drugs was there, but it was subtle: unless you knew what you were looking for, you wouldn't see anything at all.

Six years later, nothing has changed. There's a Chinese girl in the corner with a blissed-out grin on her face, rubbing her hands up and down her torso.

A large percentage of the clubgoers are sipping from bottles of mineral water instead of beer or cocktails. The water costs almost as much: thirty yuan, or almost $4, twice the daily income of the waiters at a Beijing restaurant.

When I go to the bathroom, a French man with a shit-eating grin, pissing wildly into the urinal, turns to me and asks, "What are you on? Only alcohol? I'm on Ecstasy! It's so good and cheap in Beijing!"

□ □ □

TWO HOURS LATER, there's still no sign of Ralf. Lao Wei and I are feeling buzzed; we're drinking pricey Jägermeister shots along with our Carlsberg and talking about old times.

The crowd in Tango has gotten even bigger, even crazier, and even druggier. The music's gotten louder, too, and our conversation has evolved into a series of basic shouts and exaggerated gestures.

"Where the fuck is Ralf?" I scream over the music.

Lao Wei shrugs, and we head through the crowd towards the bar, dodging a pair of hammered, fresh-faced American college kids with skinny ties and shaggy hair. They look like they just stepped out of an NYU dorm. A new DJ appears on the stage, and the music changes to a more hard-edged, tribal brand of electronica.

□ □ □

THE FIRST WESTERN-STYLE bars in Beijing were housed in international hotels. In the early nineties, when well-connected Chinese entrepreneurs realized the potential of the city's growing, thirsty expatriate population, a throng of individually-owned bars began to pop up, mostly on a street called Sanlitun near the Worker's Stadium in the city's Chaoyang embassy district.

The original Sanlitun joints were initially very popular. But they were not fashionable. They were not cool; they were just the only places outside of hotels where you could get a cocktail.

And then, towards the end of the decade, China's economy entered the first stages of its dizzying boom, and everything changed. Young Chinese who had been abroad to study in the West returned to their homeland, and the foreign population started to swell as multinational corporations rushed to open branch offices in Beijing.

The conditions were right for a nightlife explosion. Beijing's first international-style disco, Banana, opened on the ground floor of the Traders Hotel. Soon, bars and discos were opening everywhere in town. Some of these joints were Irish and British and Aussie-style pubs, with draft Guinness and overpriced, greasy bar food that catered to foreigners. Others were karaoke-and-salty-snack places that appealed to Chinese. Still other bar owners tried to cater to a mixed crowd by blending Western and Chinese ideas. Divey places with cheap drinks for exchange students opened in the university district, by Wudaokou in the north of Beijing.

Henry Li, a Shanghai native, returned from studying in Australia and opened up Public Space, a Western-style café and lounge, on the Sanlitun strip.

Of all the bars in Beijing, Public Space was the first one that had "it": the stylish, minimal coolness favored by jet-setters and the international hipoisie. Competitors rushed to open imitation joints, but Henry Li himself was always behind the best spots: he would open the uber-hip Club Vogue and the stylish Neo Lounge not long after.

Vogue was Beijing's first true international nightclub, attracting the best-looking and most in-the-know people in town, as well as setting the bar in providing international-standard, competent and professional service in a nightclub setting. Later, the Neo Lounge, a beautiful club decked out entirely in velvet and mirrors, was used as the set for the night-club scene in Quentin Tarantino's 2002 movie *Kill Bill.*

□　□　□

IN CHINA, EVERYONE always seems to be late to meet you. Ralf, who adapted to this tradition well, also developed quite a fond-ness for chain-smoking joints laced with hashish, and he wasn't even punctual before starting this habit.

But it's getting really late. I'm starting to feel like Vladimir to Lao Wei's Estragon. I picture Ralf, sitting on his couch watching old episodes of *Dr. Who*, checking his watch, and rationalizing, "Oh, I'll just leave in five more minutes . . ."

Lao Wei and I leave the dance floor and adjourn to a lounge-like anteroom where we can talk without having to shout. We reminisce about the old days when we would step out of Club Vogue, where regular-sized beers cost upwards of thirty yuan, and make our way over to the little *xiaomaibu*—family-run convenience store—next to the club. We would sit on empty plastic beer cases, drink large bottles of Yanjing for one and a half yuan, and shoot the shit about the state of the world with the chubby, amiable proprietor who slept in the store and thus spent the night shift dressed in his pajamas.

It was a strange contrast—Club Vogue, a symbol of the new, stylish, international face of the city, sitting right next to the *xiaomaibu*, a symbol of its grimy, crude, and charac-ter-filled past. The designer clothing of the club patrons next to the dirty undershirt of the proprietor. The Ecstasy flown in from Amsterdam next to the not-cold-enough bottle of Yanjing beer. The future next to the past.

◻ ◻ ◻

BY NOW, THE IDEA of what it takes to make a successful club—stylish décor, international-quality DJs, and effective service—has been firmly implanted in the consciousness of a solid number of Beijingers, and international-standard clubs open and close on a regular basis. It's almost impossible to keep up; every couple months there's a new hotspot.

Nightclubs are a fickle business; they're always shutting down, especially in Beijing. In addition to the cash flow problems that usually lead to a club's closure, in Beijing enormous chunks of the city are being destroyed and rebuilt in preparation for the 2008 Olympics. Both Vogue and Neo Lounge were casualties of this reconstruction.

Other Beijing nightlife institutions adapt to the changing times; when their current location is knocked down to build something else, the bar owners simply move the place somewhere else. Live music standby Yugong Yishan moved from its former digs just inside the gate of the Worker's Stadium to the space which used to house Henry Li's artfully designed Rui Fu.

The owners of Yugong Yishan's ex-neighbor, a strange bar constructed from the decrepit hulk of sewn-together buses known casually as "the Bus Bar," have moved their structure, which serves as a meeting ground for underage hormones and dollar shots, several times over the past few years; they are again looking for a new location.

Hundreds of *xiaomaibu* were also lost to the wrecking ball; they have been replaced by brightly lit, 7–Eleven style convenience stores which offer way more products and way less charm.

□ □ □

IT'S PAST OUR bedtime, and we're jet-lagged; by now, Lao Wei and I are talking to people we don't know, trying to make second- and third-degree connections: the game of do-you-know-Daniel? and oh-I'm-friends-with-Xiao-Liu-also. We've had a few drinks, but unlike most everyone around us, our mental fenceposts are still firmly planted in the world of sanity.

Someone knows Ralf, and mentions that he doesn't usually show up until very, very late.

Lao Wei and I look at each other; we're having a good enough time that complaining doesn't seem in order, but this is ridiculous.

Also, we're beginning to slip into the bizarre hyper-reality that results from being a little bit too buzzed in a Chinese dance club.

Suddenly I'm grabbed from behind and I find myself lifted off the ground. "You fuckers!" says Ralf, putting me down and embracing me, then Lao Wei.

His eyes sparkle; it's a joyous occasion. We're happy to see each other. "You ready to party tonight?" he asks us. Ralf has always been a tall, slim and handsome guy; his blonde hair has grown even longer than normal, down to the middle of his back. He's wearing a lot of beaded necklaces and bracelets and loose-fitting hemp clothing. He looks like a cross between a hippie and a Viking.

"We've been partying already," I tell him.

"I want to tell you how crazy this place is!" Ralf screams, his eyes wide with excitement, and dilated by god knows what.

We talk, and dance, and leave the club and go to another one, and don't head for home until the morning heat of Beijing has already begun to stifle the city.

ACKNOWLEDGMENTS

FIRST, I MUST THANK Sonny, Elvira, Mark, and Janice, without whom none of this would have been possible.

When I met with Karen Zarker and Sarah Zupko of PopMatters, this book was just a half-baked idea. Had they not been enthusiastic, it would have remained that way.

Actually writing the book took me much longer than I anticipated; if not for the invaluable work of Karen Zarker, my editor at PopMatters Books, it would have never reached completion. Karen was patient when I needed patience. When I needed someone to stand behind me and crack the whip, she did that, too.

Thanks to Richard Nash and everyone at Soft Skull Press for believing in this idea.

Thanks to Benno and to Li Du for your years of friendship and assistance. I love you both like brothers.

Thanks to "Brandon" Pu Ming, for being my surrogate father, and for the years of excellent meals.

Thanks to Laozi and Zhuangzi and Buddha for the ideas, and thanks to Peter Hessler and Karl Taro Greenfeld for inspiration.

In China, thanks to Maohair, Zhou Xingping, Shao Xiaoli, Hongfeng, Mary Jones, Liang Kegang, the Dongsi Shitiao crew and Su Pei, Liu Jianfeng, Hassan, Huan Huan, Sam Xiatian Deris and Xingxing, Rongjie and Xinmin, A King, Zhang Xin, Gong Jiaju, Fengfeng at the Phoenix, Sasha Matuszak, Jarrett Wrisley and Candace, Rindy and Xianyi Portfolio, Michael Ferchak, Christine Huang, Mia Jiang, Lao Wang, Lao Zhang and Doudou, Wang Gang, Brad "The Terror" Turley, Mian Mian, Wang Chunmeng, Joshua Lipes, Dalong, Paal Aune and Yuanyuan, Gao Yang, Jeremy Goldkorn, Eli Kislevitz, Bill Isler, the whole Chaoyang Gardens crew: Deng Sheng, Xiao Pang, etc, the Qingdao skinny-dipping crew, and everyone I left out.

In America, thanks to Alex, Jolie, Daisy, Scarlett, Bruce & Judy, and everyone else, to Anna Ansari, Mary O'Brien and Macayla, Matt Dugan and the crew at the Arrow, Tom Kelly, Domenick Cimino, Will Glass, Johnny Mays, the Bunny, and the Octagon, Yoav Kipnes, Humi Kobayashi, Carlo Schiano, Billy Jones, and all the good people at Pianos, thanks to Jasper Coolidge, to Graham Smith/Kleenex Girl Wonder for writing the soundtrack to this trip, the men of Stay Fucked, the men of Sam Champion, the men of the Nice Jenkins, Russell Baker, Joe Petrucelli, John Costantino, Eli Kagan, Kaben Schwartz, Lauren Glick, and Eddie Hale. Thanks to Steven Post for the advice. Thanks to Ringo for the haircuts. Thanks to my awesome landlord David Chen and all the Chinese teachers I've ever had.

And of course, the most special gratitude is reserved for Heidi: thanks for coming to visit, and thanks for sharing your life and your love with me.